The Economics of Copyright

For Pauline Gloria Marcus Gordon, with love.
                                        WJG

For Marta, with all my love.
                                        RW

The Economics of Copyright

Developments in Research and Analysis

Edited by

Wendy J. Gordon

Professor of Law and Paul J. Liacos Scholar in Law, Boston University School of Law, USA

and

Richard Watt

Professor of Economic Theory, Universidad Autónoma de Madrid, Spain

Edward Elgar
Cheltenham, UK • Northampton, MA, USA

Published by
Edward Elgar Publishing Limited
Glensanda House
Montpellier Parade
Cheltenham
Glos GL50 1UA
UK

Edward Elgar Publishing, Inc.
136 West Street
Suite 202
Northampton
Massachusetts 01060
USA

A catalogue record for this book
is available from the British Library

Library of Congress Cataloguing in Publication Data
The economics of copyright : developments in research and analysis / edited by
    Wendy J. Gordon and Richard Watt.
        p. cm.
    1. Copyright—Economic aspects. I. Gordon, Wendy J., 1949– II. Watt,
Richard,   1963–

K1420.5.E28 2003
346.04'82—dc21

                                                                    2003051334
ISBN 1 84376 263 3

Printed and bound in Great Britain by MPG Books Ltd, Bodmin, Cornwall

Contents

Contributors

Jorge Alonso is a Ph.D. student at CEMFI (Centre for Monetary and Financial Studies) in Madrid (Spain). He has completed his undergraduate studies in economic theory with distinction at the Universidad Autónoma de Madrid.

Paul Belleflamme is Associate Professor in Economics at CORE and IAG, Université Catholique de Louvain, Belgium. From September 1997 to the end of August 2002, he was Lecturer in Economics at Queen Mary's, University of London. He has a Ph.D. in economics from the University of Namur (Belgium) and an M.A. in economics from Columbia University. His research interests include several areas of industrial organisation and applied game theory, with a special emphasis on information products and technologies. He has published articles in the *International Journal of Industrial Organization*, in *Games and Economic Behavior*, in the *Journal of Urban Economics* and in the *European Journal of Political Economy*.

Ben Depoorter is an Olin Fellow at the Center for Law, Economics and Organization at Yale University, School of Law and Junior Faculty at Ghent University, School of Law. He holds a J.D. from Ghent University, an LL.M. from Yale University and a Ph.D. in law and economics from Ghent University. He is a recipient of a BAEF and Fulbright fellowship. Among his published books are *Telecommunications and the Internet: The Changing Boundaries of Law*, with Guy Schrans (Mys & Breesch, 2001) and *The Law and Economics of the European Union*, with Paul Stephan and Francesco Parisi (Lexis, 2003). He has authored thirty papers in the field of law and economics and comparative legal theory. He currently serves as Co-Editor of the *Review of Law and Economics* (The Berkeley Electronic Press Journals), Guest Editor of the *International Review of Law and Economics* and Secretary of the European Association of Law and Economics.

Joëlle Farchy is Assistant Professor at the University of Paris Sud and a member of the Center of Research Matisse, Paris 1. In 1990, her Ph.D. in economics was about the French film industry. She now teaches both in the University of Paris Sud and Panthéon Sorbonne (Paris 1). She has published several papers on cultural industries. Her last book entitled *The end of the* *cultural exception?* in 1999 deals with the consequences of digital innovations on cultural industries.

Wendy J. Gordon is Professor of Law and the Paul J. Liacos Scholar in Law at Boston University School of Law. A member of the Editorial Board of the *Encyclopaedia of Law and Economics* (Edward Elgar) and a former Chair of the Intellectual Property section of the Association of American Law Schools, she is best known for uniting economic and philosophic inquiries in her studies of copyright and intellectual property theory. Her 1982 piece 'Fair Use as Market Failure' (*Columbia Law Review*) was one of the first legal articles to introduce systematic economic theory into the analysis of copyright doctrine. Her more than two dozen articles include 'An Inquiry into the Merits of Copyright' (*Stanford Law Review*), 'A Property Right in Self-Expression: Equality and Individualism in the Natural Law of Intellectual Property' (*Yale Law Journal*), 'On Owning Information' (*Virginia Law Review*), 'Toward a Jurisprudence of Benefits' (*University of Chicago Law Review*), 'Excuse and Justification in the Law of Fair Use: Commodification and Market Perspectives' (in *The Commodification of Information*, Kluwer), and 'Copyright' (with Robert Bone, in the *Encyclopaedia of Law and Economics*). She has been the Visiting Senior Research Fellow at Oxford's St. John's College, a Visiting Fellow at Oxford's Centre for Socio-Legal Studies: Programme in Comparative Media Law and Policy, a Fulbright Scholar, a resident at the Rockefeller Foundation's Bellagio Center, and the recipient of various other grants and awards. She is currently the General Secretary of SERCI.

Stan Liebowitz was trained at Johns Hopkins (B.A.) and UCLA (Ph.D.). He is currently a Professor of Economics in the School of Management at the University of Texas at Dallas after having been on the faculty at the University of Western Ontario, University of Rochester, and a Faculty Fellow at the University of Chicago. In addition to five books, he has published over sixty articles in journals including the *American Economic Review* and the *Journal of Political Economy*, as well as more popular outlets such as the *Wall Street Journal* and *CIO Magazine*. He is on the Editorial Board of the *Journal of Network Industries* and the Advisory Board for the Digital Economy Center of the Heartland Institute. Professor Liebowitz's research interests include the economic impact of new technologies on copyright owners, the economics of networks, pricing issues, and antitrust. He is best known for his work (with Steve Margolis) on network effects and lock-in, culminating in two books, *Winners, Losers & Microsoft* (Independent Institute, 1999) and a collection of academic articles on that subject in *The Economics of Qwerty* (NYU Press/Palgrave, 2001, edited by Peter Lewin). His most recent book titled *Rethinking the Network Economy* was published by the American Management Association in the fall of 2002. His work has been the focus of articles in *The Economist*, the *Wall Street Journal*, the *New York Times*, the *Financial Times*, and a programme on the BBC. He has consulted and testified in the United States and Canada on issues related to technology and intellectual property.

Francesco Parisi is a Professor of Law and Director in the Law and Economics Program at George Mason University School of Law. He received his D.Jur. from the University of Rome 'La Sapienza', an LL.M. and a J.S.D. and an M.A. in economics from the University of California at Berkeley and a Ph.D. in economics from George Mason University. Among his published books are *The Law and Economics of the European Union*, with Paul Stephan and Ben Depoorter (Lexis, 2003); *Economic Foundations of Private Law*, with Judge Richard A. Posner (Edward Elgar, 2002), *Law and Economics* (3 volumes), with Judge Richard A. Posner (Edward Elgar, 1997), *Liability for Negligence and Judicial Discretion* (California, 1990; 2nd ed., 1992), and *Il Contratto Concluso Mediante Computer* (CEDAM, 1987). Additionally, he has authored over one hundred papers in the field of law and economics and comparative legal theory. Professor Parisi is currently serving as Editor of the *Supreme Court Economic Review* (Chicago University Press) and Co-Director of the Program in Economics and the Law at the J.M. Buchanan Center for Political Economy and he is a member of the Board of Editors of the *International Review of Law and Economics*, the *American Journal of Comparative Law*, and the *Social Sciences Research Network*.

Giovanni Battista Ramello is Assistant Professor of Economics at the Università Carlo Cattaneo – LIUC, Italy. He received an education both in economics and in computer sciences in Italy (Università degli Studi di Torino, Università Bocconi di Milano) and in France (Université Jean Moulin – Lyon 3 and CNSM, Lyon). He has been research fellow at the Fondazione Giovanni Agnelli, Torino (Italy), at the Banff Centre for the Arts (Alberta, Canada), and has served as an advisor for the Forum for the Information Society, Presidency of the Ministers' Council, for the Federation of the Italian Universities (CRUI), and in some Italian antitrust cases. His main research interests concern industrial organisation, antitrust, economic analysis of law, intellectual property and information goods. He has published a number of papers in these fields in national and international journals and books.

Tobias Regner is a Ph.D. student in economics at the University of Bristol, UK where he is also a member of the Centre for Market and Public Organisation. His undergraduate degree is from the University of Munich, Germany. Primarily he is interested in contract theory and behavioural economics, both in the context of the digital age.

Fabrice Rochelandet is Assistant Professor at the University of Paris Sud. He received his doctorate in economics from the University of Paris Pantheon-Sorbonne. His thesis addressed the question of copyright in view of the technological changes in the cultural industries. He has taught courses and seminars on public economics, copyright economics, and heritage and copyright. His current research centres on the economic impact of digital technologies through topics such as electronic commerce of cultural goods, intellectual property and digital divide. He has written and published several articles on the protection of copyrighted content in the digital era, the efficiency of copyright collecting societies and the European copyright harmonisation.

Lisa N. Takeyama received her Ph.D. in economics from Stanford University in 1992. She is currently employed as an Assistant Professor in the Department of Economics at Amherst College. Prior to this, she was employed for four years as an Assistant Professor of economics at the University of Oregon. Her primary work on piracy and intellectual property has been published in the *Journal of Law and Economics* and the *Journal of Industrial Economics*. She has also published other work in the *Journal of Industrial Economics*, the *European Economic Review*, *Economics of Innovation and New Technology*, and *Economics Letters*. In 1997, she was named among the top 15 economics scholars at the Assistant Professor rank at liberal arts colleges (*Journal of Economic Education*).

Ruth Towse is Reader in Cultural Industries at the Department for the Study of the Arts and Culture at Erasmus University Rotterdam, the Netherlands. She works in cultural economics and the economics of copyright, specialising in performers' rights and the music industry. She was Joint Editor of the *Journal of Cultural Economics* from 1993–2002. She has authored a number of articles on copyright and artists collected in *Creativity, Incentive and Reward* (2001), published by Edward Elgar, and edited several recent books on the economics of intellectual property and cultural economics, all published by Edward Elgar; *Cultural Economics* (1997), *Economics of Intellectual Property* (with Rudi Holzhauer) (2002) and *Copyright in the Cultural Industries* (2002).

Richard Watt is Professor of Economic Theory at the Universidad Autónoma de Madrid. After completing a Bachelors and a Masters degree in economics at Canterbury University in New Zealand, he earned his doctorate in economic theory from the Universidad Autónoma de Madrid in 1990. His interest in the economics of copyright is manifested in his book *Copyright and Economic Theory: Friends or Foes?* (Edward Elgar, 2000). He is also actively researching the economics of risk bearing and risk sharing. He has published several papers in international journals on this topic, as well as on the theory of oligopoly. He is currently the President of SERCI.

Preface

Richard Watt

The Society for Economic Research on Copyright Issues (SERCI)[1] was founded with the general objective of providing a solid academic platform from which the economic dimension of copyright can be studied, debated, and in general analysed, and from which the results of such study can be distributed as widely as possible. In particular, SERCI is concerned with researching how copyright can be efficiently and effectively administered, managed, protected, and rewarded. As an integral part of SERCI's activities, an annual congress is held at which economists, lawyers and other copyright professionals from all over the world present their research, and at which this research is actively debated. When a group of academics from such diverse backgrounds meets to discuss topics such as 'equity' and 'efficiency' in copyright administration, the positive externalities that constantly flow from one group to the other can only help in our overall understanding of such a complex and stimulating area of research.

The present book contains a refereed selection of papers from the SERCI annual congress that was held in Madrid on June 3rd and 4th of 2002. The papers that have been selected cover several of the main fields that are currently at the forefront of the copyright research agenda. They not only show how fruitful the study of copyright from an economic theory perspective has been, but the papers also clearly indicate the directions (and analytical tools) that will be of principal interest over the next few years, as research in this area flourishes.

Our most sincere gratitude goes to the people and institutions that have, collectively, made the book possible. First and foremost, we are most appreciative to the Spanish Author's Society (SGAE) for their belief in, and support of, the SERCI project. SERCI, and therefore the annual congress and this book, would not exist without their generous support. In particular, we would like to thank Eduardo Bautista, Rubén Gutierrez and Rufino Sánchez for their surprisingly adept ability to attend, understand, appreciate, and in all respects offer support for, the seemingly unconventional environment of pure academic work. Above all, we hope that the final output is useful as a bridge between academia and the day-to-day practice of copyright administration, at least offering useful suggestions, stimulating ideas, and directions of thought.

A debt of gratitude is owed to all of the team at Edward Elgar Publishers, above all for their patience and understanding as far as deadlines on a collectively authored project are concerned.

All of the papers that are contained in this volume were revised by their respective authors, based on both the lively discussions at the congress and on the comments that derived from the referee process. Given this, I would like to express my gratitude to all of the participants at the 2002 SERCI congress. The combined efforts of these academics have undoubtedly led to a far better final product. Special appreciation, however, is due to my co-editor, whose tireless work into the small hours of the morning on many occasions, and whose insightful comments on almost all of the papers in this volume, have improved the final quality of this book by an incalculable degree.

A GENERAL OUTLINE OF THE BOOK

The papers are ordered in such a way that the reader interested in a general knowledge of how economic theory can be of use in dealing with the most pressing issues for copyright administration can start at the beginning and read each chapter in order, and yet readers interested in particular issues can read separate chapters in any order. Nevertheless, I strongly recommend all readers to begin with Wendy Gordon's introduction, which does a marvellous job of introducing us to the economics of copyright by going right back to the origins of economic theory itself.

The first three chapters of the book proper (Liebowitz, Belleflamme, and Takeyama) can be grouped under the general heading of 'the economics of copying' and the next three chapters (Towse, Alonso and Watt, and Regner) consider the types of contractual relationships that occur between creators and distributors. Following that, the next two chapters (Ramello, and Farchy and Rochelandet) turn to economic analyses of the legal environment of copyright, and the final two chapters (Parisi and Depoorter, and Rochelandet) analyse the particularly important issue of collective administration of copyright.

The first chapter, written by Stan Liebowitz, offers a particularly good foundation upon which the rest of the book can build, since it not only does an excellent job in surveying the principal routes along which the economics of copyright has travelled, but it also sets the stage for many of the following chapters by pointing out the issues that constitute the central stage of the copyright dilemma currently. In particular, Liebowitz analyses the effects of digital distribution of music over the internet, both historically in comparison with other similar issues in the past (for example photocopying of written works in the 1970s, and video-taping of movies in the 1980s), and in the aftermath of the Napster revolution (peer-to-peer file sharing). Liebowitz, who is very well known for his pioneering work adapting the theory of price discrimination (under the title of 'indirect appropriability') to study alternatives to copyright, sets out to see if the new copy and diffusion technologies afforded by the internet have indeed been harmful to copyright holders. He finds sufficient evidence to conclude that copyright holders' fears of the internet, in contrast to previous technical developments that are frequently cited as having been harmful when in fact they were not,[2] may be well founded. This chapter is followed by two papers that consider different issues relating to the economics of copying. In chapter 2, Paul Belleflamme walks us through a wonderful mathematical model of copying that, without being overly complicated, clearly points out several very important results on how pricing strategies by copyright holders can be considered as an alternative to legal protection. In chapter 3, Lisa Takeyama follows up on some earlier work of her own concerning the true economic effects of the existence of copying on the welfare of copyright holders by showing how important it is to take asymmetric information into account. Underlining previous results, we find that, contrary to what is constantly claimed by copyright lobby groups, a certain degree of copying may have beneficial effects for copyright holders.

Following up on the economics of copying, the next three chapters consider the contractual relationships between creators and distributors of copyright products. Once again, in order to set the stage, we begin with Ruth Towse's particularly clear analysis of the relationships between copyright law and administration, and of the ensuing labour supply by creative individuals. In particular, Towse discusses in detail copyright policy's relationship to artists' efforts in the creation of cultural assets, paying special attention to the effects on both earnings and employment. She points out where current analysis has been lacking, and where research could be fruitfully directed. This is followed by a paper by Jorge Alonso and Richard Watt that analyses the efficiency of commonly used royalty contracts. In this paper, it is shown that the commonly used royalty contract format is highly likely to be inefficient (in the sense of diverging from the contract curve of the relationship between the participating parties), and even for the cases in which it is not inefficient, the commonly used royalty percentages are difficult to defend as the solution to a bargaining game. The suggestion is that current contractual relationships may benefit from the advice that economic theory is able to offer. Finally, in this group of papers, Toby Regner discusses the optimal distribution of ownership of copyright between creators and distributors, especially as distribution channels change with the introduction of new technologies. The prediction is that as technology develops, we should see creators retaining a greater share of ownership, and searching for new methods of distribution.

In chapters 7 and 8, the legal environment in which copyright is set is analysed using the type of tools that economic theory offers. Giovanni Ramello begins by analysing the relationship between copyright and competition law, paying special attention to the elements of conflict that have repeatedly emerged from recent antitrust cases in both the United States and Europe. In particular, the thesis argued is that the framework of intellectual property rights is crucial to antitrust evaluations because of the deterministic relation which exists between property rights on the one hand, and market structure and modes of competition on the other. In chapter 8, Joëlle Farchy and Fabrice Rochelandet study some of the more traditional alternatives that have been forwarded as substitutes for copyright in the digital age as possible barriers to trade. At the top of this list of such alternatives are the technological protection systems designed to allow content producers the ability to appropriate value in an environment of digital copying quite independently of copyright law. However, as the authors point out, such protection systems may be contrary to the interests of artists and users.

The final two chapters of the book consider the important issue of the collective administration of copyright. In chapter 9 Francesco Parisi and Ben Depoorter discuss the complementary nature of the way many intellectual property products are marketed, and they show how a market based on an oligopoly for such products can be in fact less efficient socially than a monopoly. The case of copyright collectives, an obvious example of a monopoly selling a blanket licence for complementary products, is discussed in detail. Finally, in chapter 10, Fabrice Rochelandet analyses some of the principal collectives in Europe, and subjects them to a comparative analysis according to certain common efficiency criteria. In particular, the collectives are analysed under both common accounting criteria, and using the now popular Data Envelopment Analysis technique (DEA).

NOTES

1. See the society's web page on http://www.serci.org.
2. Examples include photocopying, cassette recording, and VHS.

Introduction

Wendy J. Gordon[1]

The economic problems faced by creative persons – and by those who want access to their output – can be conceptualised in many ways. Consider, for example, this excerpt from Adam Smith's *The Wealth of Nations:*

> The labour of some of the most respectable orders in the society . . . like that of menial servants . . . does not fix or realize itself in any permanent subject, or vendible commodity, which endures after that labour is past, and for which an equal quantity of labour could afterwards be procured . . . . In the same class must be ranked, some both of the gravest and most important, and some of the most frivolous professions: churchmen, lawyers, physicians, men of letters of all kinds; players, buffoons, musicians, opera-singers . . . Like the declamation of the actor, the harangue of the orator, or the tune of the musician, the work of all of them perishes in the very instant of its production.[2]

Smith called all such labour 'unproductive' because it was consumed at the moment of exertion, leaving nothing tangible that could later be sold.

Today's technology would seem to remedy the lack that Smith perceived. A host of modern media – film, tapes, CDs, web pages – preserve the comedian's act, the orator's speech and the opera singer's vibrato. Devices for recording and transmission, listening and replaying, allow performers and their backers to obtain money at places and times far distant from the initial expenditure of labour.

Absent a technology for recording, amplifying or broadcasting sound, the creative productions mentioned by Smith were little marked by the traits that economists associate with 'public goods'. That is, they were characterised by neither significant inexhaustibility nor a significant inability to exclude free riders. A concert hall or theatre has some range before it fills to capacity, but the congestion point comes fairly quickly. Unamplified sound reaches a certain distance, then fades, and cannot be infinitely recreated from the unaugmented memories of auditors. As for excluding non-payers, in the ordinary eighteenth-century instance that problem was easily solvable:

persons who had not paid for admission (or whom the host had not invited) were stopped at the front gate. Perhaps some of the value might sneak out the door if the audience contained an inordinately skilful mimic, but the actor, singer or orator was providing value to persons in his immediate vicinity.

With microphones and broadcasting towers, tapes and CDs, the limitations of the concert hall lost their constraining power. With technology came the ability to give value to persons far distant from the performance. And with the technologies came inexhaustibility and the possibility of free riding. Artistic performance had become a 'public good'.

For generations prior to Smith, this transformation had already begun for traditional copyrightable subject matters: the collocation of words and symbols that could be written or printed. Yet it is intriguing to focus on the transformation of performance into 'vendible commodity'[3] for it is recorded performance[4] that drives the most interesting of recent copyright problems – the Napster phenomenon – as our keynote address by Liebowitz explores. Making the return to history allows us to stress that becoming a public good was not a 'problem'. It was an opportunity. The promise of inexhaustibility meant that authors could turn to audiences rather than to patronage for support, and that a wide public could share in what only a few had enjoyed before.

The question became how best to handle the technology that makes it possible for orchestral sound to come into ordinary homes, and movies to play on demand in children's bedrooms. Word can spread not just in its message but also in its form. Copyright deals with all these modes of spreading value.

However, lack of recording technology could not have been Smith's only concern. In the passage quoted, Smith groups 'men of letters' with performers, as if writers were as unable as performers to fix their labour in 'vendible commodities'. Yet by 1776, the year *Wealth of Nations* was first published, authors had long surmounted the technological barriers that still faced acrobats and musicians. Not only had ancient bards and story-tellers come to learn the technique of writing by hand, thus preventing their work from 'perish[ing] in the very instant of its production', but by 1776 the printing press had been in use for centuries. By the late eighteenth century, then, an author's particular ordering of words (whether sermon or essay, dictionary or philosophic treatise) could be fixed and reproduced in copies, and each copy could be sold as a book or pamphlet – a 'vendible commodity' if there ever was one.

So why would Smith group 'men of letters' with persons whose art was then incapable of tangible fixation? Apparently, Smith thought that a literary author like a performer could not expect much future income to flow from his present efforts. This interpretation is supported by a phrase that Smith elsewhere uses to describe men of letters: he describes them as, 'That unprosperous race of men.'[5]

Why would Smith have been so pessimistic about the chances for literary remuneration? One might have speculated that part of the reason was lack of copyright. In the absence of legal protection, a writer might be afraid of showing his manuscript to a publisher lest it be copied without payment, and even if that were surmounted, a publisher might be wary of paying the author much for a manuscript that, should it prove successful, others could copy at will. Without copyright, the situation could resemble a prisoner's dilemma: although two publishers could each do moderately well paying royalties to their own authors, a publisher who paid royalties could be ruinously undersold if other publishers felt free to copy without paying. So a lack of copyright might lead to a lack of payment and incentives for authors, and thus to underproduction.

However, a lack of copyright could not explain Smith's pessimism, for copyright had come to England in 1710. Admittedly, copyright was then fairly short – a fourteen year term renewable for another fourteen should the author survive – but its comparative brevity does not fully explain why so many authors found their writing produced insufficient means of support. Smith himself shared revenues with his publisher in an unusual arrangement that probably served Smith better than the way in which many of his contemporaries were served by their publishers.[6] Yet Smith had, and seemed to require,[7] a number of sources for remuneration other than writing: university teaching, serving as tutor to a duke followed by receipt of a ducal pension for life, and a position as commissioner of customs.

In this need for supplemental income he was typical. The late eighteenth century was a time of transition for authorship as a profession. Literacy was fairly low, and the cost of books was high (as was the cost of the cloth that made the rags that made the paper that made the books).[8] Apparently sharing among the populace via cafés and libraries made it possible to sell at least some copies at high prices,[9] but publishers rather than authors seemed to reap the largest share of what income books were capable of generating.[10] Thus, the primary responsibility for authors' woes seems to have rested mainly upon the state of the world, affected only in part by the state of the law.

As publishing industrialised, and as new media were developed, a now familiar set of problems and opportunities arose together. Authors were freed of the necessity to please patrons, but pleasing the public had its own constraints. As the value of the 'vendible commodities' increased, so did the complexity of policy issues that copyright law had to face.

If it was clear that the public needed more authorship, then copyright could encourage authorship by allowing creators and their authorised publishers to capture a return above the marginal cost of physical replication.

If only one source can print a given work, that publisher typically will charge a price above marginal cost. Ordinarily, this is the profit-maximising strategy, and the revenue it generates allows a publisher to pay something to the author for the initial work of creation. However, pricing above marginal cost results in fewer copies being purchased than if the book were sold at the lower competitive price: some persons who value copies above marginal cost will instead purchase things they value less. As a consequence of this reduced access to the work, copyright produces deadweight loss.

However, no other institutional arrangement has the clear advantage: not perfect competition, not non-copyright modes of attaining market power, and not price discrimination. Consider first the supposed ideal, perfect competition. Eliminating copyright could in the abstract eliminate deadweight loss if the lack of legal protection led to perfect competition, but under perfect competition, the resulting low prices would eliminate the possibility of payment for initial creation and thus would threaten authorial incentives. If eliminating copyright led instead (as is more likely in a real world) to imperfect competition, where factors such as lead time advantage, retributive editions, and encryption could raise some prices above marginal cost, then some deadweight loss would remain. In addition, revenues would be likely distributed in a manner that would be only loosely correlated with authorial quality, and self-help measures could waste much of whatever profits were earned.

Perfect price discrimination holds out abstract promise – since if a publisher had perfect knowledge and could costlessly bar all arbitrage, he could sell each copy to each customer at the maximum price the customer would bear, simultaneously expanding quantity, eliminating deadweight loss, and serving incentives.[11] But even if the result were normatively acceptable (involving as it does the elimination of consumer surplus), sellers have neither perfect knowledge, nor the ability to costlessly transact with each customer individually, nor the ability to costlessly prevent low-value buyers from reselling to high-value ones. Moreover, price discrimination sometimes makes matters worse.[12] Further, copyright already embodies a large degree of price discrimination,[13] yet no one believes that deadweight loss has vanished.

The usual way of addressing the trade-off is stated by Landes and Posner:[14] 'For copyright law to promote economic efficiency, its principal legal doctrines must, at least approximately, maximize the benefits from creating additional works minus both the losses from limiting access and the costs of administering copyright protection...' However, more research is needed to determine how much new authorship the public does indeed desire.

For example, a work distributed in expensive form to five people is less socially valuable than the same work distributed not only to those five, but also to a thousand more in an inexpensive edition. However, as technological change enables the cheap distribution of copies, is it always most productive to see the authorial work as having become more valuable? Or might it be the technology or the copies to which the increased value should be attributed?[15]

Admittedly, recycling Homer's 'Odyssey' would not render James Joyce's 'Ulysses' superfluous, nor would fans of Akira Kurosawa's film 'Ran' be satisfied with re-reading Shakespeare's 'King Lear' in the original. Nevertheless, it may be that few new authors, and many inexpensive copies of existing work, would best satisfy the public – in which case, a brief and narrow copyright providing few rewards might be in order. A brief and narrow copyright might also be desirable if the incentives that drive the most valued authors are non-pecuniary. Such questions are among the most important, but most difficult to research empirically.

Western nations came to recognise that technology enabled us to do something we had not done before: We could reward creativity not just through patrons and not just through church, government and university appointments. Society could reward creativity through harnessing the desires and purchasing power of audiences. This, in turn, meant that the kind of creativity would be more responsive to popular tastes and, hopefully, popular needs. It was to harness the extra value enabled by technology that copyright was invented.

However, once we recognise the possibility and desirability of having audiences pay the creative labourer long after the labour is complete, a new generation of questions arises: What is the best way of having audiences pay? How much recompense is enough to ensure an efficient level of creativity – and how much payment might be too much, inducing rent dissipation or unduly restraining the development both of new technology and future authorship? How much and what kind of copyright protection would be required to achieve sufficient recompense, and are related laws (perhaps affecting authorial bargaining power) likely to be productive or counter-productive? Are some particular rights or subject matters particularly apt targets for copyright, and, conversely, are there some rights or subject matters that should be kept exempt from copyright protection? Do there exist alternative institutions or mechanisms under which creativity can be sufficiently rewarded, and if so, how does the efficiency of the alternatives compare with that of copyright protection? Are there forms of technological protection, or licensing, that the law should prohibit or subject to mandatory limitation, and if so, why? These (and others) are typical of the types of question that are addressed in the present volume.

COPYRIGHT AND ECONOMICS

The familiar tropes of copyright economics arrive draped in technical language. For example, we are told that, 'Giving an author exclusive rights over reproduction solves a "public goods" problem.' But the lawyers and economists who go beneath the labels make the most progress.

Copyright is a regime under which creation is stimulated, but copyright has costs: it raises the cost of products, and it also raises the cost of creation for the next generation of authors.[16] Other means of collecting revenues may not impose these costs – but may impose others. One task is common to the economist, lawyer and entrepreneur: exploring and comparing alternatives.

Economists study trade-offs. As far as the production and distribution of cultural intellectual property is concerned, any protection mechanism implies both efficiency gains and losses.

Economists are in general agreement that in the absence of intellectual property rights, intellectual product markets are inherently inefficient, both in private and social terms. Economists also agree that copyright law is only capable, at best, of going part of the way towards achieving a proper balance between the sometimes contradictory interests of copyright holders and the public of users.[17] Unauthorised copying can sometimes increase social benefit.[18]

New technological developments, both in communications media and in copy technologies, are constantly upsetting the balances between incentive and access, the costs of copyright administration and costs of self-help. As we move further into the twenty-first century, copyright will evolve as well. We must search for relevant methods of administration and reward, appropriate boundaries between protection and the public domain, under which copyright can be of most benefit to the public.

The research agenda that has been followed by economists concerning copyright has revealed that it can be effectively studied using many tools of economic theory. For example, in studying copyright fundamentals, one typically invokes economic principles and models such as:

1. welfare maximising behaviour in general (both in production and in consumption),
2. social choice and the efficiency trade-off between social and private costs and benefits, in particular the theory of externalities and public goods (and so the Coase theorem and the concept of free-riding are of direct relevance),
3. the theory of monopoly,
4. optimal regulation of monopoly activities,
5. price discrimination,

6. the economic analysis of decision making under risk and uncertainty,
7. asymmetries in information,
8. asymmetries in transaction costs (relating again to the Coase theorem),
9. game theory, in particular the prisoner's dilemma, coalition formation and bargaining.

This short-list of economic principles makes it clear that economists in general, and applied microeconomic specialists in particular, are certainly in a position to be able to provide many useful insights as to how copyright can be properly shaped and efficiently administered. It is hoped that the papers included in this volume will at least prove to be thought provoking for copyright professionals (both legal professionals, as well as those in positions of responsibility in relevant administrative bodies) and economists in general, and that the papers will also help to point future academic research in a fruitful direction.

NOTES

1. My appreciation is owed to Richard Watt for his invaluable comments and suggestions on this introduction, and (if it's not improper for one co-editor to show her awe at the other's efforts) for his labours on this book as a whole. Thanks are also due to Robert Bone, Keith Hylton and Mike Meurer for their keen observations on the introduction, and to Fred Moses for coffee and all that goes with it.
2. Adam Smith, *An Inquiry into the Nature and Causes of the Wealth of Nations* (Book II, chapter III, paragraph II.3.2), available on http://www.econlib.org/library/Smith/smWN.html.
3. Whereas in the nineteenth century copyright's subject matter was confined to such things as 'musical works' and 'literary works' (where the sequence of notes and words is written down and protected), technological advances have significantly expanded the set of subject matters, which now includes such things as 'sound recordings'. Not all subject matters receive the same treatment. The desirability of giving differing forms of protection to differing types of works provides obvious fodder for both the theoretical and empirical economist.
   For example, United States copyright law denominates the sound recording as a type of 'work of authorship', see 17 U.S.C. §102(a)(7), but treats it differently from the underlying musical composition. See, e.g., 17 U.S.C. §§106(4) and (6). Many other nations do not call the sound recording an authorial work at all, but instead address it under a separate category, such as 'neighbouring rights'. See Lionel Bently and Brad Sherman (2001), *Intellectual Property Law*, Oxford: Oxford University Press, pp. 28–48.
4. Typically, a recorded performance contains two copyrights: one in the underlying musical work, and one in the sound recording.
5. Adam Smith, *An Inquiry into the Nature and Causes of the Wealth of Nations* (Book I, chapter X, paragraph I.10.93), available on http://www.econlib.org/

library/Smith/smWN.html. In this section, Smith discusses two types of 'men of letters': teachers and authors. Smith argues that an oversupply of persons educated for the church had reduced the wages available to teachers – yet notes that in comparison with authorship, teaching 'is still surely a more honourable, a more useful, *and in general even a more profitable employment* than that other of writing for a bookseller, to which the art of printing has given occasion.' *Id.* at paragraph I.10.94, emphasis added.

6. Victor Bonham-Carter (1978), *Authors by Profession, Vol. One*, Los Altos, William Kaufmann Inc., p. 26.
7. Smith's need for cash may not have stemmed from typical authorial difficulties. Evidence suggests that 'Smith did not hang on to his considerable income, and disbursed much of it in charitable acts.' Ian Simpson Ross (1995), *The Life of Adam Smith*, Oxford: Clarendon Press, p. 354.
8. Bonham-Carter, *supra*, p. 30; Lee Ericson (1996), *The Economy of Literary Form: English Literature and the Industrialization of Publishing 1800–1850*, Baltimore, Johns Hopkins University Press, at 3–8; Diane Leenheer Zimmerman (2003), 'Authorship without Ownership: Reconsidering Incentives in a Digital Age', *DePaul Law Review*, forthcoming.
9. Bonham-Carter, *supra*, p. 31.
10. Bonham-Carter, *supra*, p. 32; also see Catherine Seville (1999), *Literary Reform in Early Victorian England: The Framing of the 1842 Copyright Act 101–05*, Cambridge: Cambridge University Press. Note, however, that Seville believes that 'By the eighteenth century the profession of letters was well established.' *Id.* p. 101.
11. Harold Demsetz (1970), 'The Private Production of Public Goods', *Journal of Law and Economics*, **13**, 293–306.
12. It is the current fashion to assume that price discrimination will increase equilibrium output under monopoly, but that is not necessarily the case. The interested reader can consult Jean Tirole (1990), *The Theory of Industrial Organization*, Cambridge (Mass.): MIT Press (chapter 3).
13. The various exclusive rights granted to copyright owners can be seen simply as the law's way of facilitating price discrimination among the purchasers of copies. Consider the following examples. (a) The writer initially wants to discriminate between someone who wants to read her book, and someone who wants to reprint it and sell the copies. The 'exclusive right of reproduction' allows her to distinguish between the two classes, and to charge a much higher price to the second class of user. The 'exclusive right of reproduction' also makes arbitrage between copiers and others virtually profitless. (b) Similarly, the composer wishes to discriminate between someone who buys her sheet music to play on the living room piano and someone who buys it to perform in a concert hall; the 'exclusive right of public performance' allows her to distinguish again between the two classes. The exclusive rights force most high-value users to identify themselves (lest they be sued for copyright infringement), and approach the copyright owner with offers. See Wendy J. Gordon (1998), 'Viewing Intellectual Property as a Mode of Price Discrimination: Implications for Contract', *Chicago-Kent Law Review*, **73**, 1367–1390.

The lawyer acculturated to copyright parlance will object that this is not price discrimination, since the copyright owners in the examples are selling different 'things' to each customer. In selling a copy of her book to the ordinary consumer, the writer is selling 'only' a copy, while she is selling the potential republisher a 'right to publish'. Similarly, the acculturated lawyer will say that the composer is selling 'only' a copy to the home user, and 'a right to publicly perform' to the orchestra. These locutions are reinforced by the fact that these 'things' called copyright licences are often sold separately from the physical objects: one buys the book and the music score at an ordinary store, and purchase the 'licences' through discussions with the copyright owner or her agent.

Yet using an acid bath, and eliminating the customary language of 'licences' and 'valuable intangibles', what is happening? Simply, persons' use of physical things is being affected. The copyright owner is able to charge differing prices to users of copies who have different valuations.

14. See William Landes and Richard Posner (1989), 'An Economic Analysis of Copyright Law', *Journal of Legal Studies*, **18**, 325–366.

15. Ronald Coase's observation that causation is reciprocal arose in the context of nuisance law, where two parties' interaction caused a loss of value. It is equally relevant where two or more parties' interaction causes new value to arise, as frequently occurs in the realm of copyright. R.H. Coase (1960), 'The Problem of Social Cost', *Journal of Law and Economics*, **3**, 1– 44.

16. Increasing the payments that one generation of authors receives can increase the costs that the next generation of authors will have to bear, see Landes and Posner, *supra*, and can even result in altogether barring some routes to subsequent creativity. Each generation of artists needs to use what came before. If a prior generation has a broad copyright of long duration, then later generations will have the substantial burden of seeking licences. Such licences may not be granted at all, or may be granted only after substantial transaction costs are borne and high licence fees are paid by the later generation artist.

17. Although a work of authorship has its own defining characteristics, it is nevertheless a type of information product. Where information is concerned, economics shows a 'constant interplay between market imperfections'. See Joseph E. Stiglitz (2001), 'Information and the Change in the Paradigm in Economics', Nobel Prize Lecture, p. 491, available at http://www.nobel.se/economics/laureates/2001/stiglitz-lecture.pdf.

18. Many people may find it surprising that unauthorised copying can in fact be socially valuable, but there exist several studies that show that this may indeed be the case. For a summary of this literature, see Richard Watt (2000), *Copyright and Economic Theory: Friends or Foes?*, Cheltenham and Northampton, MA: Edward Elgar (chapter 2).

1. Back to the Future: Can Copyright Owners Appropriate Revenues in the Face of New Copying Technologies?

Stan Liebowitz

For economic incentives to work appropriately, property rights must protect the rights of capital assets....At present...severe economic damage [is being done] to the property rights of owners of copyrights in sound recordings and musical compositions...under present and emerging conditions, the industry simply has no out...Unless something meaningful is done to respond to the...problem, the industry itself is at risk. (Alan Greenspan)

1.1 INTRODUCTION

The above quote appears to be taken from today's headlines. Yet this quote has nothing to do with digital copying and predates MP3 files by a very considerable margin. The quote is from 1983, before Alan Greenspan became chairman of the Federal Reserve.[1] His concern was with the spectre of home audio taping, but he was writing as a paid consultant to the recording industry which perhaps explains his bit of hyperbole. Time has shown that the industry did not fail. As we all know, LP records morphed to a digital format now known as CDs, and the industry continued in good health. Although one can debate whether copying technology hurt copyright owners to any measurable extent, it certainly did not undo the industry.

In this paper I wish to focus on the impact of copying on copyright holders, their ability to appropriate revenues, and our understanding of the economics of this relationship. It is a subject that has become increasingly newsworthy as intellectual property assumes a greater share of the economy and as technologies for copying these properties become increasingly efficient at doing so.[2]

These new copying technologies appear to open a Pandora's Box of copyright questions. Can copyright continue to provide ample incentives for artistic creation? Will authors be able to appropriate more or less of their works' value than they have in the past? How does digital storage change the balance between authorised and unauthorised use? What legal rules strike the best balance between consumptive efficiency and productive efficiency? What pricing schemes are likely to arise? That is, how do we maximise use and creation at the same time? And a question I find increasingly puzzling: why hasn't the rampant downloading of MP3 files, which would otherwise seem to actually surpass legitimate sales, had more of an impact on CD sales? I will return to this later.

For perspective, we should remember that copying technologies have been in existence for several generations. It is useful, to understand any real world phenomenon, to know something of its history. For those relatively new to this subject, I present a little history of the economic analysis involved, which naturally also has at least a slight involvement with what was going on in the world.

1.2   WHAT DO WE KNOW OF THE ECONOMIC IMPACTS OF COPYING?

Not as much as we would like to.

The issue at the heart of copyright, indeed of all intellectual property law, is the degree to which the copyright owner can appropriate the value produced by the consumption, or appreciation, of his work by others and the degree to which this appropriation hinders consumption.[3]

The correct level of appropriation is at the centre of many disputes, both current and historical. How much appropriation is the right amount?[4] Is it possible to have too much appropriation? What impact do technologies have on appropriation? Economists studying the impacts of copying were at first mainly interested in determining the amount of harm to copyright owners, and whether copying would engender any net harm at all to the rest of society. Later, the question of whether the copyright owner would be harmed was itself questioned.

The 'old' literature

Economists examining the impacts of copyright have tended to focus on the trade-off between consumption efficiency (maximising the net value consumers get of any produced intellectual product) and production efficiency (preserving incentives to create these products efficiently). On the one hand, if the copyright holder could not appropriate any revenues, the creators of intellectual properties would be expected to produce too few intellectual products, probably far fewer than would be optimal.[5] On the other hand, by providing some degree of control over the use of these products to copyright owners by restricting others' ability to make copies, consumption of these products is decreased from 'ideal' levels.[6]

In reality, the 'monopoly' conferred by copyright is no greater than the monopoly that each worker has on his or her efforts, or that each firm has on products bearing its name. Still, monopoly power or not, the ideal number of reproductions of a public good (a public good being defined as a good that does not get used up when consumed, what is called non-rivalrous consumption) would require a quantity of reproductions above the level that copyright owners would find in their best interest to produce, and thus too few reproductions would be created.[7]

In this trade-off between consumption and production efficiency, copying was not an issue. The choice was one between lengthier or shorter copyright protection, and as such I believe the analysis of these trade-offs is correct.

Cheap and convenient copying required a new analysis. The early articles on the subject are Ordover and Willig (1978), a comment on them by Liebowitz and Margolis (1982), Liebowitz (1981), Johnson (1984), Novos and Waldman (1984), and Liebowitz (1985).[8] These papers had different models of how copying harm might be modelled. Of course, this is a relatively small literature that has barely made its way out of the rather narrow circle of economists who study the issue.

Ordover and Willig provided a model where libraries can perfectly appropriate value from readers and where publishers can price discriminate between libraries and individuals. Although this is not exactly the same as copying, the sharing of goods in the library is certainly a close cousin. Ordover and Willig claimed that it is efficient for libraries to impose a usage fee on library patrons instead of perfectly appropriating funds through lump sum levies. This is counterintuitive, and the Liebowitz–Margolis comment claimed that it was also incorrect. The library usage fee, if paid to the publisher, can be interpreted as the imposition of a copyright royalty, which is one linkage to the copying/copyright literature.

Novos and Waldman modelled a variant of the under-production and under-consumption trade-off and reached conclusions that they claimed are quite different from the traditional trade-off notions mentioned above. To my mind, however, Novos and Waldman generated their results more by altering the definitions of the trade-off than by any new insights. The typical under-production/under-consumption trade-off is in terms of quantity of intellectual property titles created and quantity of the duplicates made from each title. Novos and Waldman modelled quality, not quantity, and their results are not comparable to the traditional findings. Many results in economics that hold for quantity do not necessarily hold for quality. For example, monopolists reduce quantity but they do not necessarily reduce quality. So it isn't clear that their results run counter to any previously held findings.

Novos and Waldman do add into their model the fact that the copyrighted item can be illicitly copied. In their model, consumers can switch back and forth from being legitimate purchasers to larcenous copiers. This was certainly a useful novelty to the model. There is also the assumption that copying is a less efficient technology than producing originals and so a new form of welfare loss is possible when copies replace originals and the production costs rise above efficient levels. Johnson, as did Novos and Waldman, models social welfare when potential consumers copy instead of purchase a product. His emphasis is on the cost differential between the commercial publisher of originals and, in his model, the inefficient home copier. Both models concluded that copying harms the copyright owner, and are mainly concerned with whether society is harmed or not. The answer, in both cases, was maybe.

The break with the claim that copying necessarily harms copyright owners starts with my 1981 study for the Canadian government. I borrowed a theoretical model of the market for new and used goods from Benjamin and Kormendi and applied it to the case of copying (several years later Besen and Kirby extended this work). The major insight was an understanding that the price of the original might go up if copies can be made since consumers of originals value the ability to make copies (as CD producers are likely to discover if they implement their anti-copying technology in a serious way). If the amount of copying is fairly uniform, the copyright owner merely has to raise the price of the originals to capture this value. If the amount of copying is variable, then the copyright owner would need to charge higher prices to those consumers of originals making the most copies, in other words, he needs to be able to price discriminate. In my 1985 paper I used the term 'indirect appropriability' to describe this situation.[9] The idea often seems somewhat unlikely to occur, but I think that it has greater applicability than generally understood. And unlike many other models, it has empirical work to support its basic conclusions.

My 1981 and 1985 papers also used the term 'exposure effect' to describe an instance of sales going up because copying allowed users to become familiar with products that they might eventually buy. This concept plays an important role in the defence made by Napster, although the concept now goes by the name 'sampling'. As I showed in my 1981 paper and repeat below, however, sampling or exposure does not have an unambiguously positive impact on the copyright owner, contrary to current claims.

The newer literature

The copying literature received a slight rekindling of interest from the network effects literature that developed and blossomed after 1985. Network effects exist when the value of a product to one consumer changes (increases) the more other consumers of the product that there are.[10] A fax machine, for example, becomes increasingly valuable when there are additional other fax machines to which faxes can be sent or from which they can be received.

If network effects exist and are strong, one can imagine that illicit copying provides value to legitimate purchasers, and it becomes conceivable that illicit copying might benefit copyright owners. This is the idea behind several papers. The key papers in this area are Conner and Rumelt, Takeyama, and Shy and Thisse.[11]

An example of network effects for products prone to piracy might be word processing software that becomes more valuable to a user the more other individuals are using the same word processor. With more users, it becomes easier to exchange files with a greater number of people. In such an instance, it is conceivable that the extra value that paying customers receive from the larger user base that is enhanced by users of pirated versions might outweigh any revenues lost by the copyright holder from being unable to prevent piracy. Conceivable, but in my opinion unlikely. For one thing, network effects for many copyrighted goods are not likely to be particularly strong. For another, it seems reasonable to assume that purchasers of legitimate copies would have stronger network effects with other users of authorised copies than with users of unauthorised copies. Finally, it seems unlikely that unauthorised users would have an impact on others' willingness to pay that is greater than would be their own willingness to pay if they couldn't use unauthorised copies.

If the prevention of copying would result in few former pirates paying the asking price, the prevention of unauthorised copying would prove financially harmful to the interests of the copyright owner. Of course, if all or enough of the pirates were to become purchasers of authorised versions when pirating was no longer possible, then the prevention of piracy would still be remunerative for the copyright owner even in the presence of network effects.

Note that models where network effects make authors better off are still clearly models where appropriability is diminished since there is no appropriation of the value generated directly by the illicit copiers' use of the product.[12] In terms of a simple analogy, if we increase the size of the pie, even a smaller share might lead to a piece that is of larger absolute size. In such a case, the copyright owner would still suffer harm compared to an instance where appropriability was kept constant (unless it were impossible to increase the size of the pie without also decreasing the share going to the copyright holder).[13] This distinction is relevant to discussion of the impact of technologies on the financial remuneration achieved by copyright holders.

1.3   ECONOMIC FACTORS THAT MIGHT AMELIORATE THE IMPACT OF COPYING TECHNOLOGIES

The basic concern that copying is likely to be harmful should probably be assumed to be correct in most circumstances. What I describe below are the exceptions to the more general rule that allowing potential consumers to pirate copies of a work is likely to reduce the revenues available to the copyright owner. It is an empirical question just how likely.

Indirect appropriability

As noted, sometimes copyright owners are able to collect revenue from unauthorised copiers by charging higher prices for the originals from which the unauthorised copies are made – indirect appropriability. The basic mechanism is simple: if the copyright owner knows which originals will be used to make copies, a higher price can be charged for them, allowing the copyright holder to capture part, all, or more of the revenue than might have been appropriated through ordinary sales if unauthorised copying could be prevented.

This can be made clear with a simple example. Assume that each and every purchaser of a compact disc makes a single audiocassette copy to play in their automobile. No one makes copies from borrowed CDs. Assume further that this copying, although illegal, is unstoppable. What would be the impact on the copyright holders who, in addition to selling compact discs had also planned to sell pre-recorded tapes?

Since each original CD will have a copy made from it, and since it is reasonable to infer that the consumers of originals place some value on the ability to make a copy, each consumer's willingness to pay for the original CD is higher than it would otherwise be. The copyright owner can capture some of this additional value by charging a higher price for the CD.[14] The logic here is the same as would be true for any durable good that can be resold into another market. If automobiles could not be resold, for example, the price that consumers would be willing to pay for new autos would undoubtedly fall.

Whether the copyright owner is better off or worse off in a regime of unfettered copying depends on the particular circumstances. Assume, for example, that all consumers would be willing to pay $9 for a particular CD and would also be willing to pay $4 for a cassette tape of the same music that they can play in their automobile cassette players (assume they do not have CD players in their cars). If home taping were allowed and consumers made cassettes, the sellers of CDs would discover that they could raise the price of CDs to $13 without any loss of sales (assuming zero cost for the cassette and the time to make the tape). If home taping were disallowed, under the same assumed circumstances, the seller of pre-recorded tapes could charge a price of $4 and capture this group's value. In this case (where the costs of making cassettes is assumed to be zero), the seller would be unharmed by the copying, and thus presumably indifferent (if he understands the impact of copying) to whether copying was allowed or not.

If there are costs in making copies, whether preventing taping would be profit enhancing or decreasing would depend on the relative cost between individuals and firms of making and delivering copies. If it is much less expensive to make pre-recorded cassettes commercially than to have them made at home, one at a time, then it would be inefficient to have personal copying replace commercial production and the copyright owner will not be able to net as much from the home-taping consumer (who deducts the cost of the blank cassette and time from his willingness to pay) as he would from a sale of cassettes. Note, however, that costs include shipping, inventorying, and delivery to the consumer, not just manufacturing, so that the cost advantages of pre-recorded tapes are at least questionable. Further, purchasers of pre-recorded cassettes also bear costs of time and inconvenience.

Another complicating possibility would arise if there is a sub-group of music listeners that purchases pre-recorded tapes for the home instead of purchasing CDs. If the price that had been established for this group was also $9, say, then the seller of pre-recorded tapes is in something of a bind in terms of capturing revenues from both groups of cassette listeners. If the price of pre-recorded cassettes were lowered to $4 to capture the value from the automobile cassette users, the seller would lose $5 from those individuals who would be willing to pay $9 to purchase pre-recorded tapes for home listening. If the seller keeps the price at $9 then he will sell no tapes to those who have CDs at home and wish to listen to cassettes in automobiles.

In this case allowing copying would benefit the copyright owner. Indirect appropriability would allow the seller to capture the $4 from CD purchasers by raising the price of CDs to $13, and the seller could still collect the full $9 from those who buy pre-recorded tapes for the home (the assumption that no copies are made from borrowed CDs is still in place). In this instance, allowing copying is more profitable for the seller of tapes and CDs. Of course, many other possibilities can be imagined, but the result that allowing unfettered copying may improve the revenue position of the copyright owner, is clearly feasible.

Note that indirect appropriability implies that the purchasers of CDs in the previous example actually pay copyright owners, albeit indirectly. Fair use, a defence to copyright infringement that allows copying in certain cases (discussed in more detail below), might protect the copiers from legal liability, but it does not prevent the 'fair users' from indirectly paying the copyright owners.

There is at least one documented instance where the impacts of indirect appropriability are strong and where unauthorised copying appears to have benefited copyright owners (the case of photocopying as discussed below).

The role of copying variability

Of course, just because indirect appropriability might be capable of securing profits doesn't mean that it will succeed in any particular case. An important factor that influences the likelihood that indirect appropriability might work is the *variability* in the number of copies made of each original. Note that in the CD automobile-cassette example, each CD was used to make one tape, therefore no variability existed in the number of copies per original. If each CD had been used to make two cassette copies that would not have changed the story since there still would not have been variability. But if some CDs were used to make no copies and others were used to make 1000 copies, then indirect appropriability becomes difficult or impossible.

In the photocopying case to be discussed below, the number of copies made from originals differs for two types of users since library users make many photocopies from each original whereas personal subscribers make few copies. Because the seller could distinguish between the two groups, however, and charge different prices accordingly, indirect appropriability was able to work. But the greater the variability in the number of copies made from each original, the more difficult the task becomes of identifying how many copies are made from each original and charging appropriate prices that match the number of copies made. In many cases it will be impossible to charge different prices to different users for identical originals, since sellers cannot usually identify the purchaser's copying intent when the original is purchased.

Therefore, in an atmosphere of rampant copying and variability in the number of copies made from each original, the seller will generally find it impossible to identify which originals should have the higher price and successfully charge higher prices for them. That is why instances of illicit organised copying, where a single original might be used by a copier to make thousands of copies, are so much more dangerous to copyright holders than unorganised copying where individuals make one or two copies for themselves.

Note also that when copying occurs, the least variation in the number of copies made from originals tends to occur when copying is ubiquitous and similar. Thus if some copying is difficult to stop it might be profitable for copyright owners to encourage everyone to engage in the same degree of copying because that can afford the copyright holder some degree of appropriability. This is an interesting and counterintuitive implication.

There is one other form of indirect appropriation worth noting. In some instances legislation may allow copyright owners to collect revenue in a manner other than charging for use. So, for example, a tax could be imposed on blank audiotapes or recorders.[15] Such a tax is only indirectly, if at all, related to copying. Blank recording media can be used to copy works for which copyright clearance was already given, or for copying non-copyrighted works.

We can use the term explicit indirect appropriability in this case as opposed to the implicit indirect appropriability described earlier. On the other hand, an organisation such as the Copyright Clearance Center (CCC) tries to directly appropriate revenues for the copyright owners. The CCC gathers rights from publishers and licenses libraries to make copies upon payment to the CCC – with the payment being a function of how much and what is copied based on CCC surveys of copying in the libraries.

Exposure effects

There is the possibility that peer-to-peer systems might help copyright owners by making it easier for users to sample songs. If Napster were merely used to 'try out' a song or an album, as might be done alternatively in a record store or by listening to the radio, then Napster use would be a complement to a CD purchase, not a substitute. In fact, Napster's experts in its court hearings made this claim, the evidence for which will be examined in more detail in the next section. Of course, the difference between listening to a song in a store or on the radio and listening to the song using Napster is that in the latter case an actual physical representation of the song is in the possession of the user whereas in the former cases only the memory of the tune remains in his possession.

Even if it were the case that Napster had been used merely for sampling, its impact on the CD market need not be the benevolent one espoused by Napster's supporters. The usual assumption is that if Napster merely helps people to decide which CDs to purchase, then it must be beneficial to the copyright owner. From this perspective, because of Napster consumers are better able to select songs that provide the greatest enjoyment for the time and money. It seems natural that they should then be willing to pay more for the CDs they purchase.

As appealing as this story is, however, it is not correct.[16] The fact that the consumer is better able to satiate his desire for music with the CDs that he purchases implies that the number of CDs purchased quite possibly would fall.

With better sampling, CDs purchased provide greater utility because they better fit the desires of consumers, therefore consumers initially will have a higher willingness to pay.[17] But assuming that CDs all basically meet the same need for music consumption, the CDs purchased provide greater value and do a better job of satiating the desires of the consumers. So consumers may discover that they do not need to purchase as many CDs since their thirst for music can be quenched with fewer of them.[18] Depending on supply conditions, it can be shown that the total quantity of CDs, their price, and the total revenue in the market may go either up or down.[19]

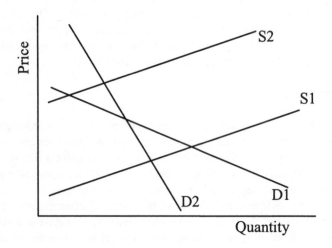

Figure 1.1 Supply and demand

This can be fairly easily demonstrated using supply and demand. In essence, the ability of consumers to better select CDs will rotate the market demand curve for CDs clockwise, from D1 to D2 in Figure 1.1. The demand curve rotates in this manner because the initial CDs purchased now provide greater utility because they better fit the desires of consumers, therefore consumers have a higher willingness to pay. But, assuming that all CDs basically meet the same need for music consumption, there is less value placed upon the purchase of later CDs since the need for music is met so well by the early CDs purchased. Depending on the position of the supply curve, the total quantity of CDs, their price, and the total revenue in the market may go either up or down.

With a supply curve such as S2, both the price and quantity of CDs purchased go up when better sampling shifts demand from D1 to D2, so that sampling would increase revenues and quantity in this instance. However, with a supply curve such as S1, lying below the intersection of the two demand curves, the quantity, price, and revenues will fall when better sampling causes demand to shift from D1 to D2. Note, of course, that the area under D2 must be greater than the area under D1 at the two intersections because greater information leads to greater efficiency.[20] Thus with S1, the quantity of CDs, the revenue generated, and the degree of appropriability all fall when sampling is enhanced.

Less exotic instances of harmless copying

Except for indirect appropriability, exposure (sampling) effects, or perhaps network effects, pirating of copyright materials would seem to be harmful to the interests of copyright owners.[21] This is because piracy is expected to prevent the copyright owner from appropriating any of the value created by his work to the users engaged in piracy. The mechanism by which unauthorised copying may harm the owners of intellectual products is straightforward enough that no detailed explanation seems necessary. Potential consumers no longer are compelled to purchase the product from the copyright owner when the option of using unauthorised copies is available to them. Defections from the legitimate market are normally expected to reduce the revenues that can be earned in the market.

There are yet some additional instances, however, where the impacts of piracy on the copyright holder's ability to appropriate will be negligible. One obvious instance is the case where the individual engaging in pirating would not have purchased an original even if pirating were not an option.[22] In this case, the prevention of piracy would provide no pecuniary reward for the copyright owner and would only diminish the gratification of the individual engaged in piracy.

1.4   THE ROLE OF THEORY VERSUS EMPIRICAL WORK

Most academic writing on this subject has been theoretical in nature – economists creating models of copying, lawyers theorising about the impacts of particular legal rules such as fair use – with but a few major attempts to empirically analyse what has actually happened and is happening in the markets. I suspect that there has been a non-optimal number of theoretical papers relative to the number of empirical studies, with the balance tipped too far in favour of theory. In part, the dearth of empirical work has been due to the difficulty in obtaining useful data sets and high cost of creating such a data set from scratch.

Governments have been at the forefront of efforts to answer some practical policy questions regarding copying. I am most familiar with two government forays along these lines. First was an attempt by the Department of Intellectual Property in Canada in the late 1970s to determine how copyright laws might be altered to respond to what were then new technologies such as photocopying and cassette recording. Second was an attempt by the US Office of Technology Assessment (OTA) in the late 1980s to determine the impact of home audio taping. Naturally, both these organisations, as a reward for their unusually productive efforts, have failed to fit into the normal government mold – each no longer exists.

The Canadian government series of papers is one that I am most familiar with since my involvement with copyright issues began as a result of being commissioned to do two of their studies, one on photocopying and the other on cable retransmission of television signals. As a part of that series they also commissioned studies on audio taping, performing rights, the term of copyright, and so forth.

The OTA studies were predicated on the creation of a large survey that described audio copying behaviour in some detail.[23] Several papers were written based on empirical examinations of the survey results. The papers tended to focus on overall welfare impacts from a ban on home taping although it wasn't clear the results were particularly robust (or in some cases, even believable). Unfortunately, in my opinion, the survey was inadequate to answer many of the questions that are at the centre of the copying controversy. Surveys of users are, in my opinion, a less than ideal methodology for answering the questions at the heart of this issue since users might not know how many CDs they buy in a year, or how many copies they make. They are certainly unlikely to know how many CDs they would buy if the price were $3 instead of $15.

What is missing is a careful and believable attempt to measure the impacts of copying on the industry whose work is being copied. This would require either a time series measuring any linkage between copying and sales in the industry, or perhaps, if a time series were unavailable, a cross section across localities with different degrees of copying. The latter approach is difficult because international differences are so vast.

Most of the empirical work that has been done in this area comes from proponents of either the copyright industry or representatives of copying-enhancing technologies, which is less than optimal when it comes to finding the truth.

What has previous empirical work told us?

Each new copying technology might appear to require fresh analysis, as each generation argues that the new technologies created during its watch require total upheavals of the status quo, whether it be the advent of sound recordings, television, photocopiers, or in the most recent instance, the Internet. But history tells us that when it comes to copyright, the more things change, the more they remain the same.. Some of the major technological challenges are listed below.

Photocopying

The ability to photocopy all books and magazines with ease might have been thought to jeopardise the livelihood of authors and publishers. After all, anyone could take a copyrighted work and make copies on the photocopier without paying the copyright owner. Yet the photocopier proved a boon to those whose works were most frequently copied.[24]

This occurred for two reasons. First, publishers were able to appropriate a portion of this additional value, thanks to indirect appropriability. Second, the convenience of being able to make copies was so great that the nature of scholarship changed among the academic communities that used so much of the copyrighted materials that were copied, and the market for journals grew relative to the market for books.

The mechanism underlying this growth in journals was indirect appropriability.[25] Publishers were able to identify those locations where photocopying copyright materials most frequently occurred – libraries and other similar institutions – and which materials were most frequently photocopied – academic journals. Publishers then began charging a much higher price for library subscriptions relative to personal subscriptions, often two, three or four times as much. The price differentials that are practically ubiquitous now among publishers of academic journals did not exist before the photocopier arrived on the scene.

Further, prior to the advent of the photocopier, researchers needed to either have a personal subscription to a journal, or to take notes in a library. Books tended to be on single topics, as opposed to journals which contained articles on varying topics which would have different levels of attraction to different scholars. Books were a key form of scholarship and were deemed of great use. Photocopying changed this relationship. The inconvenience and cost of photocopying entire books were prohibitively high so that they were rarely copied. Articles in journals, on the other hand, were well suited to the photocopier and became the major target of copying activities. Photocopying articles was fast and cheap. Subscriptions were no longer necessary except for those individuals who valued a large percentage of articles in a journal. Having a photocopy of an article was such an improvement over hand-written notes taken in the library, in terms of convenience and accuracy, that articles and journals became a far more important means of transmitting information than had previously been the case.[26]

The price discrimination that the advent of the photocopier engendered may or may not have increased overall appropriability. The evidence does not allow sufficient precision to know the answer to this question. Clearly, however, photocopying did not harm copyright owners of photocopied materials, as made clear by the growth in the number of academic journals and the financial health of the publishers. The claims to the contrary by journal publishers, and there were many, were an example of crying wolf.

Videocassette recording: the Betamax case

The 'Betamax' case (Universal Studios Inc. v. Sony Corporation of America) played a central role in the Napster defence.[27] The Supreme Court ruling allowed individuals to make private recordings of television shows on their videocassette recorders (VCRs). The Betamax case (so called because at the time the case was brought, VHS had not yet begun its obliteration of the Beta video format) represented an instance where copying was unlikely to harm copyright owners as detailed below.[28]

Almost all television viewing in the early 1980s was of advertising-supported over-the-air broadcasts, particularly those of the then big three networks – ABC, CBS, and NBC. The original Betamax had only a one-hour recording time. The major use for VCRs was expected to be the 'time shifting' of programmes for more convenient viewing. Although VCR controls made it possible for viewers to fast-forward through commercials, close attention had to be paid to avoid fast-forwarding through the programming.[29] Thus, time shifting was unlikely to significantly lower the revenues that would be derived by television broadcasters.[30] The Court concluded that time shifting was unlikely to harm copyright owners.

It was also fairly clear that the amount of time shifting would be small although the Court did not rely on this argument. For one thing, a single VCR could either make a recording or play one back, but it could not do both simultaneously. Combine this with the fact that the average household viewed six or seven hours of TV a day, including virtually uninterrupted viewing during prime time programming, and very quickly a constraint on behaviour takes hold. If a family was going to watch three hours of prime time television on Monday, say, they could not also watch a tape. If they watched a tape of the previous night's programming, they could not record the programming that was on while they watched the tape (unless they had a second VCR, which was quite rare at that time). Therefore, when it came to taping broadcast television, it was apparent that not that much taping was going to occur.

Of course, in hindsight we know that VCRs are primarily used to play back pre-recorded tapes. Ridiculing the difficulty of setting up VCRs to tape programmes unattended has become a staple of second rate comedians, and time shifting has not played the damaging role that copyright owners expected it to play. Nor is there much evidence that individuals have been copying pre-recorded video tapes to any large extent (it is the case that many pre-recorded tapes do have a fairly primitive anti-copy technology built in).

The difficulty of avoiding commercials, combined with the fact that the amount of time shifting had to be small, made it apparent that video-recording was not going to harm copyright owners substantially. Fortunately, the Court managed to get it right, albeit by a narrow, 5–4 vote. Several years later, Hollywood learned that by lowering the price of popular pre-recorded movies from $100 to $20, they could sell far more of them. Today, the sale and rental of videotaped movies generates more revenue than theatrical showings.[31] Hollywood's claim of impending doom was just another in a string of instances of copyright holders crying wolf.

Audio taping

Even without a high profile case such as Betamax, audio taping was a significant issue in the 1980s, as illustrated by the quote from Alan Greenspan at the beginning of this chapter. The basic mechanism of how indirect appropriability might work with respect to audio tapes was illustrated above.[32] As noted, controlling the variability in the number of copies made from each original was crucial if indirect appropriability was to work. It might have been the case that instances of home audio taping were common and similar enough to one another that no great harm was done to copyright owners. Despite dire predictions, the recording industry went on its merry way, appearing to merely substitute CDs for vinyl recordings as time progressed. During the period when sales of blank tapes were at their peak, the sales of albums per capita sustained their largest measurable increase in the last thirty years, from 3 to 5.5 copies per person (in the US). Inaction on the part of Congress and the presumption that most of the copying that was going on was either unstoppable and/or a legitimate exercise of fair use was almost certainly the correct decision.[33]

The US Congress, in response to the dire warnings from the recording industry, considered legislation, but it wasn't until a decade later that the Audio Home Recording Act of 1992 was passed, and it was largely concerned with digital tape recording. That act, which was considered a compromise between creators and users, allowed personal copying, but requires that recording devices include systems to prevent 'serial copying', i.e., making second generation copies, or copies of a copy. Additionally, the law had provisions requiring producers of these recording devices and recording mediums to pay a tariff for each unit produced or imported. The original target of this law, digital audio tapes (DAT), never achieved any serious market penetration. The devices that have achieved much greater penetration, CD writers on computers, are not yet considered recording devices, do not have these copy protection features, and the producers have not been paying duties. Since the anti-copying technology built into DAT players didn't envision the advent of MP3 files (which are very compressed versions of the digital file format found on CDs), the entire MP3 phenomenon would have bypassed these controls on copying anyway.

1.5   DIGITALISED NETWORKED COPYING: LESSONS FROM THE NAPSTER CASE

As we have seen, the entertainment industry has often exaggerated the damage to itself that each new copying technology would bring – from cassette tapes and videorecorders, to MP3s and Napster. Crying 'wolf' too many times, however, shouldn't by itself negate claims that a new technology will harm copyright owners. Napster and its descendants appear to be instances where real harm is a possibility.

The Napster program, created by then teenager Shawn Fanning, provided users the ability to search for songs encoded in the MP3 format and download those songs from other computer owners willing to provide those songs for transfer. Programs that allow one computer user to interact and exchange files located on other computers that are not full-time servers create a type of network that is known as peer-to-peer. Napster was a peer-to-peer based program, albeit with a central server to allow users to find one another. Napster's formal founding occurred in May of 1999.[34] Napster grew at an explosive pace and soon had tens of millions of users.[35] As Napster grew in popularity, so did potential investors, interested in the brand name and the millions of eyeballs reached by the Napster program and its website.

Some Napster supporters claimed that the online sharing of songs is a latter-day Betamax scenario. They argue that Napster users actually purchased more CDs because Napster allows listeners to sample music with which they might otherwise be unfamiliar. But given the fact that files downloaded from Napster were, or at least were soon to be, very good substitutes for the original, and since they could be 'burned' onto CDs and copied to increasingly popular MP3 players, it seems likely that these files would substitute for the actual purchase of authorised CDs.

Unlike the audiocassette example mentioned above, Napster-style copying seems unlikely to allow record companies to indirectly capture the value of the copies being made from legal originals since some originals will have dozens or hundreds of copies made, and other originals will have none. Nor does it seem likely that the amount of copying will be small – the current evidence, if it is to be believed, indicates that downloading is rampant. Finally, copies would seem likely to serve as substitutes for the purchase of originals in this case. The people making the copies are the very group that was expected to purchase originals.

The Napster evidence

In the Napster case (A&M Records v. Napster) a group of record companies brought suit in the Northern District of California against the leading online server based peer-to-peer system, Napster. The hearing occurred in the fall of 2000 and a preliminary injunction barring Napster from allowing users to download copyrighted files was granted in March of 2001. Napster shrivelled in usage and eventually declared bankruptcy, with a final dissolution occurring in the late summer of 2002.

The evidence put forward in the hearings on the preliminary injunction against Napster consisted of a set of expert reports that were mainly focused on whether or not Napster was likely to have increased or decreased sales of CDs in the market.[36]

In an attempt to demonstrate harm, the plaintiffs had as their centrepiece two reports, one that examined the pattern of CD sales in stores near college campuses (the Fine report) and the other a survey of college students asking them about their views on Napster and its impact on some of their musical habits (the Jay report).[37] The defence had its own survey of Napster users (the Fader report) and several critiques of the Fine report.

I have already expressed my misgivings with surveys. For one thing, surveys are self-reported and most Napster users were likely aware that

Napster was in legal difficulty. For this reason, survey respondents might have found it in their self-interest to minimise any evidence that Napster actually decreased their purchases of CDs. Further, even if respondents had told the truth, it is unclear they would have actually known what impact Napster had had on their behaviour. Unless they had tracked their expenses very carefully, their impressions of the impact of Napster on their behaviour may very well have been incorrect.

Statistical analysis of actual sales is really the only way to determine what Napster's impact was. Unfortunately, the statistical analysis of CD sales reported in the Fine report provided ambiguous answers. The Fine report examined sales at CD retailers near college campuses and compared the sales trends in those stores to those of other CD retailers.[38] The theory was that students at college campuses use the Internet and Napster more than do typical consumers. Therefore, any difference in the behaviour of sales between the two groups of stores was to be assigned to Napster. This focus is a very practical way of isolating the overall impact of Napster, even if imperfectly.

This particular design, although potentially useful, also had some serious problems. One major problem with the Fine study, as Napster's experts pointed out at length, was that it neglected to control for the impact that the arrival of online purchasing might have had on brick-and-mortar record stores near college campuses. It would be easy to confound the cause of decreased CD sales at local merchants if both online purchasing and downloads had occurred at the same time, which they had. Did Internet merchants such as Amazon and CDNOW increase their CD sales during the period of Napster's growth? Of course. Did college students merely shift their patronage from brick-and-mortar retail outlets to online retailers? Unfortunately, we do not know.

Unfortunately, the Fine study presents data that is very coarse: once-a-year quarterly data from the first quarter of 1997 to the first quarter of 2000. Given Napster's brief existence (it became publicly available in August of 1999) the data that is supposed to reveal Napster's influence amounts to but a single before and after snapshot of the impact of Napster.

What did the Fine study find? Fine focuses on the fact that from the first quarter of 1999 to the first quarter of 2000, a 12-month period during which Napster came into existence at about the midpoint, sales at brick-and-mortar CD stores near colleges fell by 2–3 percent but rose at other brick-and-mortar CD stores by approximately seven percent. From this Fine concludes that Napster has led to a decrease in sales of CDs. Fine's conclusions are undermined, however, by his data for earlier years. From 1998 to 1999, a year preceding Napster's existence, sales near colleges fell by about five percent while rising elsewhere by approximately three percent. Since year-to-year changes at brick-and-mortar CD retailers near colleges were not performing as well as other brick-and-mortar CD retailers prior to Napster's introduction, the fact that they continued to do relatively poorly after Napster's introduction can hardly be taken as evidence that Napster was responsible for the difference. The data, in fact, are more consistent with the theory that online sales were replacing brick-and-mortar sales than with the claim that Napster was hurting sales.[39]

Napster's experts preferred to focus on the continued robust growth of CD sales after Napster's birth. Certainly, this growth, the seven percent figure at brick-and-mortar stores reported above, is inconsistent with the idea of 'irreparable' harm claimed in the preliminary injunction, particularly considering that Napster downloads were reported to be four times as large as the number of legitimately purchased songs. But it hardly demonstrates that Napster had a benign impact on CD sales since there might well have been other factors at work and the increase in CD sales might have been even larger without Napster's impact.

All in all, the plaintiffs in the case failed to make as persuasive a case for harm as the defence did for the lack of harm.[40] But given the enormous amount of copying that Internet measurement companies reported, it should have been possible to identify a strong impact on CD sales if copying has any sort of serious impact. The alternative is to explain why copying didn't.

Since 2000, record sales have done far less well. Album units per capita fell by ten percent in 2001 and appear to have fallen another ten percent in 2002.[41] Although there are other possible reasons for this decline, the rise of MP3 downloads on the successors to Napster is the prime suspect.[42]

The reason that CD sales did not fall sooner might be because MP3 files were not initially very good substitutes for CDs since at first MP3 files could generally be played only on computers. That may help explain why Napster's negative impact on sales was not apparent. In the last few years, more computers have been equipped with CD writing hardware, allowing MP3 files to be converted back into CD formats playable through normal audio systems.

Even so, the size of the decline seems relatively small. With the number of CD-equivalent MP3s downloaded larger than the yearly sales of CDs, the recent decline still is consistent with a hypothesis that most downloaders still purchase most of their CDs.[43] That, in itself, would seem to be an interesting question to pursue.

1.6 SOME NEW HYPOTHESES WE NEED TO CONSIDER

Sometimes people don't act as we might predict. One reason could be that our economic models are just wrong about certain activities. Another possibility is that we are ascribing certain parameters to utility functions that are not appropriate.

In the case of copying, there seem to be many instances where behaviour doesn't fit nicely into our models. I am referring to the continued purchase of legitimate copies at the same time that, if the statistics are to be believed, a tidal wave of illicit copying is occurring. Even if some of these MP3s are substituting for the sale of CDs, the majority do not seem to be doing so.[44]

A fascinating experiment is being played out before us. One new factor that comes from having copying taking place over computer networks is the ability to count, with seemingly great precision, the amount of copying that is taking place. We do not yet know what the results of the massive MP3 downloading will be on the sale of CDs.[45] At this point, a negative impact appears to have finally made its presence felt, but its size implies that the copying, even of perfect duplicates, might not have the scope of negative impacts that might have been expected. Why would this be?

There are numerous possible reasons for this. I list some of them below. They suggest future research directions if we wish to discover more about this important topic.

1. The living room/computer dichotomy perseveres and is due more to the time and inconvenience costs of creating CDs than to the lack of CD burners. MP3s need to be converted back to native CD format for most CD players to read them. This might mean that MP3s are not such good substitutes for CDs. In this case, the record industry can be thankful for the inherent laziness of consumers.
2. People are honest and want to purchase legitimate CDs even when they have MP3s.
3. This degree of copying has gone on for a long time (with cassettes) so nothing is new. The only difference is that we now have a better measurement of how much copying is actually occurring. One problem with this hypothesis is that per capita sales of pre-recorded music went up rapidly during the heyday of audiocassettes.
4. Use of MP3s is a form of sampling for most users. This really only begs the question of why they are not used as a substitute, however.
5. A small number of individuals do a disproportionately large amount of copying and the reduced legitimate purchases from this group are too small to notice.

6. Copying is of oldies and hard to find songs, and is temporarily as high as it is because copiers have 40 years of old songs to dig up. It will eventually return to much lower levels.

1.7 CONCLUSION

The impact of pirating has often been misunderstood and copyright owners have frequently claimed harm when little or none was occurring. Economists have been good at theorising about these issues but much weaker at bringing data to bear on them.

Inexpensive copying technologies, which have been with us for at least 40 years, do not as yet appear to have caused great damage to copyright owners. Current damage estimates from MP3 downloads are still incomplete although evidence of harm is mounting. The magnitude of the harm is still far short of the magnitude of the copying and far from the theoretical predictions that might have been expected from all this copying.

Our understanding of why this is so, or if it is really so, leaves much to be desired. Our understanding of when copying might not be harmful would lead us to believe that use of MP3 files downloaded in peer-to-peer networks must be harmful. Although it is possible that the current generation of copying technologies will in fact live up to the dire predictions of doom forthcoming this time not only from the copyright owners but from theoretical models, the evidence doesn't yet support that claim. This issue will soon come to a head. It is important that we discover if there is something important going on in these markets that we have not put in our models.

NOTES

1. From Greenspan's testimony in 1983 on the Home Recording Act. Hearings before the Subcommittee on Patents, Copyrights and Trademarks, October 25, 1983.
2. Using share of GDP to measure importance can lead to very misleading results for goods that are inexpensive but nevertheless valuable. The diamond-water paradox, the fact that water is so important for life but so inexpensive, is a nice illustration of this potential problem. In the current instance, people listen to almost an hour of pre-recorded music a day yet spend very little of their money on pre-recorded music. The surplus is presumably very large.
3. This focus leaves aside the *moral rights* to that value that are so important under Napoleonic legal systems, but is in keeping with the practical purpose of intellectual property laws in countries such as the US.
4. One school of thought at the extremity of these debates is populated by those who believe that no copyright is required at all for an efficient functioning market for artistic and creative goods. The members of this group believe either that being first in the market provides sufficient appropriability that no additional legal protection is required, or, that

sufficient incentive to produce these products exists with other forms of remuneration, perhaps of a non-pecuniary nature, such that legal rules restricting the control of these products to their creators is unnecessary. The former strand of belief is represented by Arnold Plant, 'The Economic Aspects of Copyright in Books' *Economica* (May 1934): 167–95, and R. Hurt, and R. Schuchman, 'The Economic Rationale of Copyright,' *American Economic Review*, May 1966. The latter strand is represented by organisations such as the Free Software Foundation (at http://www.gnu.org/fsf/fsf.html).

5. In truth, there is virtually no empirical evidence on the extent to which copyright owners require remuneration to create their artistic works. However, the claim that production requires, to at least some extent, remuneration of the producers, is fully consistent with the usual market principles adduced from numerous other instances. Adam Smith's famous quote about how production doesn't come from the 'benevolence' of butchers, bakers, or candlestick makers, but instead derives from their self-interested behaviour, certainly has a plethora of empirical evidence to support it.

6. This restriction in use is sometimes carelessly referred to as a loss due to the 'monopoly' of the copyright owner. As Edmund Kitch correctly points out, providing property rights does not confer economic monopoly – which would imply that consumers have only a small number of alternative products that are not very good substitutes. See Edmund W. Kitch, 'Elementary and Persistent Errors in the Economic Analysis of Intellectual Property,' 53 *Vanderbilt Law Review*, November, 2000, p. 1727.

7. There are actually two definitions of public goods in the economics literature. The first defines them as goods with non-rivalrous consumption, as in the text. The other, more prevalent definition, is due to Paul Samuelson. It has an additional component to the non-rivalrous consumption assumption. The additional component is the inability to exclude individuals from consuming the good, as would be the case for national defence or any good without defined property rights. I believe this latter definition to be far less useful since it conflates two independent ideas that need not have anything to do with one another. Any good for which non-excludability is a property will not be efficiently produced in markets. And non-excludability usually has more to do with the laws and technology than with the good itself.

8. I include the number of cites to indicate just how small this literature is. Ordover, J.A. and R.D. Willig 'Optimal Provision of Journals Qua Sometimes Shared Goods,' *American Economic Review* 68 (3): 324–338, 1978 [17 cites]; Liebowitz, S.J. and Stephen E. Margolis, 'Journals As Shared Goods: Comment,' *American Economic Review*, June, 1982, pp. 597–602 [1]; Liebowitz 1981, see footnote 9 [9]; Novos, Ian E. and Michael Waldman, 'The Effects of Increased Copyright Protection: An Analytic Approach,' *Journal of Political Economy*, April 1984, pp. 236–246, Vol. 92, No. 2 [21]; Johnson, William R., 'The Economics of Copying,' *Journal of Political Economy* 93 (February 1985): 158–74 [22]; Liebowitz 1985, see footnote 9 [30].

9. The concept of indirect appropriability was first propounded in my 1981 monograph for the Canadian government 'The Impact Of Reprography On The Copyright System,' Copyright Revision Studies, Bureau Of Corporate Affairs, Ottawa, 1981 but the actual term 'indirect appropriability' was coined in my 1985 paper 'Copying And Indirect Appropriability: Photocopying Of Journals,' *Journal Of Political Economy*, October, 1985, pp. 945–957. The 1981 monograph is available at http://papers.ssrn.com/sol3/papers.cfm?cfid=5654230&abstract_id=250082

10. See, for example, Stan J. Liebowitz and Stephen E. Margolis 'Network Effects and Externalities' entry in *The New Palgrave's Dictionary of Economics and the Law*, Macmillan, 1998, Vol. 2, pp. 671–675.

11. See Lisa N. Takeyama, 'The Welfare Implications of Unauthorized Reproduction of Intellectual Property in the Presence of Demand Network Externalities,' *Journal of Industrial Economics*, 42, 1994, pp. 155–166; K.R. Conner and R.P. Rumelt, 'Software Piracy – An Analysis Of Protection Strategies,' *Management Science* 37 (2): Feb. 1991, pp. 125–139; Oz Shy and Jacques-Francois Thisse, 'A Strategic Approach to Software Protection,' *Journal of Economics and Management Strategy*, 8, 1999, pp. 163–190; Bakos

Y., E. Brynjolfsson and D. Lichtman, 'Shared Information Goods' *Journal Of Law & Economics* 42 (1): 117–155, Part 1, April 1999.

12. One could, however, alter the nature of imperfect appropriation before the advent of illicit copying so that after the network effects kicked in, appropriation from legitimate purchasers went up, but this would be a narrow theoretical possibility inconsistent with the flavour of this model.

13. This might seem to complicate the policy issues, but it actually simplifies them. If a technology decreased appropriability but increased payments to copyright holders, then it would both provide greater incentives to create the copyrighted material and also provide greater value to consumers who get to keep the non-appropriated value. Removing this technology would decrease value regarding both the number of titles and value received for each produced title, and couldn't be economically beneficial.

14. Unless, that is, the extra value that the marginal purchaser of originals receives is zero. This would seem unlikely, however.

15. Such payments are quite common and can be found in many countries including Canada and much of Europe. These payments would normally go to an organisation or collective representing copyright owners.

16. A typical view is espoused in the expert reports put forward by Napster in its defence. One of those reports, by Robert Hall, states on page 2: 'the exchanges of music facilitated by Napster stimulate the demand for the plaintiffs' CDs by allowing consumers to sample CDs and develop interest in CDs that they subsequently purchase.' The reports from Napster's experts can be found at: http://napster.com/pressroom/legal.html. Several, but not all, of the RIAA's reports can be found here: http://riaa.com/napster_legal.cfm.

17. In essence, the ability of consumers to better select CDs will rotate the market demand curve for CDs clockwise.

18. Another way of looking at this is to imagine that some CDs that are now purchased are 'mistakes' due to insufficient information. With the additional information provided by the Napster experience, fewer of these mistakes are made and fewer CDs are purchased.

19. By analogy, it is as if CDs were chocolate bars (or light bulbs). These bars are bought in order to eat the chocolate. If each bar were to contain more chocolate (or each bulb were to last twice as long), holding the price of a bar constant, the number of bars sold could go up or down depending on the elasticity of demand for the underlying product of interest, chocolate (or bulbs). If the elasticity of demand for chocolate were greater than one, the now lower effective price of chocolate would lead to an increase in total revenue spent on chocolate and with the price of bars constant the number of bars sold would increase. But if the demand for chocolate were inelastic, the number of bars sold would decrease. Although it could be argued that the demand for any particular CD is elastic, since otherwise the seller would find it profitable to raise its price, it need not be the case that overall demand for CDs is elastic. CD prices are not set individually (see Silva and Ramello in footnote 32) and CDs often would seem to be close enough substitutes for one another as to be classified in the same market.

20. The area under these demands measures total value, and better sampling increases the total value for any given number of CDs purchased.

21. For a review of the economic impacts of copying see Richard Watt, *Copyright and Economic Theory: Friends or Foes?*, Cheltenham, Edward Elgar: 2000. This is the most thorough review of this material that I have found. My only quibble is that he attributes most of the modelling that was originated in my 1981 monograph (see footnote 8) to Stanley Besen and Sheila Kirby, 'Private Copying, Appropriability, and Optimal Copying Royalties,' *Journal of Law and Economics*, 32, 1989, pp. 255–280.

22. One neglected point here is the price that is proffered to the pirate that would lead to his decision to forgo the product as opposed to making a legitimate purchase. So long as transaction costs do not make a market impracticable, see Wendy J. Gordon, 'Fair Use as Market Failure,' *Columbia Law Review*, 82, 1982, pp. 1600–1657, there is presumably some price above zero at which the pirate would make a purchase when confronted with this choice. The ability to price discriminate is crucial here and generally important in judging the impact of copying.

23. See 'Copyright and Home Copying: Technology: Challenges the Law,' October 1989, available at: http://www.wws.princeton.edu/~ota/ns20/year_f.html.
24. The claims in this section are documented in Liebowitz (1981, 1985).
25. It is also true that the Copyright Clearance Center (CCC) came into existence to allow copiers to make direct payments to copyright holders. But the improvement in the economic well-being of journal publishers occurred quite independent of the CCC, since the CCC was not organised until well after the market for journals had experienced enormous growth. See Liebowitz (1981) p. 64–68.
26. Book expenditures were more than three times that of periodicals from the 1940s until the 1960s when the ratio began to fall dramatically and fell to about 1:1 in the early 1980s (Liebowitz, 1985). In 1996, expenditures on serials outpaced that of books and bound periodicals by 8:5. See table 11 in 'The Status of Academic Libraries in the United States,' US Department of Education; Office of Educational Research and Improvement; NCES 2001–301; May 2001.
27. Universal Studios Inc. v. Sony Corporation of America, 1984. The original district court ruling was in 1979.
28. This material is based on Stan J. Liebowitz, 'The Betamax Case,' 1984, unpublished manuscript to be available on the Social Science Research Network (www.SSRN.com). I would like to express my gratitude to Wendy Gordon for finding an old copy of the paper.
29. It was also the case that remote controls at the time were tethered by wires to the VCR, thus making their use not very convenient.
30. Defendants in the Napster and MP3.com cases argued that their products 'space-shifted' music from a CD to a computer, a putative analogy to the time shifting that occurred in the Betamax case. A problem with this analogy is that without indirect appropriability, space shifting would decrease revenues to copyright owners, a result not analogous to that of time shifting since the VCR users still were exposed to commercials. A more important defect with this analogy in the case of Napster, is the fact that what Napster does is not actually space shifting. Since Napster users do not download their own files into their computer, but instead download files from others, it is better described as user shifting than space shifting. User shifting could, in other circumstances, be considered a euphemism for 'theft' except that the theft is from the copyright owner in the form of a lost potential sale, rather than the user who voluntarily provides the original to be copied.
31. According to the 2001 US Statistical Abstract, table 909, theatrical movie revenues were $32 per person per year in 1998 whereas revenues from pre-recorded movies were $92 per person.
32. Note that if unauthorised copying were prohibited, copyright holders might actually be worse off. In a world with no copying, record producers might find that consumers would be unwilling to pay as much for CDs, lowering revenues and profits (it is not clear how many, if any, of the former copiers would purchase legal copies). Silva and Ramello argue that unauthorised home taping helped producers largely by allowing low-valuation consumers to become music listeners and that these users later became the high-valuation listeners that record producers wanted. This would be a particularly slow type of exposure effect. Francesco Silva and Giovanni B. Ramello, 'Sound Recording Market: the Ambiguous Case of Copyright and Piracy,' 9 *Industrial and Corporate Change*, 2000, pp. 415–442.
33. See Stan J. Liebowitz, 'Record Sales, MP3 downloads, and the Annihilation Hypothesis' working paper available at http://wwwpub.utdallas.edu/~liebowit/knowledge_goods/records.pdf.
34. According to the February 12, 2001 issue of the Industry Standard available at: http://www.thestandard.com/article/display/0%2C1151%2C22139%2C00.html.
35. In February of 2001 2.8 billion files were downloaded, the peak number in its history. By April, after Napster was ordered to stop allowing copyrighted music to be transferred, the number had fallen to 1.6 billion. See 'Napster Downloads Drop 36 Percent,' *Reuters*, May 2, 2001.
36. These expert reports were conducted for the purposes of the hearing on the preliminary injunction to stop Napster from transmitting copyrighted materials and not for a complete

trial. Therefore, it is to be expected that these reports might not have the level of sophistication and completeness that might come about in a full case. Nevertheless, the hearing on the injunction had very high visibility and several of the experts were quite well known.

37. These reports are so named in the 'Memorandum And Order Re Admissibility Of Expert Reports' issued by the trial judge. Plaintiffs also had a declaration by Charles Robbins, a store owner claiming that Napster had largely destroyed his business, but this report was thoroughly discredited by the Fader report (mentioned below) who pointed out that the store had changed locations and switched from selling new CDs to selling used records and CDs during the period that its sales declined.

38. Actually, the Fine study looks at three groups of brick-and-mortar retailers: the overall set, a set of retailers near the 40 most heavily wired college campuses, and a set of retailers near college campuses that have banned Napster. Napster's expert Hall makes much of the fact that this latter group of retailers shows the same decrease in sales as the others, claiming that for this group sales should improve if Napster were having a negative impact on sales. Such a claim is unwarranted since we do not know how long Napster had been banned at these campuses and how successful the ban was.

39. The court also was aware of these problems: 'The Court finds some aspects of the Fine Report troubling – especially the fact that its shows a decline in retail sales prior to the launching of Napster. This limitation, combined with Fine's decision not to track Internet music sales, reduces the study's probative value.'

40. The judge's readings of the reports seem, to me, to have been biased against Napster even though I think her decision was in the end correct even if not supported by the evidence at hand.

41. See my working paper: 'Record Sales, MP3 downloads, and the Annihilation Hypothesis,' available at the Social Science Research Network.

42. Some other possibilities are: a) music is undergoing a period of artistic funk as happens from time to time; b) underground bands are taking a larger share of the market and their albums are not tracked by official RIAA statistics; c) consumers would rather play video games and watch movies, although my working paper argues that this is not the case; d) the recession, although my working paper demonstrates no relationship between record sales and income.

43. At its peak Napster downloads were estimated to be in the vicinity of 2.8 billion files per month, which would roughly be the equivalent of 250 million CDs per month. According to the Fine report, US national sales ran approximately 60 million CDs per month. So even with the slow bandwidths, the potential impact may have been large. See 'Music Downloads Soar,' *Reuters*, September 6, 2001, available at: http://news.cnet.com/news/0–1005–200–7080479.html.

44. The current numbers seem to indicate that each 6 or 7 CDs worth of MP3s might convert to reducing the sales of CDs by one unit.

45. The number most widely seen is on the order of 3 billion MP3 songs downloaded per month. Assuming ten songs on a CD, that works out to more than 3 billion CDs in a year. According to the IFPI, total sales of CDs world-wide are less than two and a half billion.

2. Pricing Information Goods in the Presence of Copying

Paul Belleflamme[1]

2.1 INTRODUCTION

Information can be defined very broadly as anything that can be digitized (i.e., encoded as a stream of bits), such as text, images, voice, data, audio and video (see Varian, 1998). Information is exchanged under a wide range of formats or packages (which are not necessarily digital). These formats are generically called *information goods*. Books, movies, music, magazines, databases, stock quotes, web pages, news all fall into this category.

Most information goods are expensive to produce but cheap to reproduce. This combination of high fixed costs and low (often negligible) marginal costs implies that information goods are inherently *nonrival*.[2] Moreover, because reproduction costs are also potentially very low *for anybody other* than the creator of the good, information goods might be *nonexcludable*, in the sense that one person cannot exclude another person from consuming the good in question.

The degree of excludability of an information good (and hence the creator's ability to appropriate the revenues from the production of the good) can be enhanced by legal authority (typically by the adoption of laws protecting intellectual property) or by technical means (e.g., cable broadcasts are encrypted, so-called 'unrippable' CDs have recently been marketed). However, complete excludability seems hard to achieve: simply specifying intellectual property laws does not ensure that they will be enforced; similarly, technical protective measures are often imperfect and can be 'cracked'. As a result, *illicit copying* (or piracy) cannot be completely avoided.

Over the last decade, the fast penetration of the Internet and the increased digitisation of information have turned piracy of information goods (in particular music, movies and software) into a topic of intense debate. A selection of news headlines gathered recently (February–March 2002) illustrates the current extent of the debate. These headlines are about (i) a proposed anti-piracy bill in the US that would ultimately require computer and consumer electronics companies to build piracy-prevention software into their products, (ii) a man facing jail in California for Web sales of CDs, (iii) the release of new peer-to-peer file-sharing softwares aiming to replace Napster, (iv) music distributors estimating that retail sales may be down as much as 10 percent during the past year as consumers shift to new technologies like copying CDs and downloading songs, (v) music companies settling a lawsuit with a CD consumer who alleged that the CD she purchased did not meet consumer expectations because it could not be played on a computer, or (vi) a Taiwanese Web site that offers access to a huge library of films for just $1 each (and which, understandably, has drawn Hollywood's ire).[3]

Not surprisingly, economists have recently shown a renewed interest in information goods piracy. Here follows a selection of recent working papers, which investigate a number of topical issues. Gayer and Shy (2001a) show the inefficiency of using hardware taxation to compensate copyright owners for infringements of their intellectual property (IP). In another article (Gayer and Shy, 2001b), the same authors investigate how producers of digital information goods can utilise the Internet's distribution channels, such as peer-to-peer systems, to enhance sales of their goods sold in store. The welfare implications of peer-to-peer distribution technologies are also the concern of Duchêne and Waelbroeck (2001); they show that the losses generated by illegal copies can be offset by the introduction of new products, which creates a positive surplus for their creators, as well as consumers. The idea that copyright infringement could be strategically promoted by creators is also explored by Ben-Shahar and Jacob (2001); they show, in a dynamic model, that creators might favour selective copyright enforcement as a form of predatory pricing in order to raise barriers to entry. Turning to policy matters, Harbaugh and Khemka (2001) argue that copyright enforcement targeted at high-value buyers raises copyright holder profits but, at the same time, increases piracy relative to no enforcement; therefore, they contend that either no enforcement or relatively extensive enforcement is the best policy against Internet piracy. In the same vein, Chen and Png (2001) examine how the government should set the fine for copying, tax on copying medium, and subsidy on legitimate purchases, while a monopoly publisher sets price and spending on detection. They conclude that government policies focussing on penalties alone would miss the social welfare optimum. Yoon (2001) also aims at determining the optimal level of copyright protection for an individual producer and for society as a whole. Finally, Hui *et al.* (2001) provide one of the rare attempts to estimate empirically the actual impact of piracy on the legitimate demand for information goods. Using international panel data for music CDs and cassettes, they find that the demand for both goods decreased with piracy.

These recent contributions revive the literature on the economics of copying and copyright, which was initiated some twenty years ago.[4] The seminal papers discussed the effects of photocopying and examined, among other things, how publishers can appropriate indirectly some revenues from illegitimate users (Novos and Waldman, 1984, Liebowitz, 1985, Johnson, 1985, and Besen and Kirby, 1989). The economics of IP protection was then addressed more generally by Landes and Posner (1989) and Besen and Raskind (1991). Both papers discuss the following trade-off between *ex ante* and *ex post* efficiency considerations. From an *ex ante* point of view, IP protection preserves the incentive to create information goods, which (as argued above) are inherently public (absent appropriate protection, creators might not be able to recoup their potentially high initial creation costs). On the other hand, IP rights encompass various potential inefficiencies from an *ex post* point of view (protection grants de facto monopoly rights, which generates the standard deadweight losses; also, by inhibiting imitation, IP rights might limit the creators' ability to borrow from, or build upon, earlier works, and thereby increase the cost of producing new ideas). A third wave of papers paid closer attention to software markets and introduced network effects in the analysis. Conner and Rumelt (1991), Takeyama (1994), and Shy and Thisse (1999) share the following argument: because piracy enlarges the installed base of users, it generates network effects that increase the legitimate users' willingness to pay for the software and, thereby, potentially raises the producer's profits. Finally, and more closely related to this paper, Watt (2000) has surveyed – and extensively supplemented – the literature on the economics of copyright.

The aim of the present paper is to address several of the themes studied so far in the literature within a simple and unified model. Like a number of recent papers, we use the framework proposed by Mussa and Rosen (1978) for modelling vertical (quality) differentiation: copies are seen as lower-quality alternatives to originals (i.e., if copies and originals were priced the same, all consumers would prefer originals). In a benchmark model, we consider the market for a single information good. A monopolist must set the price for the original good, taking into account that consumers can alternatively acquire a lower-quality copy at a constant cost. The optimal strategy for the monopolist can usefully be described by using Bain's (1956) taxonomy of an incumbent's behaviour in the face of an entry threat. Unless the quality/price ratio of copies is very low (meaning that copying exerts no threat and will therefore be 'blockaded'), the producer will have to modify his behaviour and decide whether to set a price low enough to 'deter' copying, or to 'accommodate' copying and make up for it by extracting a higher margin from fewer consumers of originals. Whatever the producer's optimal decision, we show that copying reduces the producer's profits but increases consumer surplus more than proportionally: as a result, copying (which amounts here to the provision of a cheaper and lower-quality alternative to a monopolised good) enhances social welfare.

The previous conclusion simply restates the *ex post* efficiency consideration of the traditional economic analysis of copying: if the information good was (legally or technically) better protected, the producer would fully enjoy his monopoly position and social welfare would be reduced. As argued above, such *ex post* inefficiency has to be balanced against *ex ante* considerations relating to creation costs. To incorporate this dimension, we extend the benchmark model by considering an arbitrary number of information goods. The Mussa-Rosen framework continues to apply for each information good. Moreover, to focus on the effects of copying, we assume that copying is the only source of interdependence between the demands for the various information goods. In particular, the goods are completely differentiated and consumers are assumed to have a sufficient (exogenous) budget to buy them all if they so wish.

Whether demands are interdependent or not depends on the nature of copying technology. In the spirit of Johnson (1985), we examine two extreme scenarios: the copying technology involves either a constant unit cost and no fixed cost, or a positive fixed cost and no marginal cost. In the former case, demands for originals are completely independent of one another: all producers act thus like the single-good monopolist of the benchmark model. Assuming a fixed creation cost that varies through producers, we can derive the number of information goods that are created at the long run, free-entry, equilibrium. Obviously, copying reduces this number. We can then balance *ex ante* and *ex post* efficiency considerations and show that copying is likely to damage welfare in the long run (unless copies are a poor alternative to originals and/or are expensive to acquire).

The picture changes dramatically when the copying technology involves only a positive fixed cost. The demands for originals now become interdependent because consumers base their decision to invest in the copying technology on the cost of this technology and on the prices of *all* originals. Therefore, copying introduces strategic interaction between the producers of originals whom everything else otherwise separates. This strategic interaction makes the producers' pricing behaviour (which takes the form of a simultaneous Bertrand game) more interesting – but also much more intricate – to analyse. Due to the complexity of the system of demands, we are unable to provide a complete characterisation of the set of Bertrand-Nash equilibria. We shed, nevertheless, some light on symmetric equilibria in which copying is either blockaded, deterred or accommodated. We show, in particular, that the latter two equilibria rely on a set of rather restrictive conditions, as the incentives for unilateral deviation are high: producers tend to free-ride (by setting higher prices) when it comes to deterring copying, or they tend to undercut when it comes to accommodating copying.

The rest of the chapter is organised as follows. In Section 2.2, we lay out a benchmark model with a single information good and we analyse the short-run welfare effects of copying. Then, in Section 2.3, we extend the benchmark model towards a multi-good setting in two different ways. First, we assume that copying involves a constant marginal cost and no fixed cost. Under this assumption, we examine the long-run welfare effects of copying. Second, we assume instead that copying involves a positive fixed cost and no marginal cost. Due to the intricacies of the model under this alternative assumption, we leave welfare considerations aside and try instead to unravel the complex situation of strategic interaction that copying induces between producers of originals. We conclude and propose an agenda for future research in Section 2.4.

2.2　　A SIMPLE SINGLE GOOD MODEL

We start by considering a very simple market for an information good supplied by a single producer.[5] We use the framework proposed by Mussa and Rosen (1978) for modelling vertical (quality) differentiation. There is a continuum of potential users who are characterised by their valuation, θ, for the information good. We assume that θ is uniformly distributed on the interval [0,1]. Each user can obtain the information good in two different ways. One possibility is to *buy* the legitimate product (an 'original') at price p. Originals are produced by a single producer at zero marginal cost. The alternative is to acquire a *copy* of the product at a cost $c \geq 0$ (in both cases, each user consumes at most one unit of the information good). The two variants of the information good are indexed by their quality: let $s_o > 0$ denote the quality of an original and s_c (with $0 < s_c < s_o$), the quality of a copy.

The cost c can be thought of as the price of an illegitimate copy sold by some large-scale pirate, or as the cost of the copying medium. We discuss the precise nature of this cost at the end of the present section (for the moment, we refer to any means of using the information good without buying an original as 'copying'). The assumption that the quality of a copy is lower than the quality of an original ($s_c < s_o$) is common (see, e.g., Gayer and Shy, 2001a) and may be justified in several ways. In the case of analog reproduction, copies represent poor substitutes to originals. For instance, even the best photocopying loses information such as fine lines, fine print and true colour images. Furthermore, copies of analog media are rather costly to distribute. Although this is no longer true for digital reproduction, originals might still provide users with a higher level of services, insofar as they are bundled with valuable complementary products which can hardly be obtained otherwise.[6]

Accordingly, a user indexed by θ has a utility function defined by

$$U_\theta = \begin{cases} \theta s_o - p & \text{if buying an original,} \\ \theta s_c - c & \text{if copying,} \\ 0 & \text{if not using the information good.} \end{cases} \quad (2.1)$$

We assume that $c < s_c$, so that the user with the highest valuation for the product is better off copying than not using the product (otherwise, copying would trivially not be an issue).

Users' behaviour

A user indexed by θ will buy the legitimate product under the following two conditions. First, buying must provide a higher utility than not using: $\theta s_o \geq p$. Second, buying must provide a higher utility than copying: $\theta s_o - p \geq \theta s_c - c$, which is equivalent to

$$\theta \geq \theta_1 \equiv \frac{p-c}{s_o - s_c}.$$

Clearly, the latter inequality cannot be met if originals are too expensive (if $p > s_o - s_c + c$, $\theta_1 > 1$ and no user buys an original).

On the other hand, the user θ will copy the product if the previous condition is reversed ($\theta < \theta_1$) and if copying provides a higher utility than not using: $\theta s_c - c \geq 0$, or

$$\theta \geq \theta_2 \equiv \frac{c}{s_c}.$$

These two inequalities are incompatible, meaning that no user finds it profitable to copy, if the price of originals is low enough. Indeed,

$p \leq \overline{p} \equiv cs_o/s_c$ implies that $\theta_1 \leq \theta_2$. Note that the 'limit price' $\overline{p}$ decreases as copies become relatively more attractive (i.e., as c and s_o/s_c decrease).

There are thus three demand regimes. First, if the price of the legitimate product is too high (if $p \geq s_o - s_c + c$), then no user will buy the legitimate product.[7] Second, for intermediate prices (i.e., for $cs_o/s_c \leq p \leq s_o - s_c + c$), users indexed on $[\theta_1, 1]$ buy the legitimate product, users indexed on $[\theta_2, \theta_1]$ copy the product, others do not use. Finally, for low prices (i.e., for $0 \leq p \leq cs_o/s_c$), users indexed on $[p/s_o, 1]$ buy the legitimate product, whilst others do not use. Collecting the previous results, we can write the demand function for originals

$$D(p) = \begin{cases} 0 & \text{for } p \geq s_o - s_c + c, \\ 1 - \dfrac{p-c}{s_o - s_c} & \text{for } \dfrac{cs_o}{s_c} \leq p \leq s_o - s_c + c, \\ 1 - \dfrac{p}{s_o} & \text{for } 0 \leq p \leq \dfrac{cs_o}{s_c}. \end{cases} \tag{2.2}$$

Producer's behaviour

The producer's problem is to choose the price p of the legitimate product so as to maximise profits, $pD(p)$, with demand given by expression (2.2). The producer's problem is complicated by the fact that some users are better off copying the product once the price exceeds some threshold. There is thus a kink in the demand curve and the producer has to choose in which segment of the demand curve to operate. By analogy with Bain's (1956) taxonomy of an incumbent's behaviour in the face of an entry threat, we will say that the producer is either able to 'blockade' copying, or that he must decide whether to 'deter' copying or 'accommodate' it. Let us now define and compare these three options.

The producer blockades or deters copying. By setting a price sufficiently low, the producer can eliminate copying. The producer's maximization program is then

$$\max_{p} \pi(p) = p\left(1 - \frac{p}{s_o}\right) \text{ s.t. } p \leq \frac{cs_o}{s_c}. \tag{2.3}$$

The unconstrained profit-maximising price and profits are easily computed as

$$p_b = \frac{s_o}{2}, \pi_b = \frac{s_o}{4}.$$

This solution meets the constraints if and only if $c \geq s_c/2$. In this case, we can say that copying is actually *blockaded*: the producer safely sets his price as if copying was not a threat. Otherwise, copying cannot be blockaded but the producer modifies his behaviour to successfully *deter* copying: he will choose the highest price compatible with the constraints, i.e.

$$p_d = \frac{cs_o}{s_c}, \text{ which implies } \pi_d = \frac{cs_o(s_c - c)}{s_c^2}.$$

The producer accommodates copying. The other option is to set a higher price and tolerate copying. The producer's program becomes

$$\max_p \pi(p) = p\left(1 - \frac{p - c}{s_o - s_c}\right) \text{s.t.} \frac{cs_o}{s_c} \leq p \leq s_o - s_c + c. \qquad (2.4)$$

Here, the unconstrained profit-maximising price is equal to

$$p_a = \frac{s_o - s_c + c}{2}, \text{ which implies } \pi_a = \frac{(s_o - s_c + c)^2}{4(s_o - s_c)}.$$

This solution satisfies the constraints if and only if

$$\frac{s_o - s_c + c}{2} \geq \frac{cs_o}{s_c} \Leftrightarrow c \leq \frac{s_c(s_o - s_c)}{2s_o - s_c}.$$

If the latter condition is not met, it is easily checked that the corner solution is equivalent to copying deterrence.

Blockade, deter or accommodate? Collecting the previous results, we observe that the producer's optimal strategy depends on the relative attractiveness of copies (i.e., for a given value of s_o, on the values of c and s_c), as summarised in Proposition 2.1 and illustrated in Figure 2.1 (for $s_o = 1$).

Proposition 2.1 The producer's profit-maximisation price is

$$p_b = \frac{s_o}{2}, \qquad \text{for } \frac{s_c}{2} \leq c \leq s_c \qquad \text{(copying is blockaded)},$$

$$p_d = \frac{cs_o}{s_c}, \qquad \text{for } \frac{s_c(s_o - s_c)}{2s_o - s_c} \leq c \leq \frac{s_c}{2} \qquad \text{(copying is deterred)},$$

$$p_a = \frac{s_o - s_c + c}{2}, \qquad \text{for } 0 \leq c \leq \frac{s_c(s_o - s_c)}{2s_o - s_c} \qquad \text{(copying is accommodated)}.$$

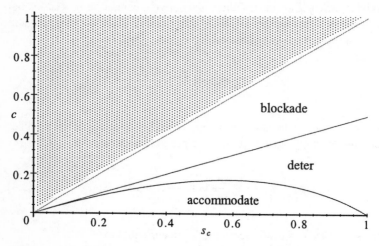

Figure 2.1 Producer's optimal strategy in the single-good model with $s_o = 1$

Welfare effects of copying in the short run

Now that we have characterised the producer's pricing behaviour, we are in a position to examine how copying affects welfare. Our *benchmark* is a hypothetical economy where copying would be infeasible; in this case, the producer would act as an unconstrained monopolist, which corresponds to the case of blockaded copying (defined above by the condition $c \geq s_c/2$). Consumer surplus (S_b) and social welfare (W_b) in this hypothetical economy are readily computed as follows

$$S_b = \int_{p_b/s_o}^{1} (\theta s_o - p)\, d\theta = s_o/8,$$

$$W_b = \pi_b + S_b = 3s_o/8.$$

Copies are relatively unattractive. If $s_c(s_o - s_c)/(2s_o - s_c) \leq c \leq s_c/2$, we know that the producer prefers to *deter* copying. In this case, the only effect of copying is to force the producer to set a lower price than the one he would set if copying exerted no threat ($p_d < p_b$). Although more users buy the legitimate product, the producer's profit falls, meaning that copying hurts him ($\pi_d < \pi_b$). However, the consumer surplus clearly increases and this increase offsets the reduction in profit, which results in an increase in social welfare (computed as the sum of consumer surplus and producer's profit): $W_d = s_o(s_c^2 - c^2)/2s_c^2 > W_b = 3s_o/8$. The possibility of making copies can be seen as a potential competition that disciplines the producer of the legitimate product in a welfare-enhancing way.

Copies are relatively attractive. For lower values of c (i.e., $c \leq s_c(s_o - s_c)/(2s_o - s_c)$), copying is *accommodated*. The welfare analysis becomes a bit more complicated and also more instructive. There are now users who get a positive surplus by copying the legitimate product and they have to be taken into account in the welfare analysis. Consider first the producer. Being just a threat (as in the previous case) or an actual fact (as here), copying has the same effect on the producer's pricing behaviour: price has to go down (though less than under the deterrence option, $p_d < p_a < p_b$) and the increased demand this generates is not enough to prevent profit from falling ($\pi_a < \pi_b$). So, as in the previous case, the producer of the legitimate product suffers from copying. It can be argued that, from a social point of view, there is no reason to worry about the previous result: copying has the advantage of breaking down the monopoly the producer would enjoy otherwise. As we have just shown, copying leads to a lower price and a higher quantity consumed: legitimate users enjoy thus a larger surplus. Moreover, if we also incorporate the surplus enjoyed by illegal users, we find again *that copying has a positive impact on welfare*.

To establish this result, we compute the surplus for legitimate and illegitimate users when copying is accommodated respectively as

$$SL_a = \int_{\frac{p_a-c}{s_o-s_c}}^{1} (\theta s_o - p_a)\, d\theta \text{ and } SI_a = \int_{c/s_c}^{\frac{p_a-c}{s_o-s_c}} (\theta s_c - c)\, d\theta.$$

We then compute social welfare as $W_a = \pi_a + S_a$, with $S_a = SL_a + SI_a$, and we observe that

$$W_a - W_b = \frac{1}{8} \frac{(4s_o - s_c)c^2 + s_c(s_c - 2s_c)(s_o - s_c)}{s_c(s_o - s_c)} > 0. \quad (2.5)$$

We record the above two findings in the following proposition.

Proposition 2.2 So long as it cannot be blockaded, copying improves social welfare in the short run.

The intuition underlying Proposition 2.2 is obvious. By introducing a cheaper imperfect substitute for originals, copying reduces the monopoly power of the producer and, thereby, increases social welfare. This result must, however, be qualified in one important way. Most generally, the creation of information goods involves substantive fixed 'first-copy' costs. So far, we have abstracted this fixed cost away by assuming implicitly that the producer could cover it even when he had to accommodate copying. That is, noting the fixed creation cost by F, we have assumed that $\pi_a > F$. It is only under that assumption that the above result holds. Indeed, if we had instead that $\pi_b > F > \pi_a$, the producer would not create the information good if he had no other choice than to accommodate copying. In such a case, copying would clearly reduce social welfare.

2.3   THE LONG-RUN PERSPECTIVE WITH MULTIPLE GOODS

In this section, we examine the previous issue more closely by considering a multi-product framework. More precisely, we extend the benchmark model by assuming that users now have the possibility to consume from a set G of information goods (with $|G| \geq 2$). As before, consumers choose, for each product, to either buy an original, make a copy, or not consume at all. We make the following assumptions about these three possibilities.

- *No use.* As before, the utility from not consuming any variant of a product is normalised to zero.
- *Originals.* Each original is produced by a separate producer, at zero marginal cost. All originals are assumed to be (i) of the same quality (indexed by $s_o > 0$) and (ii) perfectly (horizontally) differentiated. Hence, if consumer θ buys a unit of each product in the subset $M \subseteq G$, her utility is given by $m\theta s_o - \sum_{i \in M} p_i$, where $m = |M|$ and p_i is the price charged for product i.
- *Copies.* As for originals, all copies are assumed to be (i) of the same quality (indexed by $0 < s_c < s_o$) and (ii) perfectly (horizontally) differentiated. Regarding their cost, we consider, in the spirit of Johnson (1985), two extreme scenarios: the copying technology involves either a constant unit cost ($c > 0$) and no fixed cost ('*variable copying cost*' model), or a fixed cost ($C > 0$) and no marginal cost ('*fixed copying cost*'

model). Supposing that consumer θ copies a unit of each product in the subset $M \subseteq G$, her utility is given by $m(\theta s_c - c)$ in the variable copying cost model, and by $m\theta s_c - C$ in the fixed copying cost model.[8]

It is important to note that, in order to focus on the effects of copying, we assume that copying is the only potential source of interdependence between the demands for the various information goods: as just mentioned, the goods are completely differentiated; moreover, we have implicitly assumed that consumers have a sufficient (exogenous) budget to buy all information goods if they so wish.

We examine the variable and fixed copying cost models in turn. As will become apparent, the two models lead to very different results. In the former model, the demands for any particular original are completely independent from one another; we can therefore replicate the analysis of the single-good model. On the other hand, as noted by Johnson (1985), the fixed cost of the copying technology introduces some interdependence between the demands for originals: consumers will indeed base their decision to invest in the copying technology on the cost of this technology and on the prices of *all* originals.

Multiple goods and variable copying costs

We first analyse the pricing game between an arbitrary number of producers. As will be shown, with perfectly differentiated information goods and variable copying costs, the analysis remains very simple. That allows us to analyse the entry game by incorporating a fixed creation cost. Considering the equilibrium of this two-stage game, we calculate the (long run) welfare implications of copying.

The pricing game. When the copying technology involves a constant unit cost per copy, it is easily seen that the producers of originals act independently of one another, in accordance with the optimal behaviour derived in the single-good model. To see this more clearly, let us define the condition for a typical consumer to buy an original of good i:

$$\text{Consumer } \theta \text{ buys good } i \in G \Leftrightarrow$$
$$\theta s_o - p_i + \sum_{j \neq i} \max\{\theta s_o - p_j, \theta s_c - c, 0\} \geq$$
$$\max\{\theta s_c - c, 0\} + \sum_{j \neq i} \max\{\theta s_o - p_j, \theta s_c - c, 0\}.$$

In words, the condition says that consumer θ must be better off purchasing good i (and choosing whichever use is the most profitable for the other goods) than copying or not using good i (and still choosing whichever use is the most profitable for the other goods). Because originals are perfectly differentiated and because each copy of an additional good costs the same constant amount, the 'whichever use is the most profitable for the other goods' does not depend on which use is made of good i. Therefore, the above condition boils down to $\theta s_o - p_i \geq \max\{\theta s_c - c, 0\}$, which generates the same demand schedule as in the single-good model, as given by expression (2.2). It follows that, because all producers set the same price, users decide either to buy all information goods or to copy them all (or not to use any). To ease the exposition (and without loss of generality), we set $s_o = 1$ for the rest of this section.

Entry game. Now, let F_i denote the fixed creation cost faced by producer i. We assume that the cost of creation differs among producers (some producers are more efficient at creating equivalent works than others). Specifically, we assume that F_i is drawn from some cumulative distribution function $H(F)$. This function is assumed to be smooth and increasing on the interval $[\phi, \phi+1]$, with $0 < \phi < \pi_b = 1/4 < \phi+1$, $H(\phi) = 0$, and $H(\phi+1) = 1$. For given gross profits π, only the producers with $F_i \leq \pi$ will create their information good. Hence, the total number of works created, $n(\pi)$, is endogenously determined as

$$n(\pi) = \begin{cases} H(\pi) & \text{if } \pi \geq \phi, \\ 0 & \text{otherwise.} \end{cases}$$

Clearly, $n(\pi)$ is an increasing function of π. Therefore, we now have a better picture of the social trade-off that copying induces: on the one hand, copying increases social welfare per work (as demonstrated by (2.5) above) but, on the other hand, copying reduces profits per work and, thereby, the number of works created.

Welfare effects of copying in the long run

We now investigate how these two effects balance when copying is either deterred or accommodated. Global welfare (denoted Ω) is now defined as welfare per work (i.e., producer's net profit plus consumer surplus) multiplied by the number of works created (if any). To ease the computations, we make the simplifying assumptions that the fixed cost of creation is distributed uniformly and that there is a unit mass of potential producers. We have thus that $n(\pi) = \max\{\pi - \phi, 0\}$. Global welfare is then computed as (with $k=b, d, a$)

$$\Omega_k = \max\left\{\int_0^{\pi_k} (S_k + \pi_k - F)\, dF,\ 0\right\}$$
$$= \max\left\{\tfrac{1}{2}(\pi_k - \phi)(2S_k + \pi_k - \phi),\ 0\right\}.$$

Copying is deterred. In the region of parameters where copying is deterred, we find that the difference $\Omega_d - \Omega_b$ is equivalent in sign to $4c^2 - 2s_c(3 - 2\phi) + s_c^2(1 + 2\phi)$. Solving this polynomial for c, we find two positive roots for all admissible values of s_c and ϕ, the large root being larger than $s_c/2$ (above which copying is blockaded). We can therefore conclude that copying deterrence improves global welfare when c is larger than some threshold, $c_d(s_c, \phi)$, which can be shown to be an increasing function of s_c and ϕ.

Copying is accommodated. A similar conclusion is drawn in the region of parameters where copying is accommodated. A few lines of computations establish that *it is only when the relative quality of copies is low enough that copying improves global welfare*. More precisely, for having $\Omega_a > \Omega_b$, c must be larger than some threshold value, $c_a(s_c, \phi)$, which can also be shown to be an increasing function of s_c and ϕ. Moreover, if s_c is larger than some lower bound (which decreases with ϕ), $c_a(s_c, \phi)$ is larger than the boundary $s_c(1 - s_c)/(2 - s_c)$ and, therefore, cannot be reached.

The previous results are loosely recorded in the next proposition.

Proposition 2.3 When copying involves a constant unit cost and no fixed cost, copying (be it accommodated or deterred) damages welfare in the long run, unless copies are a poor alternative to originals and/or are expensive to acquire.

The intuition behind Proposition 2.3 goes as follows. When copies are a poor alternative to originals and/or are expensive to acquire, (actual or threatening) copying erodes only slightly the monopoly power of the producers. Hence, there is only a small reduction in the number of works created, which is more than compensated by the increase in the consumer surplus per work. Yet, the opposite prevails as soon as copies become more attractive. Figure 2.2 illustrates these results. In areas D_1, D_2 and D_3, producers limit price to deter copying. Copying deterrence improves global welfare in area D_1, but deteriorates it in areas D_2 and D_3 (worse, in area D_3, the supply of creative works is zero when copying has to be deterred). In areas A_1, A_2 and A_3, producers accommodate copying. Similarly, copying accommodation improves welfare in area A_1, but deteriorates it in areas A_2 and A_3 (with no work created in area A_3). Figure 2.2 is drawn for $\phi = 0.05$; if we increase ϕ , the curves separating the A and D areas shift up, which reduces the region of parameters where copying has a positive long-run effect on welfare.

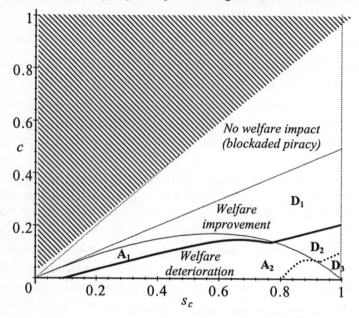

Figure 2.2 Long-run welfare effects in the variable copying cost model

Multiple goods and fixed copying costs

When copying involves a fixed cost rather than variable costs, the demands for originals become interdependent since consumers base their decision to invest in the copying technology on the cost of this technology and on the prices of *all* originals. To see the difference with the previous case, recall the condition for consumer θ to purchase an original of good i. The condition is still that consumer θ must be better off purchasing good i (and choosing whichever use is the most profitable for the other goods) than copying or not using good i (and still choosing whichever use is the most profitable for the other goods). What changes is that the most profitable uses for all other goods does now depend on whether the consumer copies good i or not: if she does, then the cost of copying any number of other goods is zero instead of C.

Users' behavior

What is the utility consumer θ can obtain depending on her use of good i? Suppose that $n \geq 2$ goods are available and let p_i denote the price of good i. Since we will be looking for symmetric Bertrand-Nash equilibria, we assume that all other goods are priced the same: $p_j = p \ \forall j \neq i$. To restrict slightly the number of cases to consider, we make the following assumptions

$$s_c < C < ns_c \tag{2.6}$$

$$ns_c > s_o \tag{2.7}$$

Assumption (2.6) simply says that no consumer will invest in the copying technology if it is to copy only one original ($\theta s_c - C < 0 \ \forall \theta$), but that some consumers might invest if it is to copy all n originals ($\exists \theta \text{ s.t. } \theta ns_c - C > 0$). According to assumption (2.7), the quality differential between originals and copies is not too large (in particular, n copies are worth at least one original).

We can now determine the most profitable use for the other goods depending on the use made of good i. If the consumer either purchases or does not use good i, it is easily seen that the consumer will treat all the other goods alike: she will either buy, copy or not use them all, leaving her respectively with an additional utility of $(n-1)(\theta s_o - p)$, $(n-1)\theta s_c - C$ or 0.[9] On the other hand, if she copies good i, not using the other goods clearly becomes a dominated option (because the copying technology has been purchased). Hence, the consumer will either purchase or copy all other goods, leaving her respectively with an additional utility of $(n-1)(\theta s_o - p)$ or $(n-1)\theta s_c$. Putting these findings together, we summarise the user's behaviour in the following lemma.

Lemma 2.1 Facing a price vector $(p_i, (p_j = p)_{j \neq i})$ and a copying technology described by (2.6), a consumer of type θ purchases original i if and only if

$$\theta s_o - p_i + \max\{(n-1)(\theta s_o - p), (n-1)\theta s_c - C, 0\}$$
$$\geq \max\{(n-1)(\theta s_o - p), n\theta s_c - C, 0\}. \tag{2.8}$$

The next logical steps would be, first, to use condition (2.8) to derive the demand for original i, and next to use the demand function to maximise firm i's profit and, thereby, derive firm i's reaction function. Though feasible, this task turns out to be extremely cumbersome (an idea of the intricacies involved is given below). We thus renounce to try and give a complete characterisation of symmetric Bertrand-Nash equilibria in the model with fixed copying costs. Instead, we provide conditions under which some specific equilibria might (or might not) occur. The price vectors we investigate correspond to the three patterns examined in the model with variable copying costs: blockaded, deterred and accommodated copying. At the end of the section, we emphasise the effects of strategic interaction by comparing the symmetric Bertrand-Nash equilibria with the outcomes that would be observed under collusion (or if we were in the presence of a multiproduct monopolist).

Blockaded copying

As before, copying is blockaded if market conditions are such that copying exerts no threat on producers of originals even when each of them behaves as an unconstrained monopolist. Because, when there is no threat of copying, the demands for the n originals are completely independent of one another, each producer chooses p_i so as to maximise $\pi_i = p_i(1 - p_i/s_o)$. That is, each firm charges $p_b = s_o/2$. The next proposition states under which condition this behaviour constitutes a Nash equilibrium.[10]

Proposition 2.4 (Blockaded copying) Each firm charging the monopoly price, $p_b = s_o/2$, is a Nash equilibrium of the game with fixed copying costs if and only if $C \geq (n/2)s_c$.

The message of Proposition 2.4 is clear: if the most eager consumer needs to copy more than half of the available originals to recoup the fixed cost of the copying technology, then copying exerts no threat on the producers of originals, who can safely charge the monopoly price.

Let us now turn to the situations where copying *cannot* be blockaded; that is, we assume that $C < (n/2)s_c$. In these situations, copying becomes an actual threat and producers of originals have to decide whether it is more profitable for them to deter or to accommodate copying. As already stressed, the increasing returns to scale in the copying technology transform the choice between copying deterrence or accommodation into a problem of *interdependent* decision making.

Deterred copying

To deter copying of its product, firm i must find the 'limit price', $\bar{p}_i$, under which all consumers find the original product relatively more attractive than the copy. In the simple model of Sections 2.2 and 2.3, firm i could solve this problem in total independence: for consumers to prefer copying to both purchasing and not using, it had to be the case (respectively) that $\theta < (p-c)/(s_o - s_c)$ and $\theta \geq c/s_c$. Clearly, any price below $\bar{p} = cs_o/s_c$ made the joint satisfaction of the two conditions impossible and, thereby, deterred copying.

Now, when copying involves a fixed cost, firm i's limit price will clearly depend on the prices set by the other firms. Intuitively, copying should be harder to deter (in the sense that firm i will have to decrease its price further) the higher the price set by the other firms, and conversely. Indeed, if the other firms set a relatively high price, consumers will have more incentive to invest in the copying technology and, because of increasing returns to scale, they will tend to copy product i along with the other products, unless the price of i is considerably lower.

To formalise the intuition, we first determine firm i's limit price supposing that all other firms charge the same arbitrary price p. That is, we characterise the function $\bar{p}_i(p)$. We then look for a fixed point of this function and determine under which conditions all firms charging the corresponding price is a Bertrand-Nash equilibrium, in which copying is (collectively) deterred.

Individual limit pricing. Suppose $p_j = p \ \forall j \neq i$. We want to determine the limit price $\bar{p}_i(p)$ under which no consumer finds it profitable to copy product i. Note that firm i is concerned only by deterring the copying of its own product. Yet, as we will see, its behaviour will depend on whether consumers copy or not the other products.

Using the analysis of the user behaviour (summarised in Lemma 2.1), let us define the utility for user θ of, respectively, buying or copying product i

$$U_B(\theta, p_i, p) = \theta s_o - p_i + \underbrace{max\{(n-1)(\theta s_o - p), (n-1)\theta s_c - C, 0\}}_{MB}$$

$$U_C(\theta, p_i, p) = \theta s_c - C + \underbrace{max\{(n-1)(\theta s_o - p), (n-1)\theta s_c\}}_{MC}$$

By comparing the exact values of *MB* and *MC*, we can express the precise form of the condition $U_B(\theta, p_i, p) \geq U_C(\theta, p_i, p)$ for all configurations of prices and parameters. The next step consists in deriving for which values of

p_i the condition is always met in the corresponding region of parameters. Straightforward computations establish the results of this two-step procedure. Lemma 2.2 states firm i's limit pricing behaviour.

Lemma 2.2 To deter copying of its product, firm i needs to set its price as follows

$$p_i \leq \bar{p}_i(p) = \begin{cases} \dfrac{(s_o - s_c)C}{(n-1)s_c} & \text{if } p > \dfrac{s_o C}{(n-1)s_c}, \\[3mm] C - \dfrac{ns_c - s_o}{s_o}p & \text{if } p \leq \dfrac{s_o C}{(n-1)s_c}. \end{cases}$$

Lemma 2.2 confirms our intuition. When the other products are relatively expensive ($p > s_o C/[(n-1)s_c]$), firm i must price much lower than the other firms ($\bar{p}_i(p) = (s_o - s_c)C/[(n-1)s_c] < p$) in order to discourage copying of its product. On the other hand, as the other products become cheaper, the constraint on i's price relaxes: for $p \leq s_o C/[(n-1)s_c]$, $\bar{p}_i(p)$ decreases with p, and eventually becomes lower than p.

   Symmetric limit pricing. The previous findings illustrate how firms tend to free-ride on each other when it comes to deterring copying.[11] The only situation for which no free-riding is observed is when all firms charge the *symmetric limit price* defined by $\bar{p}_i(p) = p$, i.e.,

$$p = p_d \equiv \frac{Cs_o}{ns_c}.$$

This symmetric limit price appears as a likely candidate for an equilibrium with deterred copying. In the next proposition, we state the conditions under which this conjecture proves right. We first define the following threshold

$$C_d \equiv \frac{n^2 s_c (s_o - s_c)}{(n+1)s_o - ns_c}. \tag{2.9}$$

Note that $C_d < (n/2)s_c \Leftrightarrow ns_c > (n-1)s_o$.

Proposition 2.5 (Deterred copying) Each firm charging the symmetric limit price, $p_d = (C s_o)/(n s_c)$, is a Nash equilibrium of the game with fixed copying costs if and only if $n s_c > (n-1)s_o$ and $C_d \leq C < (n/2)s_c$.

The intuition behind Proposition 2.5 goes as follows. Suppose the other firms charge the symmetric limit price and consider the 'would-be pirates' (i.e., those users for whom $n\theta s_c > C$). We want to determine how those users maximise their utility when they do not purchase product i. Actually, their behaviour depends on the relative quality of copies. When the quality of copies is relatively low ($n s_c \leq (n-1)s_o$), the would-be pirates prefer not using i and purchasing all other products, rather than copying all n products. Hence, there is no threat of copying for product i and firm i sees no reason to limit its price. On the other hand, when the quality of copies is relatively high ($n s_c > (n-1)s_o$), the would-be pirates become actual pirates if they decide not to purchase product i. To deter them to do so, firm i must therefore set a low enough price. How low this price should be depends on the fixed copying cost. If this cost is high ($C > (n/2)s_c$), firm i can free-ride on the other firms' effort and set the monopoly price. If the copying cost is low ($C < C_d$), the opposite prevails: firm i must set a limit price below p_d. Finally, for intermediary fixed copying costs, firm i optimally deters copying by charging the same price as the other firms.

Accommodated copying

We now look for a symmetric Bertrand-Nash equilibrium in which producers find it optimal to tolerate copying. If all originals are priced the same, users will treat all goods alike. That is, the market will be segmented as in the variable copying cost model: low-θ users will not use any good, intermediate-θ users will copy all goods, and high-θ users will purchase all goods. We need now to determine which common price will achieve such market segmentation.

Suppose that $(n-1)$ firms charge a common price p and that firm i chooses some price p_i in the vicinity of p. To derive the demand facing firm i, we need to identify the user who is indifferent between buying or copying all goods. This user is identified by a value of $\tilde{\theta}$ such that $\tilde{\theta} s_o - p_i + (n-1)(\tilde{\theta} s_o - p) = n\tilde{\theta} s_c - C$, that is

$$\tilde{\theta} = \frac{p_i + (n-1)p - C}{n(s_o - s_c)}.$$

Because all users with a larger θ then $\tilde{\theta}$ will buy all goods, the demand facing firm i (as long as p_i is not too different from p) is given by

$$D_i(p_i, p) = 1 - \frac{p_i + (n-1)p - C}{n(s_o - s_c)}. \qquad (2.10)$$

Maximising $\pi_i(p_i, p) = D_i(p_i, p)p_i$ over p_i yields firm i's reaction function

$$R_i(p) = \tfrac{1}{2}(n(s_o - s_c) - (n-1)p + C).$$

It is instructive to note that reaction functions are downward sloping. This means that, in the present situation, prices are *strategic substitutes* (using the terminology of Bulow *et al.*, 1985). This suggests that, when copying is accommodated, different originals are complements, whereas originals and copies are substitutes.

Our candidate for a symmetric Bertrand-Nash equilibrium with accommodated copying, p_a, must solve $p_a = R_i(p_a)$, which yields

$$p_a = \frac{n(s_o - s_c) + C}{n+1}, \qquad (2.11)$$

$$\text{and } \pi_a = \frac{(n(s_o - s_c) + C)^2}{(n+1)^2 n(s_o - s_c)}. \qquad (2.12)$$

Naturally, we need now to investigate under which conditions all firms charging p_a is indeed a Nash equilibrium. More precisely, supposing that all other firms charge p_a, we must make sure that firm i has no incentive to set a price that would bring it to a different segment of demand than (2.10). To do so, we need to determine exactly what the alternative demand segments look like and when they are observed. As before, the starting point is condition (2.8), which rewrites here as

$$\theta s_o - p_i + R_a \geq L_a,$$
$$\text{with } \begin{cases} R_a \equiv max\{(n-1)(\theta s_o - p_a), (n-1)\theta s_c - C, 0\} \\ L_a \equiv max\{(n-1)(\theta s_o - p_a), n\theta s_c - C, 0\}. \end{cases}$$

We start, in the next lemma, by discarding a whole range of cases in which symmetric copying accommodation *cannot* be a Nash equilibrium.

Lemma 2.3 If $C \geq C_d$, then all firms charging p_a is not a Bertrand-Nash equilibrium.

The result of Lemma 2.3 is not surprising. By analogy with the variable copying cost model, we expect copying accommodation to lead to higher prices than copying deterrence when accommodation is chosen as the most profitable option by the firms. That is, if accommodation is an equilibrium, then $p_a > p_d$ which is equivalent to $C < C_d$. If the opposite is true, copying is costly enough to allow firm i to behave as an unconstrained monopolist when all other firms charge p_a.

Lemma 2.3 provides a necessary condition (i.e., $C < C_d$) for a symmetric equilibrium with copying accommodation. However, this condition is far from sufficient: additional conditions have to be met to prevent unilateral deviations. Unfortunately, these conditions are very tedious to derive as they depend on the precise configuration of demand (which depends itself on the values of the parameters, in a much more complicated way than for $C \geq C_d$).

As a consequence, we shall not attempt here to give a precise characterisation of the configurations of parameters where symmetric copying accommodation is a Nash equilibrium. Instead, we will focus on one specific case and use it to illustrate the nature of unilateral deviations from the accommodation price p_a.

Let us consider an example where copies are a relatively poor, but inexpensive, alternative to originals ($ns_c < (n-1)s_o$ and $s_c < C << C_d$). In such situations, it can be shown that, when all other firms set the accommodation price p_a, the demand function facing firm i takes up to five different forms according to the range of prices. Letting the price p_i roam from s_o (above which there is no demand) to zero, we observe the following five demand segments.

- As soon as the price of original i is lower than s_o, some users are willing to purchase the good. In the first segment, the price is so high that only the most eager (i.e., high-θ) consumers purchase good i. These consumers decide whether to purchase good i or not to use it, given that they purchase anyway all the other, cheaper ($p_i > p_a$), information goods.
- The second segment, D_2, is given by expression (2.10) and is obtained when p_i is set in the vicinity of p_a. On top of the previous high-θ consumers, firm i also attracts consumers who prefer purchasing rather than copying all goods.
- By further decreasing its price, firm i manages to attract some lower-θ consumers. These consumers are resolute to copy all other goods no matter what; but if p_i is sufficiently low, they might prefer the original of good i to the copy. This generates segment D_3.

- Finally, a further decrease in p_i attracts the very low-θ consumers who decide to purchase and use only good i. Segment D_4 (resp. D_5) corresponds to the case where these consumers' second most-preferred option is to copy all goods (resp. not to use any good).

We want now to derive the profit-maximising price for firm i. To determine the global maximum, we must compare the values of the local maxima corresponding to the five different demand segments. Table 2.1 summarises the results obtained for the following specific parameter values: $n=8$, $s_o=1$, $s_c=0.5$, and $C=1.2$.

As we can see from the table, firm i *does not* respond to the other firms setting the accommodation price p_a by setting p_a as well. The firm is better off setting a much lower price, which allows it to reach a flatter segment of demand (D_4 instead of D_2). So doing, the firm attracts those consumers who are better off copying all goods rather than purchasing them all, but who are ready to purchase good i (and still copy all other goods) if it is sufficiently cheaper than the other goods. The increase in the number of users makes up for the decrease in the unit price, which makes the deviation profitable.

Table 2.1 Local maxima for given parameter values

Demand segment	Range of prices	Local maximum	Maximum profit
$D_1 = 1 - p_i$	$p_i \in [0.948, 1]$	$p_i = 0.948$	$\pi = 0.049$
$D_2 = \frac{13}{45} - \frac{1}{4} p_i$	$p_i \in [0.406, 0.948]$	$p_i = p_a = 0.578$	$\pi = 0.083$
$D_3 = 1 - 2 p_i$	$p_i \in [0.3, 0.406]$	$p_i = 0.3$	$\pi = 0.12$
$D_4 = \frac{7}{5} - \frac{10}{3} p_i$	$p_i \in [0.086, 0.3]$	$p_i = 0.21$	$\pi = 0.147$
$D_5 = 1 - p_i$	$p_i \in [0, 0.086]$	$p_i = 0.086$	$\pi = 0.078$

Comparison with the collusive outcome

To emphasise the effects of strategic interaction, let us compare the previous results with what would be observed if the n producers of information goods were able to collude. The cartel of producers would act as a multiproduct monopolist, maximising its profit by setting a price for all n information products. As in the previous section, we focus on symmetric price vectors.[12] Letting q denote the common price for the n products, it is easy to develop expression (2.8) and derive the demand function for any product as

$$D(q) = \begin{cases} 0 & \text{for } q \geq s_o - s_c + \frac{C}{n}, \\ 1 - \frac{nq - C}{n(s_o - s_c)} & \text{for } \frac{Cs_o}{ns_c} \leq q \leq s_o - s_c + \frac{C}{n}, \\ 1 - \frac{q}{s_o} & \text{for } q \leq \frac{Cs_o}{ns_c}. \end{cases}$$

The cartel therefore faces the following twofold maximisation program

- either $max_q \ nq\left(1 - \frac{nq - C}{n(s_o - s_c)}\right)$ s.t. $\frac{Cs_o}{ns_c} \leq q \leq s_o - s_c + \frac{C}{n}$,

- or $max_q \ nq\left(1 - \frac{q}{s_o}\right)$ s.t. $q \leq \frac{Cs_o}{ns_c}$.

Recalling expressions (2.3) and (2.4), it is quickly seen that this program is equivalent to the single producer's program of Section 2.2, up to the following change of variable: $C \equiv nc$. The cartel's optimal behaviour (with symmetric pricing) can thus be read from Proposition 2.1:

$$q_b = \frac{s_o}{2}, \qquad \text{for } \frac{ns_c}{2} \leq C \leq ns_c \qquad \text{(copying blockaded)},$$

$$q_d = \frac{Cs_o}{ns_c}, \qquad \text{for } \frac{ns_c(s_o - s_c)}{2s_o - s_c} \leq C \leq \frac{ns_c}{2} \qquad \text{(copying deterred)}, \qquad (2.13)$$

$$q_a = \frac{n(s_o - s_c) + C}{2n}, \qquad \text{for } 0 \leq C \leq \frac{ns_c(s_o - s_c)}{2s_o - s_c} \qquad \text{(copying accommodated)}.$$

Let us now compare the results in (2.13) with the ones recorded in Propositions 2.4 and 2.5, and in expressions (2.11) and (2.12). As far as *blockaded copying* is concerned, there is no difference: $p_b = q_b$ and these prices are optimal in the same region of parameters. This is not surprising as strategic interaction disappears when copying exerts no threat. Regarding *copying deterrence*, strategic interaction introduces a noticeable difference: it does not modify the limit price ($p_d = q_d$) but it narrows the region of parameters where entry deterrence is the optimal conduct. The latter point is established by comparing (2.9) with (2.13) and checking that

$$\frac{ns_c(s_o - s_c)}{2s_o - s_c} < C_d \equiv \frac{n^2 s_c(s_o - s_c)}{(n+1)s_o - ns_c}.$$

In other words, collusion makes deterrence of copying easier (i.e., optimal for a wider range of costs of the copying technology). This is another illustration of the free-riding problem described above.

Finally, as far as *copying accommodation* is concerned, the impact of strategic interaction appears also quite clearly. A quick comparison of (2.11) and (2.13) reveals that $p_a > q_a$. Moreover, computing a firm's profit when copying is collusively accommodated and comparing it to expression (2.12), one observes that collusion yields higher profits. To understand why, under strategic interaction, higher prices lead to lower profits, it suffices to recall from the previous section that prices are strategic substitutes under copying accommodation.

2.4 CONCLUSION

Information goods fall in the category of *public goods with exclusion*, that is, 'public goods the consumption of which by individuals can be controlled, measured and subjected to payment or other contractual limitation' (Drèze, 1980). Exclusion can be achieved through legal authority and/or technical means. However, simply specifying intellectual property laws does not ensure that they will be enforced; similarly, technical protective measures are often imperfect and can be 'cracked'. As a result, illicit copying (or piracy) cannot be completely avoided. It is therefore extremely important to understand how copying affects the demand for legitimate information goods and the pricing behaviour of their producers. It is equally important, for policy purposes, to identify clearly the welfare implications of copying.

This chapter addresses these questions within a simple, unified model of competition between originals and copies. We use the vertical differentiation framework proposed by Mussa and Rosen (1978): copies are seen as lower quality alternatives to originals. In a benchmark model, we consider the market for a single information good. We identify conditions about the relative attractiveness of copies under which the producer either can safely ignore the threat of copying, or has to modify his behaviour and decide whether to 'deter' or 'accommodate' copying. In the latter two cases, we show that the competition created by copying enhances social welfare. However, the welfare increase comes at the expense of the producer's profits, which might then be insufficient to cover the (potentially high) fixed cost of creation.

To account for this traditional trade-off between *ex ante* and *ex post* efficiency considerations, we extend the benchmark model by considering an arbitrary number of information goods. We consider two distinct scenarios. In the first scenario, we assume that the copying technology involves a constant unit cost and no fixed cost. Under this assumption, demands for originals are completely independent of one another and we can simply reproduce the results of the benchmark model. Assuming a fixed creation cost that varies through producers, we derive the free-entry number of information goods. We can then balance *ex ante* and *ex post* efficiency considerations and show that copying is likely to damage welfare in the long run (unless copies are a poor alternative to originals and/or are expensive to acquire).

The second scenario assumes that the copying technology involves a positive fixed cost and no marginal cost. The demands for originals are now interdependent because consumers base their decision to copy on the fixed cost of the technology and on the prices of *all* originals. Due to the complexity of the demand system and of the resulting strategic pricing game, we are unable to provide a complete characterisation of the set of Bertrand-Nash equilibria. However, we closely examine symmetric equilibria in which copying is either blockaded, deterred or accommodated. We show, in particular, that the latter two equilibria rely on a set of rather restrictive conditions, as the incentives for unilateral deviation are high: producers tend to free-ride (by setting higher prices) when it comes to deterring copying, or they tend to undercut when it comes to accommodating copying.

The directions for future research are twofold. First, and quite obviously, more work needs to be done on the fixed copying cost model. The characterisation of Bertrand-Nash equilibria should be completed. We need not only to characterise all symmetric equilibria in pure strategies, but also to envision asymmetric equilibria and mixed strategies. It is indeed very likely that mixed strategies cannot be dispensed with in this context: because demand functions are discontinuous, payoff functions may fail to be quasi-concave, which may lead to the non-existence of an equilibrium in pure strategies (see Dasgupta and Maskin, 1986).

The second direction for future research consists in exploiting the two versions of the model to address topical issues. For instance, we could try and assess the effects of enhancing technical protective measures for information goods. A case of interest is the so-called 'unrippable' CD. Because the technical measure seems to decrease the quality of *both* originals and copies (it is claimed that these CDs cannot be copied but, at the same time, legitimate users might not be able to play the CD on the device of their choice), it is not a priori evident that such strategy is profitable.

NOTES

1. I am grateful to Giulio Fella, Stan Liebowitz, Ruth Towse and Richard Watt for their comments and suggestions on an earlier draft.
2. Nonrivalness in consumption is usually defined by saying that the consumption possibilities of one individual do not depend on the quantities consumed by others. This is equivalent to saying that, for any given level of production, the marginal cost of providing the good to an additional consumer is zero.

3. Sources: (i) *Proposed anti-piracy bill draws fire*, by Stefanie Olsen (CNET News.com, March 25, 2002), (ii) *Man faces jail for Web sales of CDs*, by Lisa M. Bowman (CNET News.com, March 22, 2002), (iii) *Goodbye Napster, Hello Morpheus (and Audiogalaxy and Kazaa and Grokster...)* by Erick Schonfeld (Business2.com, March 15, 2002), (iv) *Digital Music Fight Traps Retailers*, by Benny Evangelista (Newsfactor.com, March 12, 2002), (v) *Consumer claims victory in CD lawsuit*, by Lisa M. Bowman (CNET News.com, February 22, 2002), (vi) *Plug pulled on site selling $1 movies*, by John Borland (CNET News.com, February 19, 2002).
4. With the notable exception of Plant (1934).
5. Yoon (2001) independently developed a similar model.
6. For instance, many pieces of software come with free manuals and supporting services, or with discounts on upgrades, all advantages that users who pirate the software will have to acquire at a positive price.
7. Although users indexed on $[\theta_2,1]$ are theoretically better off when they copy the product, copying does not appear as a feasible option when no originals circulate.
8. A more general formulation for the cost of copying would be: $c(x)=C+cx$ (with both C and c positive). It will become apparent below that the model quickly becomes hardly tractable under this general cost function.
9. To see this, let x (resp. y) denote the number of goods other than i purchased (resp. copied), with x and y comprised between 0 and $n-1$. If x is non-negative, then any situation $0<y<n-1-x$ is dominated. Indeed, $y>0$ implies that the copying technology has been purchased, meaning that copying an additional good makes the consumer strictly better off than not using this good. Now, because the utility from a purchased or a copied good is constant, any situation with $x>0$ and $y=n-1-x>0$ is also dominated. We are thus left with three possibilities: (i) $x=n-1$, $y=0$, (ii) $x=0$, $y=n-1$, and (iii) $x=y=0$.
10. The proofs of the subsequent propositions and lemmata can be found in the working paper version of this chapter (available at http://www.econ.qmw.ac.uk/papers/wp.htm).
11. Several authors have studied entry deterrence with several incumbents and investigate whether entry deterrence is a public good. The results they reach are ambiguous. As Applebaum and Weber (1992) summarise, precommitments by an incumbent impose both direct and indirect externalities on other incumbents. This explains why it is generally impossible to determine whether 'investment in deterrence' is too high, or too low relative to the collusive solution.
12. As the n products are identical, it seems natural to suppose that they are priced the same. However, we leave it to future research to establish that this is indeed an optimal strategy for the multiproduct monopolist.

REFERENCES

Applebaum, E. and S. Weber (1992), 'A Note on the Free Rider Problem in Oligopoly', *Economics Letters*, **40**: 473–480.
Bain, J. (1956), *Barriers to New Competition*. Cambridge, MA: Harvard Business Press.
Ben-Shahar, D. and A. Jacob (2001), 'Preach for a Breach: Selective Enforcement of Copyrights as an Optimal Monopolistic Behavior', Mimeo, Arison School of Business, Israel. Available at http://www.faculty.idc.ac.il/ben-shahar/papers/Preach%20for%20ª%20Breach%2020.07.01.pdf

Besen, S.M. and S.N. Kirby (1989), 'Private Copying, Appropriability, and Optimal Copying Royalties', *Journal of Law and Economics*, **32**: 255–280.

Besen, S.M. and L.J. Raskind (1991), An Introduction to the Law and Economics of Intellectual Property', *Journal of Economic Perspectives*, **5**: 3–27.

Bulow, J., J. Geanakoplos and P. Klemperer (1985), 'Multimarket Oligopoly: Strategic Substitutes and Complements', *Journal of Political Economy*, **93**: 488–511.

Chen, Y. and I. Png (2001), 'Software Pricing and Copyright Enforcement', Mimeo, National University of Singapore. Available at http://www.comp.nus.edu.sg/~ipng/research/copy_is1.pdf

Conner, K.R. and R.P. Rumelt (1991), 'Software Copying: An Analysis of Protection Strategies', *Management Science*, **37**: 125–139.

Dasgupta, P. and E. Maskin (1986), 'The Existence of Equilibrium in Discontinuous Economic Games. I: Theory', *Review of Economic Studies*, **53**: 1–26.

Drèze, J. (1980), 'Public Goods with Exclusion', *Journal of Public Economics*, **13**: 15–24.

Duchêne, A. and P. Waelbroeck (2001), 'Welfare Implications of Illegal Copies: The Case of Peer-to-Peer Distribution Technologies', Mimeo, CERAS-ENPC, Paris. Available at http://homepages.ulb.ac.be/~pwaelbro/paper11.pdf

Gayer, A. and O. Shy (2001a), 'Copyright Protection and Hardware Taxation', Mimeo, University of Haifa. Available at http://econ.haifa.ac.il/~ozshy/copyingtax15.pdf

Gayer, A. and O. Shy (2001b), 'Internet, Peer-to-Peer, and Intellectual Property in Markets for Digital Products', Mimeo, University of Haifa. Available at http://econ.haifa.ac.il/~ozshy/freeware18.pdf

Harbaugh, R. and R. Khemka (2001), 'Does Copyright Enforcement Encourage Copying?', Mimeo, Claremont McKenna College. Available at http://econ.mckenna.edu/papers/2000-14.pdf

Hui, K.L., I. Png and Y. Cui (2001), 'Copying and the Legitimate Demand for Recorded Music', Mimeo, National University of Singapore. Available at http://www.comp.nus.edu.sg/~ipng/research/copying_text_2.pdf

Johnson, W.R. (1985), 'The Economics of Copying', *Journal of Political Economy*, **93**: 158–174.

Landes, W.M. and R.A. Posner (1989), 'An Economic Analysis of Copyright Law', *Journal of Legal Studies*, **38**: 325–363.

Liebowitz, S.J. (1985), 'Copying and Indirect Appropriability: Photocopying of Journals', *Journal of Political Economy*, **93**: 945–957.

Mussa, M. and S. Rosen (1978), 'Monopoly and Product Quality', *Journal of Economic Theory*, **18**: 301–317.

Novos, I.E. and M. Waldman (1984), 'The Effects of Increased Copyright Protection: An Analytical Approach', *Journal of Political Economy*, **92**: 236–246.

Plant, A. (1934), 'The Economic Aspects of Copyright in Books', *Economica*, **1**: 167–195.

Shy, O. and J.-F. Thisse (1999), 'A Strategic Approach to Software Protection', *Journal of Economics and Management Strategy*, **8**: 163–190.

Takeyama, L.N. (1994), 'The Welfare Implications of Unauthorized Reproduction of Intellectual Property in the Presence of Network Externalities', *Journal of Industrial Economics*, **62**: 155–166.

Varian, H.R. (1998), 'Markets for Information Goods', Mimeo, University of California, Berkeley. Available at http://www.sims.berkeley.edu/~hal /Papers/japan/japan.pdf

Watt, R. (2000), *Copyright and Economic Theory. Friends or Foes?* Cheltenham and Northampton, MA: Edward Elgar.

Yoon, K. (2001), 'The Optimal Level of Copyright Protection', Mimeo, Department of Economics, Korea University. Available at http://econ.korea.ac.kr/~kiho/works/cp2_dist.pdf

3. Piracy, Asymmetric Information and Product Quality

Lisa N. Takeyama[1]

3.1 INTRODUCTION

This paper considers the potential benefits of 'unauthorised' reproduction of intellectual property when the quality of the product is *a priori* unknown by consumers. In particular, this paper explicitly considers the possibility that consumption of copies of intellectual property (e.g., pirated software) can reveal the product quality of originals when they are experience goods. If copies convey information about the quality of originals, but copies are themselves imperfect substitutes in use for originals, once a consumer has obtained full information by consuming a copy, the consumer may subsequently decide to purchase an original whenever the net surplus from doing so exceeds the value of a copy. Starting from this premise, the paper then explores the potential benefits of copying in the presence of informational asymmetries about product quality.

Surprisingly, most previous studies of unauthorised copying (e.g., Novos and Waldman 1984, Liebowitz 1985, Besen and Kirby 1989, Conner and Rumelt 1991, and Takeyama 1994, 1997) have examined the welfare implications of copying without considering the information value of reproductions. While Takeyama (1999) does consider the possibility that copies convey information, the information imperfection is symmetric across both sides of the market. Thus, the issue of adverse selection does not arise. In the present paper, this issue is of primary interest.

In this paper, the potential information value of piracy is modelled in the context of a two-period, durable goods monopoly with asymmetric information about product quality. A priori, all consumers are uncertain about the quality of the firm's product. However, consumers who pirate the good in period one become fully informed by the start of period two. These individuals may then have an increased willingness to pay for an original, conditional upon the degree of substitutability of copies for originals and the quality of the good. Consequently, copiers play a critical role: effectively, they become potential 'repeat purchasers' in a durable goods monopoly framework that does not, in general, readily lend itself to repeat purchases.

The results of the paper are as follows: first, owing to its information value, the presence of copying may not only benefit the firm, it can also produce a Pareto improvement in social welfare. In particular, the presence of copying has the potential to solve the adverse selection problem. That is, there exist conditions under which, without copying, a high quality firm is unable to earn positive profits because of uncertainty and the presence of low quality, but with copying, earns positive profits in either a pooling or separating equilibrium. The intuition is that copying generates 'repeat purchases' only when quality is high, which admits the possibility that any first-period losses from sales to uninformed consumers may be more than offset by the subsequent second-period profits from sales to the informed copiers.

Second, the paper demonstrates that because subsequent purchases of high quality originals by informed copiers is qualitatively similar to the notion of repeat purchases in a non-durable goods framework, the presence of copying can be sufficient in and of itself to induce revelation of product quality a priori. In particular, the paper considers the existence of separating equilibria that do not require wasteful expenditures (e.g., advertising) or strategic introductory pricing for support (see for example, Milgrom and Roberts 1986, and Kihlstrom and Riordan 1984).[2] In these equilibria, the presence of copying effectively 'weeds out' low quality, as producers of low quality are unable to earn positive profits with copying at any feasible price, making unnecessary wasteful expenditures or other costly signals of high quality. Consequently, copying can enable a high quality firm to produce and sell at the full information price, when without copying, the firm might not produce. At the same time, copying can preempt the introduction of low quality goods for which production is socially undesirable.

Empirically, the results of the paper are consistent with the observation that many firms do actively promote consumer reproduction of their intellectual property. For example, many software publishers distribute free 'giveaways' of scaled-down ('light') versions of their programs on the Internet. Indeed, by facilitating the ability of consumers to obtain cheap copies (at zero marginal cost to the firm), the growth and expansion of the Internet itself may also expand the possibilities for the provision of high quality intellectual property.

Perhaps more importantly, the paper suggests that standard measures of 'harm' from unauthorised reproduction of intellectual property may be overstated, as such measures do not account for the information value of copies. Without copying, high quality may be absent entirely from the market, or low quality may be produced when it is socially undesirable. Still, even if without copying the high quality firm is able successfully to signal or guarantee its product quality, any measure of the relative harm from copying should also net out the additional costs that must be spent in the absence of copying to signal or guarantee product quality. Hence, the true opportunity cost of reproductions made by consumers may very well be zero.[3]

3.2   THE BASIC MODEL WITH NO COPYING

In this section, I develop a basic two-period model for the case in which the intellectual property good is prohibitively costly for consumers to reproduce. Let q^i, $i = H, L$ represent the quality of the product, where high quality is given by $q^H > 0$ and low quality is given by $q^L = 0$. The product is produced by a monopolist who has an initial exogenous endowment of capacity for producing quality, such that the firm is either a 'high quality' type or a 'low quality' type. A high quality firm must spend an amount F^H to develop intellectual property with quality q^H, while a low quality firm must spend an amount F^L to develop intellectual property with quality q^L. Quality is exogenous in the sense that a low quality firm does not have the capacity to produce high quality and a high quality firm does not produce low quality.[4] Only the firm knows the true quality of its product (i.e., consumers do not). A firm producing a good with quality q^i has a constant marginal production cost, c^i, where no restrictions will be imposed on the relative sizes of c^H and c^L or F^H and F^L.[5]

Consumers live for two periods and arrive only at the beginning of the first period. They are homogeneous in that each consumer's per-period valuation of the durable good with quality q^i is given by V^i, where $V^H > V^L = 0$.[6] While consumers do not know prior to consumption the quality of the good, they hold a common a priori belief that the good is of high quality with probability p. Since consumers are risk neutral, the most they are willing to pay in the first period to consume the good over the two periods is $pV^H + \beta pV^H$, where β is the discount factor, common to consumers and the firm.

Although the model is cast in a two-period framework, the homogeneity of consumers and the absence of repeat purchases implies that the model in this case is essentially static. That is, the firm maximises profits by making all of its sales in the first period.[7] Regardless of whether the firm produces low or high quality, the maximal price that can be charged is $pV^H + \beta pV^H$. The corresponding profits are given by

$$\Pi^H = pV^H + \beta pV^H - c^H - F^H \tag{3.1}$$

if quality is high, while if quality is low, the firm receives profits of

$$\Pi^L = pV^H + \beta pV^H - c^L - F^L, \tag{3.2}$$

where the size of the market has been normalised to one.

Notice that when $\Pi^H > 0$ for $p = 1$, but $\Pi^H < 0$ and $\Pi^L > 0$ given consumers' actual beliefs, $p < 1$, we have the classic adverse selection problem. That is, the high quality firm will not find it profitable to produce because of uncertainty and the presence of low quality. Since the focus of this paper is on copying and its impact upon the adverse selection problem, the above conditions will be assumed.

3.3   THE BASIC MODEL WITH COPYING

I now extend the model of Section 3.2 by allowing the monopolist's product to be easily reproducible by consumers. Specifically, I assume that consumers are able to reproduce one unit of the firm's product at a common copying cost of P_c. Copies are supplied competitively, and therefore, P_c represents the marginal reproduction cost, assumed to be constant. Furthermore, I allow for the possibility that copies are imperfect substitutes for originals. Such imperfect substitutability may result from actual tangible differences (e.g., unauthorised copies of software do not come with user manuals or technical support), consumers' disutility of being dishonest, or it may result from expected consequences of being caught violating the copyright. While consumers have homogeneous valuations of originals, they have heterogeneous valuations of reproductions.[8] I now make the assumption that there are two types of consumers: copiers and non-copiers, where γ represents the fraction of consumers who are non-copiers. Let V_c^i be a copier's per-period valuation of a copy made from an original with quality q^i, where $V_c^H > V_c^L = 0$. Let $D^i = (V^i - V_c^i)$ represent the copier's one-period surplus of originals over copies when the product's quality is q^i. A copier's expected single-period differential valuation of originals over copies is therefore given by pD^H. Copiers will therefore choose to copy rather than purchase an original in period one whenever the first period price of originals, P_1, exceeds $(1 + \beta)pD^H + P_c$. That is, they receive more expected surplus from copying than purchasing.[9] Importantly, if a copier does choose to copy rather than purchase in period one, by the start of the second period, the copier knows whether the good is of high or low quality, since the copier has had the opportunity to consume the quality revealing copy in the first period. A copier may then wish to purchase an original in the second period, provided the good is of high quality and the second period price, P_2, is less than D^H.

Next, consider the pricing decision of the firm. Suppose that the firm sells only to non-copiers in period one, while the remaining consumers consume copies in the first period. In period two, the high quality firm will make sales to the informed copiers by charging them their one-period differential valuation of originals over copies, or $P_2 = D^H$. In equilibrium, the low quality firm makes no period two sales; however, in the second period, the firm continues to rationally maximise profits in any deviation from the equilibrium path. This implies that should a non-copier ever defer their purchase from period one, the low quality firm must mimic the pricing of the high quality firm or else be revealed as low quality. Therefore, in considering whether or not to defer purchasing until period two, a non-copier will rationally assume $P_2 = D^H$, regardless of whether the firm produces the low or high quality good. This implies that whenever $D^H < pV^H$ the rationally forecasted second period price is less than the consumer's one-period expected valuation of an original, and therefore, the intertemporal self-selection constraint preventing non-copiers from deferring their purchase until period two is binding. Consequently, to induce non-copiers to purchase in period one, the firm can charge a maximal first period price of $P_1 = pV^H + \beta min[D^H, pV^H]$.[10]

It can be easily shown that, given the above first period price, a sufficient condition for copiers to copy in period one rather than a) purchase in period one or b) do nothing in period one (i.e., neither purchase nor copy) together with purchasing in period two at a price of $P_2 = D^H$ is $D^H > pV^H$.[11] In other words, a copier's differential surplus of originals over copies when quality is high must exceed the expected utility of originals when quality is unknown. As will be seen shortly, this condition is also a necessary condition for the existence of a pooling equilibrium whenever $\Pi^H < 0$. Therefore, I now make the assumption that $D^H > pV^H$, which implies that the maximal first-period price is given by $P_1 = pV^H + \beta pV^H$. The discounted two-period profits for a high and low quality firm are then given by

$$\Pi_c^H = (pV^H + \beta pV^H - c^H)\gamma + \beta(D^H - c^H)(1 - \gamma) - F^H \qquad (3.3)$$

and

$$\Pi_c^L = (pV^H + \beta pV^H - c^L)\gamma - F^L \qquad (3.4)$$

respectively. Finally, in support of the pooling equilibrium, I simply assume that after the observation of any other first period price, consumers' posterior beliefs after such observation are that the good is low quality with certainty.

Provided $\Pi_c{}^H$ and $\Pi_c{}^L$ both exceed zero, neither firm then has any incentive to deviate from the equilibrium path.

Recall that I am assuming that $\Pi^H < 0$, or when there is no copying, the market is characterised by adverse selection. Notice, however, that $\Pi_c{}^H$ may in fact be strictly positive even though $\Pi^H < 0$. Although first period profits (net of the fixed cost) in (3.3) are unambiguously negative (since the first period price is equal to the price in Π^H), if the proportion of copiers $(1 - \gamma)$ and their differential valuation of high quality originals over copies (D^H) are both sufficiently large, $\Pi_c{}^H$ can exceed zero. It is also easily seen that, as mentioned previously, a necessary condition for the existence of a pooling equilibrium when $\Pi^H < 0$ is that $D^H > pV^H$. If $D^H < pV^H$, overall two-period profits for the high quality firm are necessarily non-positive.[12] Clearly, $\Pi_c{}^L$ will also exceed zero, provided c^L and F^L are sufficiently small.[13]

I conclude therefore, that if $\Pi^H < 0$, but $\Pi_c{}^H > 0$ and $\Pi_c{}^L > 0$, the presence of copying solves the adverse selection problem. Consequently, standard measures of 'harm' from unauthorised reproduction of intellectual property may be largely overstated, as such measures do not account for the informational value of copies. Without copying, high quality may be absent entirely from the market. If $\Pi^H < 0$, but the high quality firm is in fact able without copying to successfully signal or guarantee its product quality, then any measure of the relative harm from copying should also appropriately net out the additional firm costs associated with such signals or guarantees of product quality.[14]

3.4   PIRACY AND PRODUCT QUALITY REVELATION

In Section 3.3, copying enabled high quality to be produced despite the fact that product quality remained uncertain until after consumption. In this section, I consider the possibility that the presence of copying can alone be sufficient for the revelation of product quality prior to consumption by consumers. In particular, I consider the possibility that copying 'weeds out' low quality such that a high quality firm is able to produce and sell at the full information price, while a low quality firm does not produce. In other words, I consider the possibility that the presence of copying can induce a revealing equilibrium without the need for wasteful expenditures, or explicit and strategic (quality revealing) pricing by the high quality firm.[15]

If the presence of copying is to induce a separating equilibrium, the maximal price the high quality firm can charge former copiers in the second period remains as in the previous section, D^H, while the maximal price in the first period is now given by $V^H + \beta D^H$. At this point, one additional assumption is required: given these prices together with known high quality, potential copiers must receive positive single-period net surplus from consuming a copy, or $V_c^H > P_c$. If this inequality does not hold, potential copiers will not copy given the above prices and perceived high quality - they receive greater surplus from either purchasing in period one or doing nothing in period one together with buying in period two.

Given the first and second period prices stated above, together with the additional assumption that $V_c^H > P_c$, profits to the high quality firm in the separating equilibrium will be given by

$$\Pi_s^H = (V^H + \beta V^H - c^H)\gamma + \beta(D^H - c^H)(1 - \gamma) - F^H \qquad (3.5)$$

If the low quality firm mimics the high quality firm, profits to the low quality firm would be given by

$$\Pi_m^L = (V^H + \beta V^H - c^L)\gamma - F^L \qquad (3.6)$$

If the low quality firm is perceived correctly as low quality, the firm does not produce. Importantly, if the high quality firm is also perceived as low quality, the high quality firm also does not produce. Not only will non-copiers not purchase, but copiers will not copy, as they receive negative net surplus from consuming copies of originals perceived to be low quality. The firm thus receives zero revenue in both periods. Since any firm perceived as low quality will not produce, the necessary and sufficient conditions for a separating equilibrium to exist are $\Pi_s^H > 0$ and $\Pi_m^L < 0$.

If $\Pi_s^H > 0$ and $\Pi_m^L < 0$, the high quality firm's quality is immediately revealed a priori – the employment of wasteful expenditures or other costly signalling strategies are not required. In this case, the presence of copying alone 'weeds out' low quality, since only high quality firms are able to earn positive profits with copying. Intuitively, consider what happens as γ, the proportion of non-copiers, becomes smaller. While both types of firms receive lower profits in the first period, only the high quality firm realises the increase in second period profits from the subsequent and correspondingly larger proportion of purchases made by copiers. As a result, under the conditions stated above, copying makes irrational positive production by low quality firms. I conclude therefore that, when without copying, and as a result of adverse selection, neither firm produces, copying can enable high quality firms to produce and sell at full information prices without the need to employ costly signalling devices. In this case, copying clearly produces a Pareto improvement in social welfare.

Note also that the above conditions and the conditions for both firms to earn positive profits without copying (i.e., $\Pi^i > 0$, $i = H, L$) may be satisfied simultaneously. In other words, the possibility exists that low quality may be produced when there is no copying, while with copying, low quality is absent from the market. The presence of copying thus has the potential to produce yet another efficiency: it can preempt the introduction of low quality goods for which production is socially undesirable.

3.5   CONCLUSIONS

This paper has demonstrated that the information value of copying can improve social welfare over that without copying when there is asymmetric information about product quality. In some cases, the presence of copying can induce a Pareto improvement in social welfare, as it has the potential to solve the resultant adverse selection problem. Specifically, the presence of copying can generate equilibria in which both high and low quality are produced, when without copying the market may be missing entirely. Additionally, the presence of copying can also generate equilibria in which only high quality is produced. In these equilibria, high quality firms are able to produce and sell at full information prices and, in particular, without the need to employ costly signalling mechanisms. The presence of copying therefore, has the potential to 'weed out' low quality which, without copying, may be produced even though it is socially undesirable.

The results of the paper suggest that strict and absolute enforcement of copyrights can lead to missing markets and a consequent reduction in social welfare. This does not imply, however, that copyrights should never be enforced. Rather, the paper suggests an emphasis on the *ex post* remedial rather than the *ex ante* preventive role for copyright enforcement; that is, in its role to encourage copiers to subsequently purchase rather than to prevent them from copying at all. Consistent with this notion is the observation that software developers often freely distribute unabridged, fully functioning versions of their programs with an explicit suspension of the copyright for a limited period of time.

The paper also offers implications in regards to the appropriate measure of harm from copying. The first and more obvious point is that standard measures of harm from copying may be largely overstated, since they do not account for the possibility that copiers subsequently purchase. Less obvious, however, is the notion that such measures should also take into consideration possible variations in the number of existing products as well as the quality of those products between the copying and no-copying regimes. An extreme example would be one in which the measured harm for a firm from lost sales to copiers is positive, but without copying, the firm does not produce. The paper has also demonstrated that copying has the potential to preempt the production of socially undesirable low quality which may be produced in the absence of copying. Finally, even if no such variations in product quality exist between the regimes, any measured harm from copying should also account for the possibility that without copying firms must incur additional expenses to signal their product's quality, including possibly, the costly distribution of copies produced and distributed by the firm itself.

NOTES

1. I would like to thank participants at the 2002 inaugural congress of the Society for Economic Research on Copyright Issues held in Madrid, Spain for their helpful comments.
2. See also Bagwell and Riordan (1991), as well as earlier work by Spence (1973), Nelson (1974), and Schmalensee (1978).
3. For example, the absence of copying does not preclude firms from distributing their own 'copies' (e.g., abridged versions of their intellectual property). However, distribution of firm-produced copies is costly for the firm. The firm must incur a positive marginal cost for each copy distributed as well as any fixed cost required to develop the product, either one of which can limit the feasibility of such distribution. Importantly, given such distribution is feasible for and employed by the firm, the true opportunity cost of consumer copying should then be measured relative to the regime in which copies are distributed (perhaps given away) by the firm itself.
4. The assumption that quality is exogenously determined implies that the model does not consider the additional moral hazard problem that arises with endogenous quality in the presence of consumer uncertainty about product quality, although similar application of the ideas here can readily be applied to that case as well.
5. However, with intellectual property, much of the cost differential between high and low quality would be expected to be reflected primarily in the development cost, so that it is not unreasonable to suppose that $F^H > F^L$ and $c^H = c^L$.
6. The assumption of consumer homogeneity is made for simplicity at the expense of some loss of generality. In the next section when copying is introduced, consumer heterogeneity will be introduced via differential valuations of copies. Allowing heterogeneity in both valuations of originals as well as copies would introduce considerable complexity into the analysis and would not change the basic points that can be made in the present framework.
7. Note that I am implicitly assuming that there is no word of mouth advertising, so that in the second period, quality remains unknown by any and all individuals who did not consume in period one.
8. As is typical in models of unauthorised copying, the differential net return from copying across consumer types is modelled either via heterogeneous valuations of copies or heterogeneous copying costs. Such heterogeneity is required in order that equilibria exist in which some consumers copy the good while others purchase.
9. Purchasing in period one provides consumers with expected net surplus of $(1 + \beta)pV^H - P_1$, while copying provides consumers with expected net surplus of $(1 + \beta)pV_c^H - P_c$. Therefore, when $P_1 > (1 + \beta)(pV^H - pV_c^H) + P_c = (1 + \beta)pD^H + P_c$, copiers receive greater expected net surplus from copying than from purchasing. For simplicity, I assume that when the surpluses are equal, copiers choose to purchase.
10. To induce a non-copier to purchase in period one and not defer their purchase until period two, the firm faces the following constraint: $(1 + \beta)pV^H - P_1 = \beta(pV^H - D^H)$, where D^H is the rationally forecasted second-period price. Additionally, consumers must receive positive expected surplus from purchasing, or $(1 + \beta)pV^H - P_1 = 0$.
11. The expected two-period surplus for a copier from copying is given by $(1 + \beta)pV_c^H - P_c > 0$. The expected two-period surplus for a copier from doing nothing in period one (i.e. neither copying nor purchasing) together with buying in period two at the rationally forecasted price of D^H is $\beta(pV^H - D^H)$. Therefore, when $pV^H < D^H$, copiers will opt to copy or purchase

in period one. However, when $pV^H < D^H$, the maximal first–period price the firm can charge is $pV^H + \beta pV^H$. Since this price leaves consumers with zero expected surplus from purchasing in period one, but copiers receive strictly positive surplus from copying, copiers will opt to copy in period one rather than purchase.

12. The model could be extended to include upgrades, in which case the value of D^H could be made larger by the firm via increasing the quality of originals and by possibly also making partially obsolete previously sold originals.

13. Notice that, given $\Pi^H = 0$, there is no pooling equilibrium when both $c^L = c^H$ and $F^L > F^H$, since these conditions imply $\Pi_c^L < 0$. However, as mentioned previously, since intellectual property markets can typically be expected to have $c^L = c^H$ and $F^L < F^H$, the possibility that both $\Pi_c^H > 0$ and $\Pi_c^L > 0$ when $\Pi^H < 0$ is not ruled out in these markets.

14. As noted earlier, without copying, the firm could itself produce a 'copy' (e.g. an abridged version of its intellectual property) and sell it (or give it away) to all (or some) consumers in period one. As with copying, in period two, the firm receives positive profits from sales of 'originals' (e.g., fully-fledged versions) to informed consumers who previously consumed abridged versions. Given consumer uncertainty regarding product quality, the firm can charge at most for each copy the consumer's two-period expected valuation of a copy (which, given imperfect substitutability, is less than the consumer's two-period expected valuation of an original). If, for example, the maximal feasible price of a copy is below the firm's marginal cost, second period profits from sales to informed consumers may not be sufficient to outweigh these additional first period losses. Alternatively, if without copying firms do find it feasible to distribute firm-produced copies, standard measures of harm from copying that include lost 'sales' to copiers can still be overstated, since the true opportunity cost of *consumer*-produced copies should be measured relative to the regime in which the firm itself distributes (or gives away) its own copies. Furthermore, such measures of harm are similarly overstated to the extent that they do not account for the possibility that copiers subsequently purchase.

15. See for example, Milgrom and Roberts (1986) and Kihlstrom and Riordan (1984).

REFERENCES

Bagwell, K. and M. Riordan (1986), 'High and Declining Prices Signal Product Quality', *American Economic Review*, **81**, 224–239.

Besen, S.M. and S.N. Kirby (1989), 'Private Copying, Appropriability, and Optimal Copyright Royalties', *Journal of Law and Economics*, **32**, 255–280.

Conner, K.R. and R.P. Rumelt (1991), 'Software Piracy: An Analysis of Protection Strategies', *Management Science*, **37**, 125–139.

Johnson, W.R. (1985), 'The Economics of Copying', *Journal of Political Economy*, **93**, 158–174.

Kihlstrom, R. and M. Riordan (1984), 'Advertising as a Signal', *Journal of Political Economy*, **92**, 427–450.

Liebowitz, S.J. (1985), 'Copying and Indirect Appropriability: Photocopying of Journals', *Journal of Political Economy*, **94**, 822–841.

Milgrom, P. and J. Roberts (1986), 'Prices and Advertising Signals of Product Quality', *Journal of Political Economy*, **94**, 796–821.

Nelson, P. (1974), 'Advertising as Information', *Journal of Political Economy*, **81**, 729–754.

Novos, I. and M. Waldman (1984), 'The Effects of Increased Copyright Protection: An Analytical Approach', *Journal of Political Economy*, **92**, 236–246.

Schmalensee, R. (1978), 'A Model of Advertising and Product Quality', *Journal of Political Economy*, **86**, 485–503.

Spence, M. (1973), 'Job Market Signaling', *Quarterly Journal of Economics*, **87**, 355–374.

Takeyama, L.N. (1994), 'The Welfare Implications of Unauthorized Reproduction of Intellectual Property in the Presence of Demand Network Externalities', *Journal of Industrial Economics*, **17**, 155–166.

Takeyama, L.N. (1997), 'The Intertemporal Consequences of Unauthorized Reproduction of Intellectual Property', *Journal of Law and Economics*, **40**, 511–522.

Takeyama, L.N. (1999), 'The Advertising Value of Pirating Intellectual Property', Unpublished Manuscript.

4. Copyright Policy, Cultural Policy and Support for Artists

Ruth Towse

4.1 INTRODUCTION

When it was first introduced, statutory copyright law applied to literary works, with works of art and music soon being added to the list. Over the years, performers' rights and other related rights have been added to copyright law creation. By protecting the rights of authors, artists, composers and performers, copyright law has enabled them to control the exploitation of their work and thereby, in principle, to earn rewards from their creations.

Thus most of the people we call artists – those who create works of art – rely on copyright law to establish property rights to their intellectual property, which we could also think of as their human capital output. There is therefore a close connection between cultural policy, which seeks to stimulate artistic supply, and copyright and changes in copyright law – what can be thought of as copyright policy.

However, copyright policy is driven by other stakeholders, who are the publishers (the firms in the cultural industries who market artists' works – the literary and music publishers, the record, film and broadcasting companies, and so on) and consumers. Governments have to balance the interests of these groups and consider their different claims when they change copyright law.

The need for change has been driven by technological progress, which in the cultural sector has profoundly altered the way copyrighted material is created by artists and delivered to consumers. Digitalisation is a shock to the present day cultural economic system and will undoubtedly alter many aspects of the way artists and firms trade. However, it is also the case that copyright law opens up the possibility of rent-seeking by interested parties and that changes to copyright are made in response to their demands. Economists therefore have a role to play in informing policy-makers.

Much of the economic analysis of copyright has concentrated on its economic rationale in general and on its component doctrines. This analysis, of course, has some bearing on copyright policy – the stance governments take towards changing the scope and duration of copyright law. Economists have not asked 'big' questions like how does copyright impinge on creativity (always assuming that we understand what that is) in the same way they have investigated the role of patents in stimulating innovation and technical progress. Endogenous growth theorists make much of the role of human capital in economic development and vaguely call for strengthening copyright and other intellectual property (IP) right law to promote it. There has been some interesting work in economic history on creation without copyright and on artists' earnings, especially in the case of composers (Tschmuck, 2002, Scherer, 2001), and on a broader canvas David (1993) has taken an economic historian's overview of IP law. As the title of this well known article indicates, copyright law has firmly established itself like the 'Panda's thumb', which is an evolutionary aberration, so that we now face a path dependent situation in which the costs of getting rid of it are too great to contemplate, even though it may, as with the Panda's thumb, serve no purpose any longer.

The emphasis on economic rights in copyright law makes it all the more curious that little has been done to establish the extent to which it succeeds in this aim. Whereas it is to be expected that lawyers would work from first principles in analysing copyright, it behoves economists to take a more empirical approach of the effects of copyright on markets and those markets are predominantly in the cultural sector. This is the more curious in the light of the considerable (albeit inconclusive) efforts to assess the economic effects of patents on innovation, economic growth and industrial organisation. Even from economists we hear statements like 'strengthening copyright law will assist economic agents' without any consideration of what that means (supposedly broadening its scope and increasing its duration) or empirical evidence to back them up.

In this chapter, I discuss copyright policy in relation to creativity in the cultural sector and the insights into artistic supply that have come from work in cultural economics. I suggest that changes to copyright law should be informed by our understanding of the effect on the creation of content in the cultural industries. The analysis of copyright law by economists and others has tended to lose track of the effect that it has on artists' earnings and employment. There is a now extensive theoretical literature on the economic analysis of copyright and also on artists' labour markets but little empirical study of artists' earnings from copyright. I therefore begin by giving a brief summary of work by cultural economists on artists' labour markets and then go on to discuss the role of copyright policy in relation to artists.

4.2　　CULTURAL ECONOMICS AND ARTISTS' LABOUR MARKETS

Cultural economics is the application of economics to the arts and embraces 'high' and 'low' culture, that is the creative and performing arts and heritage and the cultural industries - publishing, broadcasting, film, music, computer games and other entertainment. One of the most important debates in cultural economics is the case for public support for the arts. Cultural policy in most countries is concerned with ensuring the production and consumption of good quality arts and culture and with enabling all members of the population to have access to these benefits. The creation of new art and access to the classic repertoire through exhibitions and performance are therefore fundamental aspects of cultural policy, and cultural economists have attempted to understand the supply behaviour of artists (an inclusive term that has been adopted for convenience to cover all creative and performing artists and craftspeople) by studying artists' labour markets. In that study, artists' earnings and their response to financial incentives has been an important matter since it raises the question of how creativity can be fostered by governments and other public bodies concerned with finance of culture, for example, by grants to artists or schemes to encourage arts organisations to commission work. One source of earnings is from copyright royalties and related remuneration and copyright law therefore enters the picture; not only so-called economic rights but also moral rights play a role in stimulating artistic supply (Towse, 2001b). In some countries, and the UK is a particular case in point, cultural policy avoids direct public finance of artists, taking the view that if artists' property rights are well established – and that is mainly achieved by copyright law – they can survive on the market without the need for public financial support. That view clearly begs the empirical question of how much artists earn from one source or another. Hence the need to study the labour market in which they work.

The study of artists' labour markets has not been easy because there is little satisfactory data on artists in official statistics. The definition of artists and of artistic work is difficult and is not standardised. Cultural economists by and large have had to undertake their own surveys, which are inevitably less reliable than a census. Nevertheless, surveys of artists in a number of developed countries reveal remarkably consistent results, namely that artists are mostly self-employed, work long hours on short term contracts, and experience higher than average unemployment; they are multiple job-holders in both the cultural sector and in other sectors of the economy, in which they receive below national average earnings that fluctuate from year to year, despite the fact that they are typically highly qualified. An important finding is that when earnings rise, artists react by devoting more time to arts work; the supply of arts labour is relatively elastic with respect to financial rewards and therefore creative activity can be increased by grants or other rewards to artists.

Artists' labour markets are competitive and, though trade unions and professional associations seek to negotiate minimum rates of pay, bargaining power is severely limited by excess supply of labour (often exacerbated by public finance of artistic training). Moreover, there are strong tendencies for demand to concentrate on a few superstars, who dominate markets, earning very high incomes. The result is that the distribution of artists' incomes is typically skewed. This appears to be a feature of royalty earnings too. Mass production and globalisation of the cultural industries reinforces the superstar phenomenon, though it remains to be seen whether the Internet can counteract it.

4.3 COPYRIGHT LAW AND ARTISTS' BARGAINING POWER

Artists are typically at a disadvantage in relation to firms in the cultural industries for several reasons: as individuals, artists have poor access to the capital market and therefore need to contract with a firm to distribute their work, whereas the firm, often a multinational giant corporation in an oligopolised industry has easy access. With little capital reserves, artists have to sell their work within a short time of its creation; thus their time preference rate is much shorter than a firm's; and artists have a relatively small portfolio of work and cannot pool risks, unlike a large firm with a huge portfolio of copyrighted work which it can exploit when market conditions are favourable. Another source of asymmetry is in relation to market information; artists have considerably less experience of market conditions than do firms. Moreover, individual artists cannot afford the legal costs of defending their rights in court, whereas firms can.

These asymmetries mean that legal changes are likely to affect the two groups differently. Take the simple example of extending the duration of copyright from 50 to 70 years: the economic effect of extending the life of the asset seems likely to benefit artists less than it does firms. Ample evidence of the disadvantaged bargaining position of artists when dealing with firms in the cultural industries is to be found in Caves' (2000) study of industrial organisation in the cultural industries. In this book, he applies contract theory to the bargain between artists and firms, showing that the specific features in cultural production – artists' concern about their reputation and quality of their product, differential talent between artists, radical uncertainty about the reception of novel work, that many products require the co-operation and co-ordination of many different skilled workers, the need to meet deadlines and the costs of failure to do so – conspire to cause serious contracting problems that firms deal with by incentive and option contracts to protect their investment. In the standard royalty contract, the artist receives a royalty of around 10-15 percent of sales revenue and this yields low earnings from copyright for the 'typical' artist. Firms, however, have the incentive to back superstars because there is less uncertainty about their product and the demand for it; superstars, by contrast, have a strong bargaining position and their high incomes reflect the fact. This analysis therefore contributes to explaining the widely observed skewed distribution of artists' incomes; the chosen few get very high rewards while the majority earn relatively little that is below their transfer wage.[1]

Watt (2000) provides us with the first analytical model of the royalty contract that considers the optimal contract that the creator of an original work can make with a publisher (he uses the term 'distributor'). Taking risk into account (not radical uncertainty as postulated by Caves), he concludes that the typical royalty (rental) contract to be found in the cultural industries is sub-optimal for utility maximising creators and discussed the puzzle of why they nevertheless appear to prefer such contracts.[2]

While copyright law exists to establish property rights rather than to determine the type of contract authors make with publishers, there are, as I discuss below, instances in which the law attempts to influence the contract, for example, by making rights unwaivable or specifying that they may only be assigned to copyright collectives. Economic analysis of the bargain that is struck in the contract is therefore relevant to the discussion of the role of copyright on assisting artists to earn a living from creative activity.

4.4   AUTHORS AND PUBLISHERS – HARMONY OR DISSONANCE?

Though early copyright law in England and the USA focused on artistic works, it did not, unlike Continental copyright law, confine itself solely to rights of authors but from the start also gave protection to publishers and other copyright-holders to whom authors and other creators assigned or sold rights in their works. With the focus on economic rights and the view that trading them improves authors' earning power through exploitation by specialised publishers who have better entrepreneurial skills than authors (or why else would authors contract with them?), Anglo Saxon copyright law assumes there is what has been called a harmony of interests, nowadays called synergy, between authors and publishers.

Plant (1934) is one of the few economists writing on copyright who noted conflict of interest between author and publisher. The conflict he analysed was over the price of the work (on which the author's royalty is based): whereas the author would choose the price that maximises revenue, the publisher sets the (higher) profit maximising price. It is interesting to note that the main thrust of Plant's article was whether copyright law assisted authors to earn a reasonable income and he concluded that authors would be better off without it; he therefore rejected the case for copyright law. For not only did it result in insufficient reward, it also had the unintended consequence of worsening the position of authors by increasing competition. Plant's analysis focused on the role copyright played in reducing risk, which he thought resulted in overproduction of low quality works that would not otherwise succeed on the market and this excess supply reduced prices of books (he only considered copyright in books) and therefore disadvantaged the authors of better quality products.

Apart from Plant, though, most economists writing on copyright have assumed that copyright serves the interests of both parties, authors and publishers, equally. In a general sense it does because both are assumed to want to maximise returns from their joint output – the more successful the CD, the more the composer and musicians earn. But it is also obvious that the more one of the parties earns, the lower the share of the other. If a composer gets a higher royalty, the record company gets less (unless it is able to recoup it from consumers). It is in obtaining their share of the returns that bargaining power is the issue.

The relatively weak bargaining position of most artists *vis-à-vis* firms demonstrates that there are conflicts of interest. It is interesting to note that in certain cases copyright law recognises this fact in a limited way and has attempted to rectify it. Legislators have attempted to protect artists by making their rights unwaivable. One example of this is the performer's right to equitable remuneration from rental and from the public performance of sound recordings embodied in the 1996 European Union Rental Directive; another example is *droit de suite* or artists' resale rights. It seems that by doing so, law-makers intend to tip the balance in favour of artists to enable them to earn a greater share of revenues. However, legislation and the market are very different things – what matters is the market reaction to such legal changes.

The market response may not be what the policy-maker intends. Legal changes alter market prices and may also raise transaction costs. It is possible that there may be unintended effects of well-meaning legislative changes that make matters even worse. For example, *droit de suite* is intended to assist artists to recoup the increased value of their works from later sales but it seems more likely to reduce prices for young artists and to favour only those few superstar artists whose work is sold at auction in their lifetime. Art dealers and other buyers discount the anticipated cost of the 'tax' by paying a lower purchase price. Another example is the Rental Right, which in some areas requires such high transaction costs to collect that it is not worthwhile doing so. Under the terms of the Rental Directive, the above-mentioned performers' rights were made individual and could only be assigned to a collecting society. That simultaneously raised administration costs and reduced the performers' freedom of choice (what Kretschmer, 2002, has called 'compulsory representation'). Moreover, as we see later, collecting societies do not act only in the interests of artists but often include publisher members with somewhat different interests.

The market outcome may well affect author and publisher (artists and firms) differently. 'Strengthening copyright' with the intention of helping artists could conceivably instead benefit firms even more, thus making artists' bargaining power relatively weaker rather than stronger as was the intention. Recently, Landes has specifically criticised the extension of copyright to 70 years, calling the long duration of copyright 'a major economic puzzle' (Landes, 2002, p.16). He argues that on any reasonable discount rate, the increase in value of extending copyright 70 years beyond the life of an author is trivial but that it increases access costs, which raise the costs of creativity; using a simple arithmetic example with a discount rate of 10 per cent, he shows that 93 per cent of the present value accrues within 28 years (Landes, 2000, footnote 35).[3] Thus the marginal benefit of a 70 year rather than a 28 year term is very likely to exceed marginal costs.

Moreover, as the vast majority of works are no longer still in publication when the copyright expires, there is a strong presumption that the duration of copyright is irrelevant to their economic life; in practice, most authors earn a return on most of their works over a far, far shorter period.[4] What these examples show is that copyright policy should take economic responses into account and to do so, it is necessary to have empirical evidence, something that lawyers typically do not consider and economists have been slow to provide in the cultural sector.

4.5   AN EMPIRICAL APPROACH TO COPYRIGHT LAW IN THE CULTURAL INDUSTRIES

Following on from my work on artists' earnings, I have adopted what I call a cultural policy approach to the analysis of copyright (Towse, 2001a). In Taylor and Towse (1998), Taylor and I attempted to analyse empirically the expected effect on performers' earnings of the introduction of Rental Directive performers' rights, which were new to the UK (previously, remuneration for the public performance of sound recordings had been passed by the record companies' collecting society to the Musicians' Union, who had used the income for collective benefits). Our data showed that the median performer earned only small incomes from these sources and preliminary estimates suggested that the legislative changes would not increase individual performers' earnings; they would, however, be likely to increase the transaction costs of administration. Moreover, we also pointed out that were they to achieve the result of increasing performers' payments, someone would have to pay – consumers through higher prices, record and film/video companies through lower profits or other artists (composers or authors) through a reduction in their royalties.

The discussions on the EU Rental Directive (Reinbothe and von Lewinski, 1993), however, showed no sign that such matters were taken into account. While it is true that empirical analysis of artists' earnings is not easy (I discuss some of the problems in detail below), it strikes an economist as irresponsible that market regulation is undertaken without considering incentives to economic agents and without assessing likely market outcomes.

Copyright collectives and artists

One way in which artists have strengthened their bargaining position with copyright users is through membership of copyright collectives. The high transaction costs of licensing and defending the exploitation of individual rights seem to make it very likely, if not inevitable, that collective rights management is adopted to spread administrative costs and to reap economies of scale. Collecting societies vary between countries in their constitution; most are private, non-profit co-operatives, often mandated by the state, though in the UK, where they evolved without state involvement, they are merely regulated by the state.[5] Some are state owned and run (a model that seems likely to be adopted in developing countries required by international conventions to set up copyright administration). Whatever their legal status, they nearly all have both authors and publishers as members, implying the earlier mentioned harmony of interest between them. As membership societies, they are self-governing with representation organised on the basis of the author/publisher divide. That principle may put individual artists at a disadvantage as relative economic power between publisher and author members becomes an issue. Kretschmer (2002) has argued that the transaction cost rationale for collective agency (which he rejects in favour of a property rights approach) does not merit this joint system and that it fails individual authors; he uses GEMA, the German collecting society, and the Performing Rights Society (PRS) in the UK as case studies. He suggests that European societies were in fact set up for *collective* action rather than for individual rights administration. Watt (2000) has further pointed out that blanket licensing by collecting societies makes good economic sense (on transaction cost grounds) but that a good deal of the saving on costs is dissipated in individual distributions, which, as he rightly says, destroys the original rationale of collective management. Watt does not argue for using licence fee revenues collectively (the logic of some European societies, according to Kretschmer) but that as the individual incentive has already been dulled by the blanket fee, there seems little point in incurring the considerable costs of registration and monitoring necessary to make an individual distribution to authors.

The governance of the PRS was investigated as part of the UK Monopoly and Mergers Commission's enquiry into its alleged anti-competitive practices and reforms were recommended but the principle of author and publisher membership was not disputed (Monopoly and Mergers Commission, 1996). Whatever the underlying economic rationale, it is a fact that almost everywhere collecting societies have a monopoly of administering a particular bundle of rights (the notable exception is the USA with two); they are accepted by anti-trust authorities as a natural monopoly and therefore more efficient than a competitive situation. For users, blanket licensing of rights is held to offer the most efficient administrative solution, though, as argued earlier, it may not be the most economically efficient one.

However, even with the agency of collecting societies, the vast majority of individual creators and performers earn very little from their rights, despite the large incomes of the collecting societies and the notable growth of income from secondary use of copyrights (for access to which society membership is essential). Data on distributions to individual author members shows how skewed they are (Towse, 2000). The plain fact is, therefore, that most artists are unable to obtain sufficient rewards from their work, even though copyright legislation entitles them to a 'fair return'; nor, as we have seen from studies of artists' earnings, do they do so from other sources, such as fees and sales. Thus, empirical evidence suggests that other policies are needed to support creativity in the arts.

Government policy for artists

Governments throughout the developed world have cultural policies that seek to promote creativity in the arts and they therefore need to find means of assisting artists to earn incomes that enable them to devote themselves to work in the arts. Copyright protection is viewed as one of these means. However, it does not follow that because it fails to ensure a living wage for most artists that copyright law should be abolished. What is needed is to acknowledge that the present legislation alone is inadequate for the simple reason that laws do not guarantee market outcomes. That requires persuading artists as well as policy-makers that copyright law is not the panacea they suppose it to be and, furthermore, there are unintended consequences of well-meaning copyright legislation. Because copyright law protects both author and publisher (artists and firms in the cultural industries), changes to copyright, such as increasing its duration, can, as I have argued, weaken the relative bargaining power of artists. In other respects also copyright law has unintended consequences: it creates moral hazard for firms, for example in the film and music industries, and has led to over reliance on copyright protection instead of the development of anti-copying devices and marketing strategies that allow legal use of copyright material (witness the Napster case). One of Plant's objections to copyright law, let us remember, was that it created what we now call moral hazard by reducing risk, thereby creating the 'wrong' market incentives.

If we had *tabula rasa*, what would economists recommend as a means of stimulating artistic endeavour? The Coase theorem tells us that we should recommend a situation in which property rights are established and each right is tradable, provided transaction costs are low. Even though there are high administration and compliance costs of copyright, nevertheless this strategy can be recommended as a desirable direction to take. Four types of legislative action to support creative activity may be identified: 1) creating new property rights, for example digital rights; 2) extending the scope of existing rights – the example considered here was the extension of performers' rights; 3) restricting the freedom to exercise rights – the example of unwaivable rights; and 4) altering the duration of copyright (which, as we know, has increased very much over the last three hundred years). Economic analysis of various aspects of copyright rests on the trade-off between the different interest groups, such as consumers and producers but, as mentioned before, mostly assumes the interests of the creators of content (authors of original copies) and firms who make and sell copies (publishers) are the same. Landes and Posner (1989) have argued that overly strong copyright protection (typically favoured by the publisher) *reduces* the incentive to create because the costs of access rise as the duration of copyright increases and fair use is restricted. What they call the costs of creation, for example, tracing copyright-holders for permissions, increase over time, though the benefits decline, and thus limit the duration of copyright. The policy economists would not recommend is making rights unwaivable because that interferes with the transfer of rights to the most efficient owner. As Watt points out, this is unlikely to be the individual creator because she would likely have higher transaction costs than either a firm or a copyright collective.

One strategy is to opt for alternatives to copyright law as incentives to create. Plant thought better incentives could be offered to create good quality new works by a scheme of state patronage in the form of grants or prizes to artists and that this would be a more effective means than copyright law because it would embody some form of quality control.[6] However, Plant also advocated another solution using copyright law: copyrights should be of short duration and they should return to being renewable as copyright originally was in the 1710 Statute of Anne in England (and as patents still are). Practitioners have also called for shorter renewable copyright terms; in its submission to the Monopoly and Mergers Commission 1996 enquiry mentioned above, the International Federation of Managers, representing managers of pop groups, called for 20 year copyrights that would revert automatically to the original creator and could then be renegotiated if they have future value. I concur with this proposal. It is consistent with the Coase theorem (and so makes good economic logic); though it would reduce the present value of the work at the time of its creation, the reduction would be relatively small as around 90 percent of the value of the copyright accrues in the first 20 years; it would reduce the asymmetry between author and publisher by giving the former another chance to obtain reward for valuable work (which seems 'fairer'); it would give the publisher the incentive to exploit the work in a timely way and also reduce the risk the 'second' publisher takes on unproven work, thereby increasing the incentive; and it would in addition stop the nonsense of the duration of copyright in a work vastly exceeding its economic life[7] – it has been estimated that in the US something like 85 percent of works did not have their copyrights renewed (reported in Landes, 2002, footnote 34). There are therefore compelling economic reasons that support the proposition to reduce the term of copyright.

4.6   CONCLUSION

In this chapter, I look at copyright law as a tool of cultural policy and its effectiveness as a means of raising artists' earnings. Cultural policy is concerned, among other things, with stimulating creativity in the arts and cultural industries and with ensuring that there is a supply of good quality work produced by artists. Although artists are not motivated solely by financial reward, the evidence from studies of artists' labour markets tells us that they respond positively to increases in income from their artwork and devote more time to producing it. That in itself, of course, is no guarantee of artistic quality or true creativity, something cultural economists have yet to investigate; suffice it to say that an increase in quantity at least offers the possibility of increasing quality.

Governments have various means at their disposal for assisting artists; besides copyright law, there are subsidies to artists and arts organisations.

They can make direct grants to artists and/or indirect grants via arts organisations to commission work from them or even directly commission work, for example through government agencies, such as Arts Councils. The relative effectiveness of these policies is a topic that is of great interest and importance to cultural economists and to cultural policy-makers and it merits further investigation.

As part of that investigation, I have gathered empirical and institutional evidence to test some of the propositions about copyright as a means of assisting artists. Though I have concentrated on economic rights, I recognise that moral rights may also act as an incentive and offer non-financial rewards (Towse, 2001b); however, I do not deal with that here. My interest is more about testing the actual or implied predictions made by those advocating copyright policies, such as strengthening copyright or increasing its scope, that are manifest in various recent policy proposals – introducing new rights, increasing the duration of copyright and making some rights unwaivable. These (and other) so-called improvements cannot be evaluated from first principles alone, either by lawyers or economists, and call for understanding how the markets work in the cultural sector. Legislating for higher artists' earnings from copyright cannot work if markets fail to respond in the desired way. At present, however, we have little evidence and empirical analysis to appeal to.

Hard data are difficult to obtain in this area for several reasons. First, official data on the cultural sector, for example earnings and employment, are deficient, no doubt because the arts and cultural industries are not regarded as economically significant. Data problems also affect macro estimates of the economic role of copyright, now being tackled internationally by WIPO (World Intellectual Property Organisation). A second problem, familiar to economists, is that many economic agents in the cultural industries are private organisations and have no reason to reveal information about themselves to researchers. However, some data exist and I have been able to use data from collecting societies to gain a glimpse into the value to individuals of some of their rights. Another source of potential information is official enquiries on industrial behaviour, for example, anti-trust proceedings. The UK Monopolies and Mergers Commission enquiries into the music industry and rights administration provided good institutional and statistical material for researchers. Copyright Tribunal proceedings are also publicly available. There is information for the persistent.

With information from collecting societies and surveys of artists' earnings we can establish what is anyway common knowledge – that only a few artists earn a living wage from work in the arts and that only the very small proportion of superstars make high incomes from royalties and other sources. Therefore one has to conclude that though copyright law is a necessary condition for assisting artists to earn incomes, it does not do so sufficiently. Therefore the question is how can we as a society overcome the limitations of the cultural policy tools at our disposal. It is understandable that copyright lawyers seek to improve the lot of creators through legal means; the open question is how or if it can be done. That I believe, requires the assistance of economic research and my plea is that this be taken seriously and supported by policy-makers.

One of the most serious problems I encountered in my empirical research was the impossibility of assuming *ceteris paribus; cetera non erant pares*! With digitalisation altering not only copyright law but also the way in which cultural goods are traded and how copyright is administered, it is difficult to isolate the effect of those changes from statutory changes that are also happening. To give the example of Taylor and Towse (1998): while we were trying to predict the effect of the introduction to the UK of a new performer's individual right that resulted from the EU Rental Directive – a seemingly 'natural experiment' – digitalisation was being introduced and also piracy was becoming an increasing problem! Of course, empirical testing is difficult but that is no reason to abandon it. We should better persuade governments of its potential input into policy decisions.

In this context, it is noteworthy that most other statutory law and other government policies are monitored for their effects in achieving policy objectives. Health and education policies are constantly informed by empirical results. In relation to the law, crime statistics are collected and bodies like Health and Safety Authorities monitor those regulations. But no equivalent tracking is done of intellectual property law. Economists have done a considerable body of empirical work on patents but so far, copyright has not attracted the same attention and effort. The WIPO exercise mentioned earlier is not designed to discover whether copyright law creates incentives to artists nor to discover whether the social benefits of copyright legislation outweigh the social costs. It is time this vacuum was filled.

My claim is that changes to copyright law that are expected to assist artists do not work because of the unintended consequences; for example, they strengthen the bargaining power of firms in the cultural industries more than they help artists. That is a testable hypothesis, though it would be difficult to test it. If true, it suggests that policy-makers should abandon the cry to 'strengthen' copyright law as a major part of cultural policy for stimulating creativity and instead offer direct grants or loans to artists. What would be preferable is *reducing* the term of copyright to 20 years from the date of a work's publication, which with modern IT is not so costly to register. That would enable authors to benefit more from their creations.

NOTES

1. Caves' analysis provides an explanation based on firm behaviour. Others have put forward supply-side theories and the well-known theory of superstars was first proposed by Rosen. See Towse (2001a) for a survey of these theories.
2. This accords with my own work on different types of royalty contracts, in which I considered the effect of different incentives on the quality of creative supply (Towse, 1999). My work predated both Caves and Watt and I took a less analytical approach to Watt and concentrated on one area of copyright (performers' rights – see below) as I did not have the superior evidence of Caves at my disposal.
3. It is interesting to consider whether lawyers actually understand discounting and present value. One often hears it said by lawyers and by artists' organisations that increasing the duration of copyright strengthens the artist's position. That would only be true with unlikely assumptions about economic incentives and market outcomes.
4. The 'classic' source for this information is Breyer's 1970 article (see Watt, 2000, for a discussion of Breyer). As with so many issues in the economics of copyright, there is very little empirical evidence, though that is clearly needed to dispel many of the legal myths.
5. Regulation is by the Copyright Tribunal. For an interesting discussion of the role of the economist in relation to the operations of these tribunals, see Peacock (1993) and Einhorn (2002).
6. It is notable that cultural policy concerns about artistic quality and incentives to artists to produce it have been absent from more recent economic work on copyright, though Hurt and Schuchman and Breyer both did so (see Watt, 2000). Plant was writing before the introduction of state patronage for the arts in the UK with the formation of the Arts Council in 1946.
7. Kretschmer (2002) suggests the product cycle in the cultural industries is 5–20 years.

REFERENCES

Caves, Richard (2000), *Creative Industries: Contracts Between Art and Commerce*. Cambridge MA and London: Harvard University Press.

David, Paul (1993), 'Intellectual Property Institutions and the Panda's Thumb: Patents, Copyrights and Trade Secrets in Economic Theory and History', in Mogee, M. and Schwen, R. (eds.) *Global Dimensions of Intellectual Property Rights in Science and Technology*. Washington DC: National Academy Press; 19–61.

Einhorn, Michael (2002), 'Music Licensing in the Digital Age' in Ruth Towse (ed.) *Copyright and the Cultural Industries*. Cheltenham and Northampton MA: Edward Elgar; 165–177.

Kretschmer, Martin (2002), 'Copyright Societies Do Not Administer Individual Property Rights: The Incoherence of Institutional Traditions in Germany and the UK' in Ruth Towse *op cit*; 140–164.

Landes, William (2002), 'Copyright, Appropriation Art and Borrowed Images: An Economic Approach' in Ruth Towse, *op cit*; 9–31.

Landes, W. and R. Posner (1989), 'An Economic Analysis of Copyright Law', *Journal of Legal Studies*, **18**, 325–366.

Monopolies and Mergers Commission (1996), *Performing Rights*, cm. 3147. London: HMSO.

Peacock, Alan (1993), *Paying the Piper*. Edinburgh: Edinburgh University Press.

Plant, Arnold (1934), 'The Economic Aspects of Copyright in Books', *Economica* **1**, 167–195.

Reinbothe, J. and S. von Lewinski (1993), *The EC Directive on Rental and Lending Rights and on Piracy*. London: Sweet and Maxwell.

Scherer, Frank M. (2001), 'The Evolution of Free-Lance Music Composition', *Journal of Cultural Economics*, **25(4)**, 307–319.

Taylor, Millie and Ruth Towse (1998), 'The Value of Performers' Rights: An Economic Approach', *Media, Culture and Society*, **20(4)**, 631–652.

Towse, Ruth (1999), 'Copyright, Incentives and Performers' Earnings' *KYKLOS*, **52(3)**, 369–390.

Towse, Ruth (2000), 'Copyright and the Cultural Industries: Incentives and Earnings', paper presented to the Korea Infomedia Lawyers Association, September. http://www.kafil.or.kr/seminar/17-1.PDF

Towse, Ruth (2001a), *Creativity, Incentive and Reward: An Economic Analysis of Copyright and Culture in the Information Age*, Cheltenham: Edward Elgar.

Towse, Ruth (2001b), 'Partly for the Money: Rewards and Incentives to Artists', *KYKLOS*, **54(2/3)**, 473–490.

Tschmuck, Peter (2002), 'Creativity Without a Copyright' in Ruth Towse *op cit*; 210–220.

Watt, Richard (2000), *Copyright and Economic Theory. Friends or Foes?* Cheltenham: Edward Elgar.

5. Efficient Distribution of Copyright Income

Jorge Alonso and Richard Watt[1]

5.1 INTRODUCTION

A very common aspect of the production and distribution of cultural creations is the fact that the creator does not also participate directly in the distribution or sale of the creation (more correctly, the distribution or sale of the rights in the creation). The reasons for this are, quite obviously, based on the economic theory of specialisation on the one hand, but also for the case of the reproduction and performance rights in easily reproducible creations (for example, musical compositions and written works), the transactions costs savings that accrue from having a copyright collective that deals with many similar creations is perhaps the single most significant reason for creators not dealing directly with final consumers. Naturally, when the creator does not take care of the entire production-distribution chain, the matter of how she[2] is reimbursed from the income that is generated becomes important. We shall refer to the creator's reimbursement as the 'copyright royalty'.

Clearly, there are a great many alternatives from which the formula that determines royalty payments may be selected. However, in spite of the size of the alternative set, one particular format is very much prevalent in real-world situations – the royalty is a fixed proportion of total sales revenue (see, for example, Baumol and Heim (1967), and Towse (2001), where a wealth of real-world information is given concerning royalty contracts). Assuming that each consumption unit is sold at a constant price, naturally this is equivalent to the creator receiving a fixed proportion of the sales price of each unit sold. We shall refer to this as a fixed proportion sharing rule, since independently of the amount of sales revenue that ends up being collected, the royalty percentage payment is the same. In contrast, for example, the author may be offered a lower percentage share if the sales revenue is small, and a higher percentage share for greater sales revenue outcomes. The principle objective of this paper is to investigate whether or not a fixed proportion sharing rule is indeed efficient.

The issue of efficiency will be studied quite apart from any issue regarding incentives. For example, any sharing rule that states that the creator's royalty will be calculated as an increasing function of sales income means that the creator is interested in maximising sales income, while the distributor is interested in maximising profits. Aside from the special cases of constant elasticity of demand or zero marginal costs, the two points will not (in general) coincide. Hence the pricing decision of the distributor will not, in general, coincide with the pricing decision that the creator would most prefer. In this paper, we simply take the total sales revenue as being a random variable, and we do not consider what in fact affects the values that it takes. The only question that we set out to answer is exactly how this revenue, once collected, should be shared between the creator and the distributor.

The analysis in the paper is sufficiently general to cover any type of distribution agreement. For example, if the creator is a musician, the distributor may be a record label (also often referred to as the publisher), who fixes the creation (in this case, the musical composition) onto some physical support, copies of which are then sold to consumers. The royalty contract will stipulate how much the record company must pay the musician out of final sales revenue. However, for the case of musical compositions, there is also a large market for broadcasting and public communication rights, which is typically managed by a copyright collection society. Once again, the revenues that the copyright society generates must somehow be shared among the members (the musicians and song writers), and the way that this is done is what we are calling a royalty contract here. Finally, our model also works to study the contract between a copyright collective (now thought of as the 'creator') and a broadcaster (the distributor). In general then, although different rights may be marketed and administered by different distributors, the same problem arises when the revenue that is generated must be split between the creator and the distributor, and this is the problem that we study here.

Since we want to decide how the sales revenue should be shared between the distributor and the creator under the assumption that sales revenue can take any of a set of different values, we are necessarily thrust into the realm of sharing a random variable. There is uncertainty as to the final value of sales revenue that will be available to be shared, but the contract that stipulates how the revenue will be shared in each contingency must be decided before the true state of nature has been revealed. As is natural, we shall only consider Pareto efficient sharing rules, that is, rules under which neither party to the contract can benefit from a change without making the other party worse off. Thus, we are considering a direct application of the theory of efficient risk sharing, initiated (in the modern sense) by Borch (1962).[3] However, the relevant literature has shown to be of little practical aid for real-life cases, due in no small part to the very complex nature of the subject matter. Hence, in this paper we shall concentrate on attempting to provide a simple model, with transparent results and conclusions, that we hope will be at least a first step towards characterising the type of royalty contract that should be observed in real life cases. This paper really contains no new results or theories, but rather our intention is to simplify existing theories and results in order to attempt to make them more useful to real-life situations.

In what follows, we firstly consider a very simple theory of efficient risk sharing, with the intention of finding out if indeed we can identify situations in which an efficient royalty contract will always imply a fixed proportion sharing rule, and situations in which this will never be the case. Then, we go on to analyse a particular model, the Nash bargaining model, from which an exact contract can be identified. In this case, we can consider the cases in which a fixed proportion sharing rule is always efficient, with the objective of comparing the exact contract that eventuates with the type of contract that is used in real-life royalty contracts. Section 5.4 concludes and offers certain directions for further research. Proofs of all formal results are given in the appendix.

5.2 EFFICIENT SHARING RULES

To begin with, we should consider what we mean by a sharing rule, and what we mean by an efficient sharing rule. In general, let us assume that total sales revenue is represented by the variable x. In interests of simplicity, throughout the paper we assume that x is a binomial random variable, that takes the value x_1 with probability $(1-p)$, and the value x_2 with probability p. Without loss of generality, we assume $x_2 < x_1$, that is, the bad state of the world is state 2. Both creator and distributor are fully agreed on the value of the probability p. We assume that the creator has utility function $u_c(x)$, and that the distributor has utility function $u_d(x)$, where both functions are assumed to be strictly increasing and strictly concave (i.e., both the creator and the distributor are assumed to prefer more money to less, and are strictly risk averse). For simplicity, we assume that $u_j(0) = 0$ for $j=c, d$.

A sharing rule is a function, $k(x)$, where it is agreed that the creator will receive as royalty income the amount $k(x)$, and that the distributor will receive as his payment the amount $x - k(x)$. Since we have assumed that x is binomial, we can restrict our analysis to only two numbers, $k_1 = k(x_1)$ and $k_2 = k(x_2)$.

It is interesting to note that nothing at all is gained by assuming that the contract stipulates an up-front payment and then some sharing arrangement of final revenue, as is often the case (see Baumol and Heim (1967) for a discussion of the types of contract that are often used, at least for the case of books). This is because, whatever is the initial up-front payment, say $h(0)$, and the ensuing royalty payments, $h_1 = h_1(h_0, x_1)$ and $h_2 = h_2(h_0, x_2)$, our model is simply set as $k_1 = h_0 + h_1$ and $k_2 = h_0 + h_2$. So long as the up-front option is always set efficiently, it can always be described by the simpler two payment model that we use here.

We assume that if no contract is agreed upon, both parties receive an income of 0. We also assume that both parties to the contract will act in accordance with the expected utility theory, that is, they will maximise their respective expected utility functions (see Von Neumann and Morgenstern (1947))

$$Eu_j(z^j) = pu_j(z_1^j) + (1-p)u_j(z_2^j) \text{ for } j=c, d$$

where $z_i^c = k_i$, $z_i^d = x_i - k_i$ for $i=1, 2$.

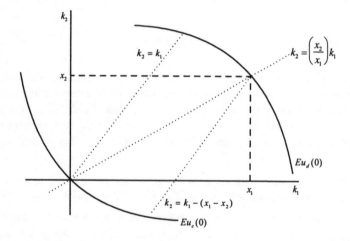

Figure 5.1 Indifference curves

Given this, all of our analysis can be set out graphically in the plane of vectors $k = (k_1, k_2)$. In this space, it is immediate that the creator's indifference curves are convex to the origin and geometrically higher curves correspond to greater expected utility, while the distributor's indifference curves are concave to the origin and those corresponding to greater expected utility values are located geometrically lower. The creator's reservation utility is given by the indifference curve that passes through the origin, while the distributor's reservation utility is given by the indifference curve that passes through the point $x = (x_1, x_2)$. This information is shown in Figure 5.1.

In Figure 5.1 we have also shown the certainty contracts for each of the two participants. The creator will receive a certain payoff whenever $k_1 = k_2$ which is a line of slope 1 that passes through the origin, while the distributor will receive a certain payoff whenever $x_1 - k_1 = x_2 - k_2$, that is, whenever $k_2 = k_1 - (x_1 - x_2)$, which is a line of slope 1 that passes through the point (x_1, x_2). Given the assumption that $x_1 > x_2$ which is referred to as the existence of aggregate risk, the certainty line of the creator is everywhere above the certainty line of the distributor. Finally, we have also shown the point that corresponds to the contracts that specify a fixed proportional share of revenue, the line $k_2 = (x_2 / x_1) k_1$, that passes through the origin and the point (x_1, x_2).[4]

An efficient contract is defined as one that satisfies Pareto efficiency. A contract $k = (k_1, k_2)$ is Pareto efficient if there does not exist any other contract $\tilde{k} = (\tilde{k}_1, \tilde{k}_2)$ such that $Eu_j(z^j(\tilde{k})) \geq Eu_j(z^j(k))$ for $j = 1, 2$ with strict inequality for at least one j. In words, a contract is Pareto efficient if and only if there does not exist another contract that is weakly preferred by both the creator and the distributor, and strongly preferred by at least one of them. As was first shown by Borch (1962), any efficient risk sharing mechanism must satisfy the condition that the marginal rates of substitution of each participant are equal. Since the marginal rate of substitution of participant j at a point k is simply[5]

$$MRS_j(k) = -\frac{\left(\dfrac{\partial Eu_j(z^j)}{\partial k_1}\right)}{\left(\dfrac{\partial Eu_j(z^j)}{\partial k_2}\right)} = -\frac{(1-p)}{p}\frac{\left(\dfrac{\partial u_j(z^j)}{\partial k_1}\right)}{\left(\dfrac{\partial u_j(z^j)}{\partial k_2}\right)} \quad \text{for } j = c, d$$

we can identify all efficient contracts as those points k that satisfy

$$u_c'(k_1)u_d'(x_2 - k_2) = u_c'(k_2)u_d'(x_1 - k_1) \tag{5.1}$$

Note that (5.1) identifies implicitly a function, $k_2 = K(k_1)$, that corresponds to all efficient (strictly interior) contracts. This function is normally called the contract curve of the problem. At any point at which the contract curve intersects the line $k_2 = (x_2/x_1)k_1$, we have an efficient contract that has a fixed proportional sharing rule. Furthermore, if the contract curve coincides with the line $k_2 = (x_2/x_1)k_1$, then *all* efficient contracts have a fixed proportional sharing rule. This is the particular case that we would like to identify. We now go on to point out some useful results concerning the contract curve.[6]

Lemma 5.1 For all $0 < k_i < x_i$, with $i=1, 2$, the contract curve satisfies $k_1 > K(k_1) > k_1 - (x_1 - x_2)$.

The intuition for Lemma 5.1 is very simple - given two strictly risk averse participants, an efficient contract can never ask that only one of them accepts all the risk. Hence the contract cannot satisfy $k_2 = k_1$ (creator suffers no risk) nor can it satisfy $x_2 - k_2 = x_1 - k_1$ (distributor suffers no risk). The particular cases of extreme values of k_i must be excluded, since these are equivalent (for one of the two participants) to not signing a contract at all. In any case, the next lemma shows why these extreme cases may be important and should be discussed separately.

Lemma 5.2 If the utility functions satisfy $u'_j(0) = \infty$ for $j=c,d$, and assuming that the values of k_i are finite, then the contract curve passes through the origin and the point (x_1, x_2).

Lemma 5.3 The slope of the contract curve at any point is

$$K'(k_1) = \frac{A_c(k_1) + A_d(x_1 - k_1)}{A_c(k_2) + A_d(x_2 - k_2)}$$

where $A_j(z) = -u''_j(z)/u'_j(z)$ is the Arrow-Pratt measure of absolute risk aversion of party j.

Corollary 5.1 $K'(k_1) > 0$.

Corollary 5.2 If both parties to the contract have decreasing (increasing, constant) absolute risk aversion, then $K'(k_1) < (>,=) 1$.

We can now state our first main result.

Theorem 5.1 The contract curve has at least one point satisfying $0 \leq k_1 \leq x_1$, such that the contract stipulates a fixed proportional sharing rule. Furthermore, if $u'_j(0) < \infty$ for both $j=c, d$, then there is a unique intersection between the contract curve and the fixed proportion sharing rule line if any of the following conditions hold

a) $A'_j(z) \geq 0$ for $j=c, d$

b) $R'_j(z) > 0$ for $j=c, d$

c) $R'_d(z) \geq A_d(z)(1 - R_d(z))$

where $R_j(z) = zA_j(z)$ is the Arrow-Pratt measure of relative risk aversion.

Perhaps the most interesting of these results is Theorem 5.1, which points out that there must always exist an efficient contract that stipulates a fixed proportional sharing rule, and that also points out a series of cases for which there is exactly one such internal contract (i.e., the contract must share the surplus between the creator and the distributor with a strictly positive share for each). Aside from constant absolute risk averse utility functions, the requisites of the theorem are also satisfied by quadratic forms (for which absolute risk aversion is increasing), both of which have been extensively used to study empirical cases, but neither of which satisfy the logical assumption that absolute risk aversion is decreasing.

There exist several empirical studies that estimate risk aversion, with a rather common result being that the degree of relative risk aversion is something that is very nearly constant and valued between 0.5 and 2.5 (see, for example, Friend and Blume (1975), Hansen and Singleton (1982), Szpiro (1986), Weber (1970)).[7] Hence, it seems that constant relative risk aversion (CRRA) is a good assumption to place upon our model. CRRA functions coincide with the case $u'_j(0) = \infty$, and hence have contract curves that pass through the two origins (i.e., there are at least two intersections between the contract curve and the fixed proportion sharing rule line). In particular, for the case of CRRA functions, we have the following result.

Theorem 5.2 If both the creator and the distributor have CRRA utility functions, then either there are no internal intersections between the contract curve and the fixed proportion sharing rule line, or the two coincide completely. The second case corresponds to both agents having identical degrees of relative risk aversion, and the first corresponds to them having different degrees of relative risk aversion.

Thus, the result that all efficient sharing rules will always correspond to a fixed proportion share of the final revenue can be seen to correspond to the case in which both the creator and the distributor have CRRA utility functions with exactly the same degree of relative risk aversion. However, note that this situation is quite delicate, since if the creator and the distributor have constant absolute risk aversion but different values of the risk aversion parameter (albeit slightly different), then a fixed proportion sharing rule is never efficient! Concretely, if we take the realistic case of $R_c > R_d$, and then consider the marginal rates of substitution of both the creator and the distributor at any point on the fixed sharing rule line ($k_2 = \delta k_1$), we have

$$-MRS_c(k) = \left(\frac{k_1}{k_2}\right)^{-R_c} = \left(\frac{k_1}{\delta k_1}\right)^{-R_c} = \delta^{R_c}$$

and

$$-MRS_d(k) = \left(\frac{x_1 - k_1}{x_2 - k_2}\right)^{-R_d} = \left(\frac{x_1 - k_1}{\delta(x_1 - k_1)}\right)^{-R_d} = \delta^{R_d}$$

But given $R_c > R_d$ and $\delta < 1$, we have $\delta^{R_c} < \delta^{R_d}$, and so we find that the indifference curve of the distributor is steeper as it passes through the fixed proportion sharing rule line than the indifference curve of the creator. Therefore, the contract curve must lie strictly above the fixed proportion sharing rule line for all contracts (except, of course, for the two contracts located at the origins). In this case, the royalty contract stipulates that the creator should get a greater share of sales revenues in the bad state (state 2) and a lower share in the good state.

The intuition for this is easy to see. Since the creator is more risk averse than the distributor, it is efficient for the latter to insure (partially) the former by offering a more stable income stream. This can be done by increasing the payment in the bad state and reducing it in the good state. Logically, the (realistically unlikely) case of $R_c < R_d$ leads to the opposite result.

It is interesting to note that certain real-world contracts that are quite often used, at least for the case of author royalties for books, involve a point that is located strictly below the fixed proportion sharing rule line. For example, Baumol and Heim (1967), p. 34, note that author's royalties are often graduated upwards, so that the royalty percentage grows as the total sales revenue grows. This implies that the royalty percentage in the good state is greater than that in the bad state, that is, a point located below the fixed proportion sharing rule line. If both the creator and the distributor have constant relative risk aversion (which is actually quite likely, as we have already noted), then such a contract can only be efficient (i.e., located on the contract curve) if the creator is less risk averse than the distributor, something that is very difficult to believe.

Surely such contracts are highly inefficient. To see this clearly, once again, take the case of music distribution. It is quite well known that record companies quite often give their artists an advance payment on royalties[8] that is, when the contract is signed, an up-front payment is made as an advance on future royalties (so that the artist will only perceive royalties in the future once the up-front payment amount has been reached).[9] This is equivalent to the distributor insuring the artist, since if the royalties due never turn out to reach the up-front payment amount, then it is the distributor that suffers the loss. In fact, an up-front royalty advance provides the equivalent of a deductible insurance contract, which is well known to be the best possible option for the insured when the premium is proportionally related to the indemnity (see, for example, Arrow (1971) for the first proof of this result). To see that this is true, simply take the maximum possible royalty payment state as being the 'no-loss' state. Then, when the royalty is high but not the maximum, a small loss has occurred, and a deductible contract will stipulate that no coverage should be paid in this case. However, when the royalty turns out to be very low (a high loss has occurred), a deductible contract will stipulate full coverage above the deductible, thereby implying that the total loss suffered by the insured cannot be any greater than the amount stipulated by the deductible. This is clearly what a royalty advance contract offers. In any case, in order for the distributor to offer insurance to the creator, it will always be necessary that the former be less risk averse than the latter (indeed, almost all insurance models assume that the insurer is risk neutral), which (assuming constant relative risk aversion) can only imply a point above, never below, the fixed percentage royalty line.[10]

The natural question is, given the knowledge that there always exist fixed proportion sharing rules that are Pareto efficient, will such a point ever be the final solution to any bargaining process designed to select a particular contract from the efficient set? Given that there may only be one such contract, it would seem nothing short of a miracle if it were to be selected out of the infinite set of options. However, if the contract curve were to coincide entirely with the line that indicates fixed proportion sharing rules, then independently of exactly which contract is used, it must share the sales revenue in the same proportion in all states, as is commonly done in the real world. We now go on to analyse exactly this case.

5.3   THE NASH BARGAINING SOLUTION

In the previous section, we have considered efficient royalty contracts between a creator and a distributor. However, there are an infinite number of such contracts (assuming perfect surplus divisibility), and so we still need to look at the mechanism under which exactly how one of these contracts is chosen over the others. Here, we take the Nash bargaining solution as being the relevant mechanism (see Nash (1950)).

The Nash bargaining solution (NBS) chooses one particular point on the contract curve (the set of efficient contracts), according to a small set of reasonable axioms that the solution should adhere to. Nash proved that his axioms can only select exactly one contract, and that particular contract appears as the solution to a very simple constrained maximisation problem, which in our case can be written as

$$max_k \, (Eu_c(k) - u_c(0))^\alpha (Eu_d(k) - u_d(0))^{1-\alpha}$$

subject to k being in the feasible set of bargains, and $u_j(0)$ is the utility that each agent achieves if no bargain is struck (that is, it measures each agent's reservation utility). In this problem, a new parameter, α, has been introduced. This parameter measures the 'relative bargaining power' of the creator. According to our assumptions, we have $u_c(0) = u_d(0) = 0$, and only two states of nature, and so in our case the NBS is the solution to the problem

$$max_{k_1,k_2} \, (pu_c(k_1) + (1-p)u_c(k_2))^\alpha (pu_d(x_1 - k_1) + (1-p)u_d(x_2 - k_2))^{1-\alpha}$$

where there is no real need to constrain the values of k_i (even though it may seem reasonable for them to be non-negative and not greater than x_i), since in principle there is no reason to assume that negative incomes for one party or the other cannot be optimal.

Taking the two first order conditions and simplifying, we get immediately to the fact that the NBS, here denoted by the vector, $k^* = (k_1^*, k_2^*)$, is found by the simultaneous solution to the two following equations

$$\left(\frac{\alpha}{1-\alpha}\right)\left(\frac{Eu_d(k^*)}{Eu_c(k^*)}\right) = \frac{u_d'(x_1 - k_1^*)}{u_c'(k_1^*)} \qquad (5.2)$$

$$\left(\frac{\alpha}{1-\alpha}\right)\left(\frac{Eu_d(k^*)}{Eu_c(k^*)}\right) = \frac{u_d'(x_2 - k_2^*)}{u_c'(k_2^*)} \qquad (5.3)$$

Combining the two first order conditions, we get

$$\frac{u'_d(x_1 - k_1^*)}{u'_c(k_1^*)} = \frac{u'_d(x_2 - k_2^*)}{u'_c(k_2^*)} \implies \frac{u'_d(x_1 - k_1^*)}{u'_d(x_2 - k_2^*)} = \frac{u'_c(k_1^*)}{u'_c(k_2^*)}$$

that is, as expected, the NBS is obviously a particular point that satisfies the contract curve for the problem.

On the other hand, given any vector $k = (k_1, k_2)$, as we have already seen above, a contract with a fixed proportion sharing rule stipulates

$$k_2 = \left(\frac{x_2}{x_1}\right) k_1 \qquad (5.4)$$

that is, there is a simple linear relationship between the two royalty payments. Thus, we are interested in knowing if the simultaneous solution to (5.2) and (5.3) will, in general, satisfy (5.4).

Since under Theorem 5.1, we know that in all cases there does exist at least one efficient contract that stipulates a fixed proportion sharing rule, in principle, we cannot ignore the possibility that, while it is not guaranteed under any case except constant and common relative risk aversion, a fixed proportion sharing rule may eventuate as the optimal contract. For example, in the case of $u'_j(0) < \infty$ for both $j=c$, d, this would only occur if the NBS locates exactly that single efficient contract that lies on the fixed proportion sharing rule line. Surely this is unlikely at best, especially when we consider that for the fixed proportion sharing rule to always eventuate under the NBS, then altering the underlying parameter set would shift the NBS to exactly the new unique point satisfying both efficiency and a fixed proportion sharing rule. Since it is clearly extremely doubtful that we will ever find such a case, we shall concentrate here exclusively on the case for which a fixed proportion sharing rule is always found as the NBS, that is, the case of constant and common relative risk aversion, $R_c = R_d = R$. In particular, since we are assuming a specific utility form, we can also locate exact solutions (numerical if we introduce numerical data for the parameters), which will allow us to get an idea as to the exact value of the royalty proportion in the solution.

For this case, it turns out that we get the following

Theorem 5.3 If both the creator and the distributor have CRRA utility functions with the same degree of relative risk aversion, then the NBS selects the royalty contract that stipulates that each party receives a proportion of sales revenue equal to his relative bargaining power.

In particular, note that the fixed proportion of sales revenue that the NBS contract locates is independent of both R and p. If we take the most traditional type of royalty contract that is signed between creators and publishers,[11] we would find that the fixed proportional sharing rule is generally set at something around 10 percent, that is, it corresponds to $\alpha = 0.1$, or the distributor has a relative bargaining power that is nine times greater than that of the creator. Is this a reasonable approximation to what real-life intuition suggests? Consider, for example, the well known fact that when the time between offers collapses to 0 in the alternating offers bargaining game of Rubinstein (see Rubinstein (1982)), its sub-game perfect equilibrium converges to the NBS defined by bargaining powers equal to the inverse of each participants' intertemporal discount factor (see, for example, Binmore (1992) for a simple proof of this). If the distributor is a large corporation (for example, a record company), it is reasonable to assume that its discount factor is equal to the interest rate, and it is also reasonable to assume that an individual creator has a discount factor that is greater than the interest rate (that is, an individual creator is certainly more impatient than a copyright collective), but nine times greater seems somewhat exaggerated.[12]

Naturally, there are other factors that may influence the value of the relative bargaining powers, and that may provide a far better defence for the creator having a relative bargaining power that is nine times smaller than that of the distributor. For example, one thing that we have completely omitted in the preceding analysis is the differences that occur both in independent wealth and in outside opportunities for each party (that is, the relative need of each for the distribution contract to exist). For the case of performance rights, as we have argued above, successfully managing the copyright to a musical composition implies such high transactions costs that it is really not feasible to administer outside of a copyright collective, and so indeed it certainly does seem reasonable that the creator's need is greater, which would be consistent with a value of α that is significantly less than one half. On the other hand, copyright collectives are not really corporations, but rather a large group of copyright holders acting together, in which case they probably will not want to exercise excessive bargaining power against individual members, which may in turn explain why individual royalty percentages for the case of copyright collectives may be as high as 90 percent.[13]

5.4   CONCLUSIONS

In this paper we have considered, in a very simple setting, efficient royalty contracts between the creator of a cultural work and its distributor. Perhaps one of the most important examples of such contracts are those signed between copyright holders (by defect, creators) and the firms that produce and sell the final consumption items. Other examples are the relationship between creators and copyright collectives, and between copyright collectives and broadcasters. Since a general characteristic of such contracts is that they have fixed proportional sharing rules (the percentage share of sales revenue is independent of the final value of sales revenue), our interest has been in considering the efficiency of such contracts.

We find that, under certain quite general conditions (increasing and concave utility for both creator and distributor), there is always at least one efficient contract that does specify a fixed proportion sharing rule, and furthermore, if marginal utility with zero wealth is strictly finite, then one can also find simple conditions such that there is exactly one such contract. For these cases, however, it seems very unlikely that the single contract (out of an infinite set) will be consistently selected as the outcome of a bargaining process, and so we have carried on to consider the case for which all efficient contracts involve a fixed proportion sharing rule.

The relevant case has been shown to correspond to constant and common relative risk aversion for both parties. For this case, independently of all parameters, all efficient contracts stipulate that the percentage shares of revenue will be independent of the state of nature that emerges. However, we also indicated the rather delicate nature of this result, since if the creator and the distributor have constant but different relative risk aversion, then no efficient contracts (except the two origins) are consistent with fixed proportion sharing rules.

We have also pointed out that, if we must assume that one of the creator or distributor is more risk averse, then it is surely most logical that the most risk averse of the two is the creator. This view is upheld by noting that it is common to see distributors offering insurance to creators through royalty advance contracts. However, such a situation also implies that any contract that stipulates that the royalty percentage increases with the amount of sales revenue, as is also often the case in real-world contracts, must be inefficient. Hence, clearly, there is a very large set of real-world contracts that are currently in use that can be improved upon.

Finally, we have considered the Nash bargaining solution as a mechanism for selection of a single contract from among the efficient set. We noted that, for the case in which all efficient contracts have a fixed proportion sharing rule, the proportional share corresponds to the relative bargaining powers of the parties to the contract. We noted that real-world contracts, in which it is frequent to see fixed proportion sharing rules with the creator retaining a smaller share of revenue, may be argued to be efficient given the relative impatience of creators compared to copyright collectives, and given the greater relative need of creators for the contract to exist. However, this becomes more difficult to defend for the cases when the creator ends up with a share that may be as low as 10 percent of total revenue.

As far as future research is concerned, there are several ways in which the current analysis can be extended and improved. It may be worthwhile to consider a more general set of states, perhaps even a continuous set of states of nature, instead of the simple two dimensional setting used here. On one hand, it is doubtful that further insights will be gained, and it is certainly true that this particular extension will imply a significant increase in mathematical complexity, but on the other hand, this extension will allow real-world data to be used and therefore, the theoretical model could be contrasted with valid empirical data. Secondly, as far as the theoretical model itself is concerned, it would certainly be interesting to include differences between the creator and the distributor on dimensions other than their pure roles within the model. Risk free wealth could be included quite simply, and may be a powerful way of explaining bargaining powers. Naturally, it would also be interesting to carry out an empirical study with the objective of seeing if the assumptions of constant and common relative risk aversion, and a relative bargaining power of about 0.1 for creators are reasonable assumptions for the case at hand.

Finally, there is a significant background risk problem that has been completely ignored in our model, in which we have studied the relationship between a creator and a distributor quite independently from all other such contracts. In particular, it is certainly true that the distributor will generally already hold a portfolio of existing contracts with other creators, to which it is considering adding the current contract. It is also true that there are likely to be significant covariance effects that may actually reduce the risk that the distributor faces. Exactly how such background risk issues will affect the characteristics of the efficient contract would be most interesting.

NOTES

1. Financial aid under research project PB98-0059 from DGES is gratefully acknowledged.
2. Throughout, we shall use the feminine pronoun to refer to a creator, and the masculine to refer to a distributor. This is purely in the interests of ease and clarity of exposition, and no further connotations should be attached to this decision.
3. See also the seminal papers of Wilson (1968) and Pratt and Zeckhauser (1989). Gollier (1991) provides a summary of the relevant literature up to 1991, and Pratt (2000) shows how certain previous results can be unified into a consistent theory.
4. We refer to this second point as the distributor's origin.
5. Note that we are assuming that the derivative of each agent's utility in k_2 is not zero. This can be guaranteed at any interior point.
6. Some of the following results are also given in Watt (2000) for a very similar setting.
7. More recently, Levy (1994) and Blake (1996), using observed portfolio choices, have found much higher values. These results, however, as well as the findings of Mehra and Prescott (1985), imply that relative risk aversion may only be as high as 47.

8. Very recently, according to publicly released information in the trade press, Mariah Carey signed with Universal with a 22 million Euro advance on royalty payments. No information at all concerning the royalty percentages as a function of sales revenue was given, however.
9. Baumol and Heim (1967) also note that such contracts are common for book publishing.
10. A second natural interpretation of contracts that stipulate a royalty that increases with sales revenue is that they are intended to provide proper incentives for problems involving asymmetric information (a case that has been simply assumed away in this paper). This option, however, begs the question as to why such contracts should locate below the fixed proportion sharing rule, since the incentive mechanism only requires that they locate below the creator's risk free locus.
11. See Baumol and Heim (1967) for the case of book publishing, and Towse (2001) for the case of music.
12. Indeed, if this were true, we would find creators rushing to take out huge loans from banks, since the interest rate seems so low to them.
13. In Spain, the creators of musical compositions receive a percentage of income generated and performance rights that is between 85 and 90 percent.
14. Other ways of writing the condition are possible, for example, the condition is equivalent to requiring that two times the distributor's absolute risk aversion is not less than his measure of absolute prudence.

REFERENCES

Arrow, K. (1971), *Essays in the Theory of Risk Bearing*, Chicago: Markham.

Baumol, W. and P. Heim (1967), 'On Contracting with Publishers: or What Every Author Should Know', *American Association of University Professors Bulletin*, **53**, 30–46 (reprinted as chapter 22 in Towse (1997)).

Binmore, K. (1992), *Fun and Games: A Text on Game Theory*, Massachusetts: D. C. Heath.

Blake, D. (1996), 'Efficiency, Risk Aversion and Portfolio Insurance: An Analysis of Financial Asset Portfolios Held by Investors in the United Kingdom', *The Economic Journal*, **106**, 1175–1192.

Borch, K. (1962), 'Equilibrium in a Reinsurance Market', *Econometrica*, **30**, 424–444.

Friend, I. and M. Blume (1975), 'The Demand for Risky Assets', *American Economic Review*, **65**, 900–922.

Gollier, C. (1991), 'The Economic Theory of Risk Exchanges: A Review', *Contributions to Insurance Economics*, G. Dionne (Ed.), Massachusetts: Kluwer Academic Publishers.

Hansen, L.P. and K.J. Singleton (1982), 'Generalized Instrumental Variables Estimation of Non-linear Expectations Models', *Econometrica*, **50**, 1269–1286.

Levy, H. (1994), 'Absolute and Relative Risk Aversion: An Experimental Study', *Journal of Risk and Uncertainty*, 289–307.

Mehra, R. and E. Prescott (1985), 'The Equity Premium – A Puzzle', *Journal of Monetary Economics*, **15**, 145–161.

Nash, J. (1950), 'The Bargaining Problem', *Econometrica*, **18**, 155–162.

Pratt, J. (2000), 'Efficient Risk Sharing: The Last Frontier', *Management Science*, **46**, 1545–1553.

Pratt, J. and R. Zeckhauser (1989), 'The Impact of Risk Sharing on Efficient Decision', *Journal of Risk and Uncertainty*, **2**, 219–234.

Rubinstein, A. (1982), 'Perfect Equilibrium in a Bargaining Model', *Econometrica*, **50**, 97–110.

Szpiro, G. (1986), 'Measuring Risk Aversion: An Alternative Approach', *The Review of Economics and Statistics*, **68**, 156–159.

Towse, R. (Ed.) (1997), *Baumol's Cost Disease: The Arts and Other Victims*, Cheltenham: Edward Elgar.

Towse, R. (2001), *Creativity, Incentive and Reward: An Economic Analysis of Copyright and Culture in the Information Age*, Cheltenham: Edward Elgar.

Von Neumann, J. and O. Morgenstern (1947), *Theory of Games and Economic Behavior*, 2nd Edition, Princeton: Princeton University Press.

Watt, R. (2000), *Copyright and Economic Theory: Friends or Foes?*, Cheltenham: Edward Elgar.

Weber, W.E. (1970), 'The Effect of Interest Rates on Aggregate Consumption', *American Economic Review*, **60**, 591–600.

Wilson, R. (1968), 'The Theory of Syndicates', *Econometrica*, **36**, 113–132

APPENDIX

Proof of Lemma 5.1. If we use $k_2 \geq k_1$, then clearly the concavity of the creator's utility function implies $u'_c(k_1) \geq u'_c(k_2)$, and so in order for (5.1) to hold, we require $u'_d(x_2 - k_2) \leq u'_d(x_1 - k_1)$. However, this requires $x_2 - k_2 \geq x_1 - k_1$, that is $k_1 - k_2 \geq x_1 - x_2$ which is impossible, since its left-hand side is non-positive, and its right-hand side is strictly positive. Similarly, if $k_2 - x_2 \leq k_1 - x_1$, that is $x_2 - k_2 \geq x_1 - k_1$, then $u'_d(x_2 - k_2) \leq u'_d(x_1 - k_1)$. Thus, we require $u'_c(k_1) \geq u'_c(k_2)$, that is, $k_1 \leq k_2$ which was just shown to be impossible.

Proof of Lemma 5.2. Put $k_1 = 0$ into equation (5.1). The right-hand side must now take the value ∞ and so in order for it to be satisfied, we require the left-hand side to also take the value ∞. This can only occur if $k_2 = 0$. Hence the contract curve passes through the origin. Secondly, put $k_1 = x_1$

into (5.1) and note that by a similar argument, the equation can only be satisfied if $k_2 = x_2$.

Proof of Lemma 5.3. First, take logarithms of each side of (5.1)

$$Ln(u'_c(k_1)) + Ln(u'_d(x_2 - k_2)) = Ln(u'_c(k_2)) + Ln(u'_d(x_1 - k_1))$$

that is

$$h(k_1, k_2) \equiv Ln(u'_c(k_1)) + Ln(u'_d(x_2 - k_2)) - Ln(u'_c(k_2)) - Ln(u'_d(x_1 - k_1)) = 0$$

Now, from the implicit function theorem, and recalling that by definition

$$\frac{\partial Ln(u'(z))}{\partial z} = -A(z)$$

we have

$$\frac{dk_2}{dk_1} = -\frac{\left(\dfrac{\partial h(k)}{\partial k_1}\right)}{\left(\dfrac{\partial h(k)}{\partial k_2}\right)} = \frac{A_c(k_1) + A_d(x_1 - k_1)}{A_c(k_2) + A_d(x_2 - k_2)}$$

as required.

Proof of Corollary 5.1. This follows immediately from Lemma 5.3 when both parties are strictly risk averse as has been assumed.

Proof of Corollary 5.2. If both parties to the contract have decreasing absolute risk aversion, then $A_j(z_1) < A_j(z_2)$ whenever $z_1 > z_2$. However, under Lemma 5.1, all points on the contract curve will satisfy $k_1 > k_2$ and $x_1 - k_1 > x_2 - k_2$. Hence, if both parties to the contract have decreasing absolute risk aversion, the numerator of $K'(k_1)$ in Lemma 5.3 must be smaller than the denominator, that is, $K'(k_1) < 1$. Similar arguments suffice to prove the other two cases.

Proof of Theorem 5.1. Firstly, for the case in which $u'_j(0) = \infty$ for at least one $j = c$, d, existence of an intersection between the contract curve and the fixed proportion line is given by Lemma 5.2. In this case, the contract curve touches the fixed proportion sharing rule line at the origin of the individual for whom $u'_j(0) = \infty$, which of course, may be for both individuals (i.e., in this case, there may be two points at which the contract curve touches the fixed proportion sharing rule line).

For the other case, $u'_j(0) < \infty$ for both $j=c$, d, we proceed as follows. Firstly, recall that all possible fixed proportion sharing rules are defined by the equation $k_2 = \delta k_1$, where $\delta \equiv x_2/x_1$. If the contract curve touches the fixed proportion sharing rule line, then by equation (5.1) we must have

$$u'_c(k_1)u'_d(\delta(x_1 - k_1)) = u'_c(\delta k_1)u'_d(x_1 - k_1)$$

Now, since $u'_j(0) < \infty$, we can define two functions as follows

$$M_1(k_1) \equiv \frac{u'_c(k_1)}{u'_d(x_1 - k_1)} \text{ and } M_2(k_1) \equiv \frac{u'_c(\delta k_1)}{u'_d(\delta(x_1 - k_1))}$$

Therefore we have

$$M_1(0) = \frac{u'_c(0)}{u'_d(x_1)} > \frac{u'_c(0)}{u'_d(x_2)} = M_2(0)$$

and similarly

$$M_1(x_1) = \frac{u'_c(x_1)}{u'_d(0)} < \frac{u'_c(x_2)}{u'_d(0)} = M_2(x_2)$$

so that $M_1(k_1)$ starts out above $M_2(k_1)$, but ends up below it. Since both are continuous functions, there must be at least one point at which $M_1(k_1) = M_2(k_1)$, i.e. it is on the contract curve. Furthermore, the relevant point must satisfy $0 < k_1 < x_1$.

Now consider when the intersection is unique, under the assumption that $u'_j(0) < \infty$ for both $j=c$, d, which (as we have already noted) implies that the function $M_1(k_1)$ starts out above $M_2(k_1)$, but ends up below it. Note that

$$M_1'(k_1) = \frac{u_c''(k_1)u_d'(x_1 - k_1) + u_c'(k_1)u_d''(x_1 - k_1)}{u_d'(x_1 - k_1)^2}$$

$$= -M_1(k_1)(A_c(k_1) + A_d(x_1 - k_1))$$

and

$$M_2'(k_1) = \frac{\delta(u_c''(\delta k_1)u_d'(\delta(x_1 - k_1)) + u_c'(\delta k_1)u_d''(\delta(x_1 - k_1)))}{u_d'(\delta(x_1 - k_1))^2}$$

$$= -M_2(k_1)\delta(A_c(\delta k_1) + A_d(\delta(x_1 - k_1)))$$

Firstly, any intersection between the two curves will be unique if $M_1(k_1)$ has strictly less slope than $M_2(k_1)$ at that point. This can be expressed as the requirement that $M_1'(k_1) < M_2'(k_1)$ whenever $M_1(k_1) = M_2(k_1)$. Using the expressions just obtained for the slopes of the two functions, we get a unique intersection if

$$-M_1(k_1)(A_c(k_1) + A_d(x_1 - k_1)) < -M_2(k_1)\delta(A_c(\delta k_1) + A_d(\delta(x_1 - k_1)))$$

when $M_1(k_1) = M_2(k_1)$. That is, at the intersection we require

$$(A_c(k_1) + A_d(x_1 - k_1)) > \delta(A_c(\delta k_1) + A_d(\delta(x_1 - k_1)))$$

Now, if each participant has non-decreasing absolute risk aversion ($A_j'(z) \geq 0$) then $(A_c(k_1) + A_d(x_1 - k_1))/(A_c(\delta k_1) + A_d(\delta(x_1 - k_1))) \geq 1$, and since $\delta = x_2/x_1 < 1$, the condition is satisfied for sure.

Secondly, the two slope equations can also be written as

$$M_1'(k_1) = -M_1(k_1)\left(\frac{R_c(k_1)}{k_1} + \frac{R_d(x_1 - k_1)}{x_1 - k_1}\right)$$

$$= -\left(\frac{M_1(k_1)}{k_1(x_1 - k_1)}\right)((x_1 - k_1)R_c(k_1) + k_1 R_d(x_1 - k_1))$$

and

$$M_2'(k_1) = -M_2(k_1)\delta\left(\frac{R_c(\delta k_1)}{\delta k_1} + \frac{R_d(\delta(x_1 - k_1))}{\delta(x_1 - k_1)}\right)$$

$$= -\left(\frac{M_2(k_1)}{k_1(x_1 - k_1)}\right)((x_1 - k_1)R_c(\delta k_1) + k_1 R_d(\delta(x_1 - k_1)))$$

Now, at any point such that $M_1(k_1) = M_2(k_1)$, clearly the requisite that $M_1'(k_1) < M_2'(k_1)$ reduces to the condition

$$(x_1 - k_1)(R_c(k_1) - R_c(\delta k_1)) + k_1(R_d(x_1 - k_1) - R_d(\delta(x_1 - k_1))) > 0$$

which is guaranteed if each participant has strictly increasing relative risk aversion.

Finally, when neither non-decreasing absolute risk aversion nor increasing relative risk aversion holds, we cannot prove uniqueness of the intersection using only the slopes of the two functions $M_i(k_1)$, $i=1, 2$. However, note that if both were strictly convex, since the first one starts off below the second but ends up above it, there can only be one intersection between the two.

With a minimal amount of effort, the second derivatives of each function can be calculated as

$$M_1''(k_1) = M_1(k_1)((A_c(k_1) + A_d(x_1 - k_1))^2 - A_c'(k_1) + A_d'(x_1 - k_1))$$

and

$$M_2''(k_1) = M_2(k_1)((A_c(\delta k_1) + A_d(\delta(x_1 - k_1)))^2 - A_c'(\delta k_1) + A_d'(\delta(x_1 - k_1)))$$

and so it suffices to show that the two terms

$$(A_c(k_1) + A_d(x_1 - k_1))^2 - A_c'(k_1) + A_d'(x_1 - k_1)$$

and

$$(A_c(\delta k_1) + A_d(\delta(x_1 - k_1)))^2 - A_c'(\delta k_1) + A_d'(\delta(x_1 - k_1))$$

are both strictly positive. However, since absolute risk aversion is decreasing, the only negative term in either equation is the slope of the distributor's absolute risk aversion. Therefore, expanding the squared term, we can impose the condition that $A_d(z)^2 + A_d'(z) \geq 0$ for any z, which will then guarantee that both functions $M_i(k_1)$ are strictly convex, and so can only have a single intersection. It is straightforward to show that

$$A'(z) = \left(A(z)R'(z) - A(z)^2\right)\big/R(z)$$

and so our condition can be written as

$$\frac{A_d(z)R_d'(z) - A_d(z)^2}{R_d(z)} \geq A_d(z)^2$$

which reduces directly to the stated condition.[14]

Proof of Theorem 5.2. Assuming that both the creator and the distributor have CRRA utility functions, with relative risk aversion parameters of R_c and R_d respectively, then we know that their utility functions are given by

$$u_j(z) = \frac{z^{1-R_j}}{1-R_j} + y_j \text{ for } j=c, d.$$

where the y_j are constants. For this function, the Arrow-Pratt measure of relative risk aversion is simply $zA_j(z) = R_j$. Marginal utility is given by

$$u_j'(z) = z^{-R_j} \text{ for } j=c,d.$$

and so in this case the two functions $M_1(k_1)$ and $M_2(k_1)$ are given by

$$M_1(k_1) \equiv \frac{(k_1)^{-R_c}}{(x_1 - k_1)^{-R_d}} \text{ and } M_2(k_1) \equiv \frac{(\delta k_1)^{-R_c}}{(\delta(x_1 - k_1))^{-R_d}}$$

Clearly, we have $M_1(0) = M_2(0) \to \infty$ and $M_1(x_1) = M_2(x_1) = 0$. Now, if the two were to also be equal at any given interior point, then it would have to be true that at that point

$$\frac{(x_1 - k_1)^{R_d}}{(k_1)^{R_c}} = \frac{\delta^{R_d}(x_1 - k_1)^{R_d}}{\delta^{R_c}(k_1)^{R_c}} \Rightarrow \delta^{(R_d - R_c)} = 1$$

Since $\delta < 1$, this can only happen if $R_d = R_c$, but in this case, it will happen at all interior points. That is, the two functions coincide exactly if the creator and the distributor have identical relative risk aversion, and they never coincide internally otherwise.

Proof of Theorem 5.3. Since for the case at hand

$$u_j(z) = \frac{z^{1-R_j}}{1-R_j} + y_j \text{ for } j=c,d.$$

and normalising (without loss of generality) so that $y_j = 0$ for both $j=c$, d, the first order conditions for the NBS are

$$\left(\frac{\alpha}{1-\alpha}\right) \frac{\left(p\left(\frac{(x_1-k_1^*)^{1-R}}{1-R}\right)+(1-p)\left(\frac{(x_2-k_2^*)^{1-R}}{1-R}\right)\right)}{p\left(\frac{(k_1^*)^{1-R}}{1-R}\right)+(1-p)\left(\frac{(k_2^*)^{1-R}}{1-R}\right)} = \frac{(x_1-k_1^*)^{-R}}{(k_1^*)^{-R}} \quad i=1,2$$

Simplifying, these two equations reduce to

$$\left(\frac{\alpha}{1-\alpha}\right)\left(\frac{p(x_1-k_1^*)^{1-R}+(1-p)(x_2-k_2^*)^{1-R}}{p(k_1^*)^{1-R}+(1-p)(k_2^*)^{1-R}}\right) = \left(\frac{k_i^*}{x_i-k_i^*}\right)^R \quad i=1,2$$

Since for the case at hand we know that $k_2 = \delta k_1$, the second equation can be dispensed with entirely, and we can simply locate the solution using the following single equation in a single unknown

$$\left(\frac{\alpha}{1-\alpha}\right)\left(\frac{p(x_1-k_1^*)^{1-R}+(1-p)(x_2-\delta k_1^*)^{1-R}}{p(k_1^*)^{1-R}+(1-p)(\delta k_1^*)^{1-R}}\right) = \left(\frac{k_1^*}{x_1-k_1^*}\right)^R$$

While this is a rather formidable looking equation, fortunately it reduces quite simply to something extremely simple and intuitive. Firstly, since $x_2 - \delta k_1^* = \delta(x_1 - k_1^*)$, we have

$$\left(\frac{\alpha}{1-\alpha}\right)\left(\frac{p(x_1-k_1^*)^{1-R}+(1-p)(\delta(x_1-k_1^*))^{1-R}}{p(k_1^*)^{1-R}+(1-p)(\delta k_1^*)^{1-R}}\right)=\left(\frac{k_1^*}{x_1-k_1^*}\right)^R$$

that is

$$\left(\frac{\alpha}{1-\alpha}\right)\left(\frac{(x_1-k_1^*)^{1-R}(p+(1-p)\delta^{1-R})}{(k_1^*)^{1-R}(p+(1-p)\delta^{1-R})}\right)=\left(\frac{k_1^*}{x_1-k_1^*}\right)^R$$

Cancelling the common term $p+(1-p)\delta^{1-R}$, we have

$$\left(\frac{\alpha}{1-\alpha}\right)\left(\frac{(x_1-k_1^*)^{1-R}}{(k_1^*)^{1-R}}\right)=\left(\frac{k_1^*}{x_1-k_1^*}\right)^R$$

With a minimal amount of effort this reduces to $k_1^*=\alpha x_1$ as required.

6. Innovation of Music

Tobias Regner[1]

6.1 INTRODUCTION

The impact of new information technologies is a hot topic in economics and business. In particular the issue of digital content is in the spotlight. This paper analyses the consequences for the music industry of the recent advances in information processing and transmission. It is based on the property rights theory framework introduced by Grossman and Hart (1986) and Hart and Moore (1990) and it studies the innovation process of music goods from an organisational point of view.

We identify as 'the agents' the artists who create music and record labels who promote and distribute it. Obviously, the result of their combined work (a song or album) is not predictable at the moment they agree to co-operate. Therefore the exact nature of the piece of music is ill-defined ex ante. The contract between artist and label cannot specify the innovation itself. According to the basic theoretical framework they can only contract on the allocation of the property rights of the innovation (the copyright).

Based on a detailed case study of the music industry we identify its two most essential business areas and relate them to the two relevant parameters of the incomplete contracts model: the relative marginal efficiency and the relative indispensability of the agents.[2] The results of the model application are in line with the incumbent ownership structure since they predict copyright of songs to be owned by the labels. However, based on the analysis we conjecture a gradual decrease of the label's power because of technological change and its impact on the industry, and therefore a change in the allocation of property rights. We also discuss new types of intermediaries in a future music market.

The structure of the chapter is as follows. Section 6.2 gives the intuition of the theoretical framework and Section 6.3 takes an in-depth look at the music industry. The historical development of the industry is illustrated and its implication on the market structure is shown. The copyright law and the payment system in the music industry are briefly explained. Moreover, two aspects of the core music business (marketing and distribution) are examined in detail and analysed with respect to the model parameters.

In Section 6.4, the recent advances in information technology and their impact on the industry are briefly explained. An outlook of possible future developments and their implications is also given. Finally, the consequences for the marketing and the distribution of music are described. Section 6.5 concludes.

6.2 THEORETICAL FRAMEWORK: PROPERTY RIGHTS THEORY

The theory of the firm and the study of its boundaries originated with the famous essay by Coase (1937). The question of why there is so much economic activity within formal organisations despite the fact that markets are such an efficient mechanism for allocating scarce resources was answered with the costs of transacting in a world of imperfect information. It may be less costly to organise production within a firm, if transaction costs of market exchange are very high.

Recently its focus shifted from the co-ordination problems towards the role of firm boundaries in providing incentives to invest, recognising the opportunistic behaviour in the 'hold-up problem' (first noticed by Klein *et al.* (1978) and modelled by Grout (1984)).

Property rights theory's basic elements are relationship-specific, non-contractable investments in human capital and the impossibility to draw up a complete contract because of uncertainty. Parties are vulnerable to hold-up as unforeseen situations are bound to arise (after their investments have been made) that require the two parties to renegotiate over the terms of their dealing. In this (efficient) ex post bargaining, a part of an agent's 'sunk' investments is expropriated by the other party. Unwillingness to invest or increased resources to protect itself against hold-up threat is the consequence and in either way, inefficiency is the result.

If no extra value is created by the particular relationship, both would be equally well off if they traded with outsiders from the spot market and the hold-up problem would not exist. In general however agents are not totally dispensable or replaceable and there is in fact some value added by their particular co-operation which results in inefficient incentives to invest. The degree of indispensability determines the extent of the inefficiency.

Property rights theory regards ownership of non-human (e.g. physical) assets as the defining characteristic of firms. Each agent necessarily owns his human capital. Ownership of the non-human assets however implies the right for the owner to exclude others from using the asset, which in turn affects the relevant payoffs for the bargaining and thus the incentives to invest in his human capital.

Then, giving more control over assets to one party strengthens its incentives to invest, but only at the expense of weakening the incentives of the other party. Thus there is a trade-off which determines the efficient allocation of ownership. The governance structure of a firm can therefore be regarded as a mechanism for dealing with hold-up problems.

In the context of the music industry the two agents are an artist and a record label. Combined they produce a piece of music, the asset being the copyright of the music. Both can improve the value of the innovation by investing in their respective human capital (writing songs and creating a promotion campaign, for instance). However – once made – the investments are specific to that very relationship. As the exact nature of the innovation is ill defined ex ante, the two agents cannot write a contract for the delivery of a specific product. In fact, the ex ante contract can only be written on the allocation of ownership of the innovation.

Since there is just one indivisible asset – the copyright of the song – two ownership structures are compared: label and artist ownership.

Owning the copyright provides high incentives to invest for the label, but gives reduced incentives to the artist (and vice versa). Two parameters influence this trade-off. As explained earlier the indispensability of an agent will affect the investment level of his partner. Furthermore, the overall payoff depends on the marginal efficiency of an agent's investment. The combination of these two parameters answers the question of optimal ownership and subsequently the relative indispensability and the relative marginal efficiency of the agents are analysed to determine if label or artist ownership is more efficient. Finally, we study the impact on the parameters induced by technological changes over time in order to explain changes in the industry structure.

6.3   THE MUSIC INDUSTRY

Music is one of the bigger consumer markets of the world with a global revenue of around $40 billion annually.[3] In most industrialised countries per capita consumption of music products is above $30 a year. Japanese, Norwegians, Icelanders and US Americans are spending even more than $50 a year on average.[4]

History

The birth of the music industry took place around the turn of the century. The development of a new technology (the gramophone) allowed re-playing of music. Records were used to save the information of music on a physical container. Consumers were then able to play them on their gramophone whenever and wherever they liked. Thanks to the mass production of records it became possible to distribute recorded music and offer it for a reasonable price. Because the incumbent companies were able to control the important retail distribution system, today's music industry is characterised by very high barriers to entry.[5]

Thus we have an oligopolistic market dominated by five record companies. The so called major labels BMG, EMI, Sony, Universal and Warner have a combined market share of approximately 80 percent.[6]

Arguably the emergence of the software Napster marked another important date for technology used in the music market. Music had already gone digital in the early 80s when Philips and Sony invented the CD which quickly replaced analogue forms of music products such as records and cassettes. Information technology like the development of the MP3 compressing format[7] by the Fraunhofer Institute and Internet broadband data transmission facilitated the exchange of music files among friends, albeit on a very small scale and certainly in the sense of fair use.[8] It was only in 1999 that file-sharing networks emerged and their huge success – epitomised by Napster – made the record industry and the public at large realise the technological possibilities of digital music in the networked age.

Therefore, this account distinguishes between the pre-Napster music industry with no or minimal and thus insignificant copying and a post-Napster music industry that features large scale copying of music files using peer-to-peer file-sharing networks.

Industry structure

A label's role in the pre-Napster music market is basically to find and finance artists, to produce and promote their songs and finally to distribute the product in the retail industry. The label functions as an intermediary between the artist and the final consumer and it services the artist in a number of ways. Two fields seem to stand out: Marketing and Distribution.[9] Promotional and distributional entry barriers are also the main reason for the current highly concentrated industry structure according to Alexander's (1994) study of the music recording industry.

Marketing. An artist's reputation is obviously very essential for the sales of a record. Naturally, good quality of previous records can build up a favourable reputation for a band since music is an experience good.[10] Also promotion in any kind of form (TV advertisements, TV show appearances, magazine advertisements, concerts to name a few) improves the sales of an artist's recordings.

Whereas the quality of songs depends mainly on the artist's effort, successful promotion is reliant on the label and its investment. Established artists will already have a certain reputation based on their quality of songs and the media promotion of a newly released record will not be all that important, although it should not be underestimated. For newcomer artists though, their own reputation clearly will not have a very high impact on record sales. Here the label's promotion of the artist in the media is the part of marketing that significantly influences sales.

Therefore, seeing the market as a whole, the label's promotional endeavour seems to be more important to sales than the effort of the artist and its effect on quality. However, by no means at all is the artist's investment ineffective. The marginal productivity of their effort varies with the level of their reputation (the quality of their previous work), but in general it tends to be lower than the marginal productivity of the label's investment into promotion.

Distribution. The main way to sell CDs and other music products is through the retail industry. Labels command a very good retail distribution network for their products. Other ways to reach the final consumer such as online shops still seem to account for negligible sales and they are mostly owned and provided with music products by the labels anyway.

There does not seem to be an alternative distribution channel to the retail distribution network, which makes the labels indispensable in the production process of music. Their distribution role is irreplaceable. They have the experience and the corporate connections to run the retail distribution of music products. Artists have no other option than to work with them in order to sell their products to the final customers of the mass market.

Legal aspects and payment. Copyright law is the legal tool that arranges property issues between artists who create music, customers who consume it and the intermediary labels.

Obviously, copyright law prohibits customers copying the artist's work unless it is for fair use. However, protection as such is not the primary goal of the idea of copyright, which goes back to the writing of the US constitution in 1787. Instead, the intention is 'to promote the progress of science and useful arts'[11] and therefore a temporary monopoly can be granted to the innovator (to motivate him). The duration of copyright is 70 years after the artist's death.[12]

Very relevant for the music industry is the 'work for hire' aspect of the copyright law: Copyright will not be owned by the artist, if – by and large – the innovation has been commissioned by a company. Examples include a journalist whose articles are owned by the newspaper that employs him, whereas the contribution of a freelance writer remains his property (due to 'work for hire').[13]

Although the contract situation seems less clear in the music market, songs are generally declared 'works for hire' and copyrights are owned by the labels. Only in some rare cases with highly successful musicians do labels agree that the ownership of the copyrights will revert to the artists after a certain period.[14]

The payment scheme of the industry is based on royalties. Artists receive a certain percentage of the revenue their songs generate. The initial rate is between 7 and 15 percent (depending on the reputation of the artist). However, a number of deductions make the final royalty percentage the artist receives (for instance 12 percent) go down to about 3 percent of sales revenue.[15]

Obviously, this is not the major piece of the profit cake. An empirical study in Towse (2001) about the distribution of royalties between individuals and record companies confirms this. The vast majority of artists earn relatively little from copyrights, whereas the large chunk of royalty income generated goes to the publishers and a small minority of high earning performers who have enough reputation and bargaining power to control their own affairs by particular contractual arrangements.

'The Economics of Superstars', originated by Rosen (1981) and extended by Adler (1985), explains the skewness of earnings in superstar dominated professions such as entertainment.

Summary. Property rights of music products are generally allocated to the labels. The 'work for hire' clause of the copyright law grants them ownership of the innovation.

An analysis of marketing and distribution in the music industry shows that relative marginal productivity and indispensability are in favour of the labels, because of their more efficient marketing and their indispensable retail distribution network. However, the reputation of very famous artists might be important enough in the production process that they can demand copyrights to revert back to them (and better contracts, of course). On the other hand, new musicians without any reputation to build on have no other choice but to rely on a label to promote and distribute their music in order to sell in the mass market.

Therefore, we conclude that label ownership is more efficient in the pre-Napster music industry. This confirms the *ex ante* allocation based on copyright law. The way profits are distributed between artists and labels in reality supports this balance of power.

However, it should be noted here that generally there will be a change of ownership, if *ex ante* allocation and optimal ownership structure are different since the *ex ante* owner gets compensated and ownership changes in order to provide the best possible investment incentives.

6.4   POST-NAPSTER SCENARIO

Technological change and future developments

Currently the music market is being thoroughly restructured. On behalf of the major labels the Recording Industry Association of America (RIAA) sued Napster for infringing copyrights. The verdict returned was 'guilty' and its centralised file service was forced to shut down in July 2001. However, other peer-to-peer[16] file trading software (like Gnutella, FastTrack – consisting of MusicCity, Kazaa, Morpheus – which in contrast to Napster operate without a central file server) have become increasingly popular. In fact, the number of people typically logged on to the FastTrack network recently surpassed Napster's record of 1.57 million users in February 2001.[17] Lawsuits of the RIAA against some of the Napster offshoots are ongoing, but it does not seem very likely that they can be stopped for good. In fact, a recent study by The Yankee Group (2002) predicts audio file downloads from file-sharing networks to increase from 5.16 billion in 2001 to 7.44 billion in 2005.

As explained earlier, technological advances had a deep impact on the industry and further developments will gradually keep on changing it. The amount of transmittable data and the density of high-speed Internet connections in the population is bound to continue to increase significantly in the near future.[18] Whereas today the download of one song is convenient (in terms of time and connection costs) only for users with cable modems or digital subscriber lines, the number of such users is certainly increasing and so downloading megabyte files should be common very soon for the broad public.

These advances in transmission technology will allow the addition of supplements to the song itself. Parts of the CD cover and its information about the album/song (like the lyrics) could be added to the music file, thus shifting more and more information from the physical containers of the product (the disc itself, the box/cover and the booklet) to a digital-only form.

Whereas today many consumers still prefer a CD (definitely the more complete product) to a file because of its design, collectability and convenience, in the future all information contained in a CD might be visualised digitally and there might even be more features added to that product that are not feasible with a CD (virtual disc or band interviews on video for instance).

Marketing

The Internet offers artists new and efficient ways to promote themselves compared to the conventional marketing.

Established artists might use their own web site, newsgroups and mailing lists to update their fans about new products. This way they can easily inform and service their already existing user base. Since these customers have already experienced the artist's music and are convinced of his quality, the necessary update to inform them about new products is very cost-efficient.

Newcomers are helped by peer-to-peer file-sharing networks where potential consumers can try and experience their products, before eventually buying them as a CD if they like it. The P2P networks serve as information transmission channels for these artists. The widespread and hardly stoppable use of the networks provides an informational externality that increases the reach of newcomer music that was not possible before.[19] The loss of control over rewarded distribution is happily given up in exchange for the exponential increase in publicity.[20]

Distribution

The labels' traditional retail distribution channels are becoming less important and may eventually fade away entirely when music is distributed entirely electronically.

Firstly, music products can be sold directly by artists in online shops, which can be set up comparatively easily. Secondly, Internet-based distribution technologies (for instance direct distribution of MP3 files) are rapidly emerging.

Still, as long as there is a significant quality difference between the traditional music product (the CD) and a digital copy there will be demand for the original product and its way of distribution, although it is more expensive. Thus, labels will by and large maintain distribution control over physical music products for quite a while. However, when it becomes technologically feasible to provide all the CD's information in digital form that is convenient to use then the traditional distribution system will cease to be useful.

Summary

Labels are getting more and more dispensable as their retail distribution network becomes replaceable due to alternative ways of distribution. Relative marginal productivity is in favour of the artists, because they are able to promote their products more efficiently themselves. However, the migration process from label ownership to artist ownership will certainly not happen overnight.

First of all it depends on the technological development as explained above. Since the CD clearly offers a quality-of-use advantage to many consumers compared to the MP3 file alone, the retail distribution system – the labels' stronghold – is necessary. In the short term it will only be challenged by online CD sales.

Moreover, artists need to recognise their option. They might have strong personal ties with agents of the labels and might prefer the incumbent situation. They also might shy away from the transaction costs of starting a business of their own, which would demand some entrepreneurial involvement.

The new opportunities for artists in the networked age bring some threats as well. Established artists now have a cost-efficient way to service their existing user base, but their superstar bonus seems to erode because of the impact of file-sharing technology.

Its impact is positive though for less known artists thanks to the information externalities created by P2P networks. However, they still have to compete for attention[21] in a seemingly abundant field of new artists who are all able to utilise these information transmission channels.

In the advanced stage of the model artists will own their innovation (the copyright of their creative work) and in theory would employ workers for the various tasks Internet-based marketing and distribution require: web services like the design and maintenance of a web site or running an online shop for CD sales, promotion services (concert agency), art design of booklet and cover. These services are not particular and workers can be replaced on the spot market.

However in reality artists would rarely run their business entirely alone, instead asking intermediaries to provide them with the necessary services (see above). Again, these intermediaries are easily replaceable as the markets for web services, promotion services and art design can be expected to be rather competitive.

The artist 'Prince' can be seen as an early precursor. He became exceptionally popular in the early 90s but feuded with his record company in the middle of a long-term contract. He reluctantly fulfilled the deal only to produce his latest album with a label he founded himself. However, his motives might not be purely based on a monetary gain, but simply because of antipathy towards music labels.

These new intermediaries in the music industry might even be the old ones if the labels restructure and refocus their business. Nonetheless, they would face tougher competition than before since agents from other markets (IT services, promotion agencies) can enter the market and their indispensability in the industry will be lost. In particular intermediaries might offer new valuable services for unknown artists targeting their 'need for attention' in the networked world.

The interaction between the model parameters – relative indispensability and relative marginal efficiency – is visualised in Figure 6.1.

Due to the high indispensability of labels and their marginal efficiency advantage artists of the pre-Napster scenario would generally be positioned in the lower right section of the diagram which represents efficient label ownership. Different parameter values for established artists and newcomers are taken into account. Technological changes as described earlier affect the model parameters and thus the position of artists in the diagram. Depending on the artist type and the exact impact of technology a move across the ownership threshold – into efficient artist ownership – appears predictable.

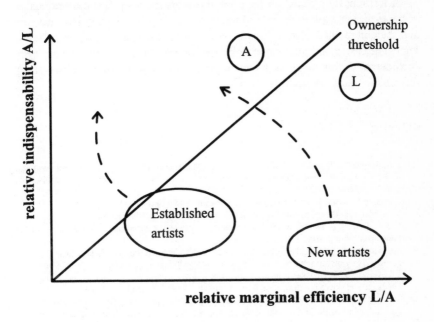

Figure 6.1 Interaction between model parameters

6.5   CONCLUSION

The property rights theory of the firm appears to be a very useful framework to understand the current ownership structure in the music market. Based on a detailed case study of the industry the findings of the model are in line with pre-Napster reality. The recent and future developments of technology in information processing and transmission suggest that the relevant parameters of the model could be affected. Therefore the paper questions whether the current industry structure of the music market – emerged and established over the course of a century – still offers the most efficient way to provide music innovations. If intellectual inputs dominate the innovation process of music sufficiently, then artists should own the music product.

This paper attempts to shed some new light on the highly interesting field of digital content in the networked age. It can only be regarded as a beginning. A recent study by Clemons and Lang (2002) generally confirms our results.[22] Alternative theoretical approaches to analyse the changes in the music industry are certainly plausible and should be encouraged by the rather open theoretical grounds of this paper.

A formalisation based on the property rights framework and an extension of the model to explain the role of new intermediaries in the industry structure and the contractual relationships between them, artists and labels will be the logical next step. A future paper will focus on this. Some issues have not been considered in this work (a payment or reward model, for instance). They remain for future research.

NOTES

1. I would like to thank Maija Halonen, David de Meza, Osiris Parcero, Mariano Selvaggi and Richard Watt, seminar audiences at Bristol and at the SERCI congress and at Kiel for inspiration and valuable comments.
2. Compare Hart and Moore (1990) and also Aghion and Tirole (1994).
3. Data from the Recording Industry Association of America (www.riaa.com).
4. Year 2000 figures from *The Economist*. Source: International Federation of the Phonographic Industry (2001).
5. See Tschmuck (2001). However, the concentration process has not been linear over the century. New manufacturing technology led to significant waves of entry (late 1910s/early 1920s and 1950s (magnetic tape recording)). Horizontal integration started again from the 1960s on and drove concentration down to today's level (Alexander (1994)).
6. See also Tschmuck (2001). Towse (2001) argues that an oligopolistic structure is very typical for industries in the cultural sector with a few multinationals dominating the market.
7. MP3 (MPEG Audio Layer 3) uses a psycho-acoustic algorithm to reduce the file size by 90 percent. Quality is reduced as well, although this is hardly noticeable for common consumers.
8. Copies for private non-commercial purposes are fair use (or fair dealing in the UK) and thus exempted from copyright infringement (see Towse (2001) for an economic analysis). Samuelson (1996) provides an in-depth analysis of the character and the importance of fair use for society.
9. Among the other core competencies of labels are their function as risk agents (at least for newcomer bands, because they own a portfolio of bands and can pool the risk), their experience in handling the stars' media affairs (a 'star agency'), the production of CDs and talent scouting. Although these are certainly necessary, they do not seem to be overly important and the model will focus on marketing and distribution.
10. Shapiro and Varian (1999) describe the properties of information goods. Music for instance is an experience good, because you have to experience it to know what it is and to be able to value it.
11. From www.riaa.com
12. Or 95 years after publication in the case of 'work for hire'; numbers for the US.
13. See King in *Wired*.

14. According to Krasilovsky and Shemel (2000) which is an excellent account of the music business.
15. Three percent deducted since the artist has to pay the producer's royalty out of his own royalty. Twenty five percent reduction for packaging (the artist's royalty is based solely on the recording itself, not on the artwork, wrapping or sales appeal added on by the packaging ingenuity of the label). Fifteen percent are reduced for free goods (labels do not pay artist royalties on records that are given away to distributors for promotional purposes (despite the name they are sold to consumers). Twenty percent reduction for CDs (labels claim they need to get reimbursed for their research and development costs for new technology). Thirty five percent reduction for reserves (artists are not paid royalties on returned (unsold) records and therefore a portion of royalties is held back as a reserve against these returns): (12%–3%)*0.75*0.85*0.8*0.65=2.98% (example from Krasilovsky and Shemel (2000)).
16. Or just P2P.
17. See Richtel in *New York Times*.
18. A recent Jupiter Research report (Mulligan (2002)) forecasts that by 2007 44 percent of European households with Internet will have a broadband connection compared to 3 percent at the end of 2001.
19. Duchene and Waelbroeck (2001) conclude that distribution in a file-sharing environment offers large advantages to new artists. The P2P network functions as an information diffusion technology. Consumers with high marginal willingness to pay for a quality product will buy the CD – after testing the song as an MP3 for free. More general accounts of this positive network effect of copying are Takeyama (1994) and Shy and Thisse (1999).
20. Also market studies seem to confirm this as a Jupiter report relates the use of Napster to increased music purchases (Sinnreich (2000)). In fact, Gopal *et al.* (2002) show strong empirical evidence that over the last decade the number of artists that have appeared in the billboard charts is statistically related to the number of Internet users. This implies that consumers become aware of more new albums that they like, thus leading to more artists being ranked in the charts because of decreased information sampling costs. Therefore, the superstar phenomenon appears to be eroded by file-sharing technologies.
21. Herbert Simon coined the term 'A wealth of information creates a poverty of attention' that is so appropriate for the informational age (from Shapiro and Varian (1999)).
22. Their strategic business area analysis based on the VERΔ Change Grid method concludes that the decoupling of value creation and revenue generation in the music industry leads to a transformation of the market structure. Famous artists will simply bypass the existing label distribution system.

REFERENCES

Adler, M. (1985), 'Stardom and Talent', *American Economic Review*, **75**, 208–12.

Aghion, P. and J. Tirole (1994), 'The Management of Innovation', *The Quarterly Journal of Economics*, **109/4**, 1185–1209.

Alexander, P.J. (1994), 'Entry Barriers, Release Behavior, and Multi-Product Firms in the Music Recording Industry', *Review of Industrial Organization*, **9**, 85–98.

Clemons, E. and K. Lang (2003), 'The Decoupling of Value Creation from Revenue: A Strategic Analysis of the Markets for Pure Information Goods', *Journal of Information Technology & Management*, **4**, 259–287.

Coase, R. (1937), 'The Nature of the Firm', *Economica*, **4**, 386–405.

Duchene, A. and P. Waelbroeck (2001), 'Welfare Implications of Illegal Copies: The case of Peer-to-Peer Distribution Technologies', working paper, CERAS Paris.

Gopal, R., S. Bhattacharjee and G. Sanders (2002), 'Economics of Online Music Sharing: Cui Bono?', working paper, University of Connecticut.

Grossman, S. and O. Hart (1986), 'The Costs and Benefits of Ownership: A Theory of Lateral and Vertical Integration', *Journal of Political Economy*, **94/4**, 691–719.

Grout, P. (1984), 'Investment and Wages in the Absence of Binding Contracts: A Nash Bargaining Approach', *Econometrica*, **52**, 449–460.

Hart, O. and J. Moore (1990), 'Property Rights and the Nature of the Firm', *Journal of Political Economy*, **98/6**, 1119–1158.

International Federation of the Phonographic Industry (2001), 'World Music Sales' in *The Economist*, May 19th.

King, B., 'Judge: If You Own Music, Prove It', *Wired*, http://www.wired.com/news/mp3/0,1285,50625,00.html

Klein, B., R. Crawford and A. Alchian (1978), 'Vertical Integration, Appropriable Rents and the Competitive Contracting Process', *Journal of Law and Economics*, **21**, 297–326.

Krasilovsky, M. and S. Shemel (2000), *This Business of Music*, New York: Billboard Book.

Mulligan, M. (2002), *European Broadband Internet Forecasts, 2001-2007*, New York: Jupiter Research.

Richtel, M., 'Free Music Service Is Expected to Surpass Napster', *New York Times*, http://nytimes.com/2001/11/29/technology/29musi.html

Rosen, S. (1981), 'The Economics of Superstars', *American Economic Review*, **71**, 845–858.

Samuelson, P. (1996), 'The Copyright Grab', *Wired*.

Shapiro, C. and H. Varian (1999), *Information Rules*, Boston: Harvard Business School Press.

Shy, O. and J.-F. Thisse (1999), 'A Strategic Approach to Software Protection', *Journal of Economics and Management Strategy*, **8**, 163–190.

Sinnreich, A. (2000), *Digital Music Subscriptions: Post-Napster Product Formats*, New York: Jupiter Research.

Takeyama, L. (1994), 'The Welfare Implications of Unauthorized Reproduction of Intellectual Property in the Presence of Demand Network Externalities', *Journal of Industrial Economics*, **17**, 155–166.

The Yankee Group (2002), 'Digital Audio: Legitimate Services Inch Forward', http://www.yankeegroup.com/public/news_releases/news_release_detail.jsp?ID=PressReleases/news_08142002_mes.htm

Towse, R. (2001), *Creativity, Incentive and Reward*, Cheltenham: Edward Elgar.

Tschmuck, P. (2001), 'Internetoekonomie und Musikwirtschaft', in *Micafocus*, http://www.mica.at/micazine/archiv.php?artid=14

7.   Copyright and Antitrust Issues

Giovanni B. Ramello

7.1   INTRODUCTION

The recent Microsoft case has brought spectacularly before the public's attention the tension which exists between antitrust and copyright law.[1] In fact intellectual property rights, even where not expressly invoked, have been the focal point of the judicial proceedings and remedies.[2] In addition, charged with anti-competitive practices, Bill Gates' company appealed directly to the exclusive rights conferred by copyright in his defence, pointing out the margin of uncertainty which exists between legitimate use of copyright and the protection of competition.[3]

An equally dramatic legal battle, in terms of intensity, unexpected reversals and duration, has been the Napster case which posed the opposite dilemma, raising the question of whether copyright enforcement, an apparently neutral and legitimate practice, can in reality become part of a strategy aimed at monopolising the market.[4] Currently the case is in the pre-trial phase and will only be heard in one year's time.[5] Nevertheless, this has been enough to fan the flames of the debate, which in less dramatic but equally impassioned tones has been continuing in various settings.[6]

Generally speaking, the difficulty in analysing the interplay between competition and copyright law lies in the fact that the two statutory frameworks contain both convergent and opposing elements, which render the final balance uncertain. The convergence lies in the stated 'common purpose of promoting innovation and enhancing consumer welfare':[7] in fact both laws are based on the microeconomic principles of efficiency and are designed to avoid specific market failures. In this respect, therefore, copyright and antitrust laws are both equally aimed at maximising social welfare. However, whereas antitrust law seeks to achieve this through the elimination of behaviours and practices that restrict competition, copyright pursues the same aim in the opposite way, by creating legal monopolies and altering the competitive paradigm. It is from the friction between these two different and opposing policies that the conflict can arise.

This chapter attempts to support the thesis that the framework of intellectual property rights is crucial to antitrust evaluations because there is a deterministic relation between property rights on the one hand, and market structure and modes of competition on the other. This consideration does not generally receive adequate emphasis in antitrust investigations. In particular, the analysis will adopt the following perspective: antitrust aims to discourage behaviours which are incompatible with the competitive game and lead to inefficient outcomes. However, if the markets in question are not efficient or competitive, due to a particular statutory framework defined *ex lege*, the entire question and its interpretation become less clear. And in this state of vagueness the distinction between what is legal and what is not becomes somewhat difficult to make. This appears to be the case for copyright because, we will argue, by defining a precise system of incentives and barriers to entry, copyright sets up a market structure characterised by behaviours and outcomes which tend to deter efficiency and competition. In such markets, as we shall detail below, competition is non-price and the industrial structure is normally that of a strongly concentrated oligopoly. In addition, there are peculiar characteristics such as network externalities on the demand side, stock and catalogue inertia effects on the supply side, which further distort the competitive game. All these aspects are in many ways deterrent and prejudicial to the existence of perfect competition, or of an innovation race in which many producers of many ideas confront each other. In fact, the configuration of such markets tends to foster not so much creative investments, as commercial investments (for instance, by means of sunk costs) which promote the emergence of dominant positions. In general, therefore, conducting a cost-benefit analysis, the outcome of copyright in terms of welfare becomes more uncertain than asserted by the traditional economic theory of intellectual property.

Antitrust can contribute to re-balancing the situation described above. For example, it can prevent the application and the extension of copyright, with its negative side effects, where it is not necessary. However, there seems to emerge a fundamental contradiction between the two statutory frameworks, which have grown out of profoundly different economic and historical contexts and operate in a completely different manner. In consequence, even though recourse to antitrust law in markets regulated by copyright can occasionally have beneficial effects, these effects are necessarily limited, and it would seem more appropriate to intervene on copyright itself, by directly altering the system of incentives which it creates.

The chapter is organised as follows: Section 7.2 examines the main features of both copyright and competition law, with an in-depth discussion of the aims, structure, scope and effects on the market configuration of each legal framework. Section 7.3 proposes an evaluation of copyright law from the standpoint of competition, paying special attention to the system of incentives and the resultant behaviours adopted by copyright owners. Section 7.4 then addresses the difficult assessment of tying in the copyright sphere, while Section 7.5 attempts to formulate some policy recommendations. Finally, Section 7.6 contains the concluding remarks.

7.2   COMPETITION AND COPYRIGHT: COMPARING TWO LEGAL PARADIGMS

The first step in a discussion of the conflict between antitrust and copyright law is to address the differences between the legal paradigms, which have distinct origins, aims and structure. In the following paragraphs we will attempt to clarify the reasons for this conflict, underlining in particular the different aspects and the – at times contradictory – impacts which these regulations can have on the economic scenario and on behaviours.

Antitrust law

It is important to note that, at the origin, the main motivation behind the institution of antitrust law was political: i.e. to curb the influence of the powerful trusts that were emerging from the burgeoning industrial development of the United States.[8]

Therefore, even though a complex and sophisticated antitrust doctrine developed over the years, at the bottom it lacked an economic theory in support of antitrust law enforcement. Only in the twentieth century – in the decades of the 1920s and 1930s – did economists undertake the study of monopolistic competition, systematising oligopoly theory and, starting in the 1950s, developing the first general model that could be used in antitrust proceedings (structure–conduct–performance).[9] Finally, during the last thirty years, with the establishment of the Chicago school, antitrust actions became dominated by the criterion of economic efficiency. We can therefore say that the branch of economics research known today as Industrial Organisation (IO) is in large part the effect, rather than the cause, of the Sherman Act.

Today, jurists and economists concur that antitrust is a tool for combating monopolistic behaviours which have the effect of excluding a segment of consumers from the market, relative to the competitive context. The law enforcement activity targets the behaviours of firms – given the structure of the markets – to induce them to engage in virtuous competition and thereby avoid a type of market failure.

However we note that economic theory has not always provided judges with effective tools for detecting and punishing certain unlawful behaviours which impact negatively on consumer welfare. One of the most important such instances is collusion: the legal action is still not adequately supported by economic tools which in fact offer judges criteria for efficiency that are still somewhat elementary.[10]

Although it recognises the importance of dynamic processes, such as technological change, economic doctrine mainly provides a consolidated theory of static efficiency, but not of dynamic efficiency. Consequently, even today antitrust policy still prevalently deals with static efficiency and markets.[11]

The long-run effects on welfare of acquisitions, joint ventures, vertical restrictions and even of certain 'abuses' of dominant position are quite uncertain, especially in new industries. And what's more, antitrust interventions are primarily referred to strategies relating to pricing. This perspective is a consequence of the law itself, but also of the economic theory, which offers models of product differentiation and non-price competition that are poorly utilisable in legal proceedings. Whereas it is known that strategies such as product differentiation and advertising, for example, characterise the competition in many markets, particularly in the service and information industries.[12]

Summing up, therefore, the first point to be noted is the structural weakness of the IO theory, with respect to the current needs of antitrust law in markets regulated by copyright. This weakness is probably attributable to the fact that this theory chiefly grew out of a study of the structure and dynamics of the manufacturing industries. And it has therefore produced analysis tools geared to that particular context.[13] Now these tools poorly apply to the markets of information goods protected by copyright, where the modes of competition differ significantly from those of the sectors which produce tangible goods.

The final observation concerns the evolution and workings of antitrust law. Over the years the US antitrust model has spread to a great many countries, starting with Europe, thereby undergoing a process of partial internationalisation – so to speak.[14] Nonetheless, the legal underpinnings and the organisation of law enforcement activities are national in scope, even though co-operation between different countries remains possible. A world-wide antitrust framework does not yet exist, nor is this in itself necessary for the individual national antitrust laws to work. The globalisation of antitrust is as yet limited, and not strictly necessary, even though it is undoubtedly important.

Copyright law

It is interesting to note that copyright shares with antitrust the political motivations for its inception. In this case, however, the purpose of the law was to control – and if necessary censor – new information before it was put into circulation (Patterson, 1968, Chap. 2).[15]

There were two guiding principles which characterised the development of copyright: technological dynamics and the evolution of markets. On the one hand, every stage of technological change has shaped the current framework of the law, which was originally conceived for literary texts, and subsequently extended to phonograms, computer programs and, most recently, to databases. On the other hand, the emergence of new economic interests has led to repeated amendments of the law, which have tended to favour the interests of producers (publishers) more than those of the authors.[16] In the past few decades there has also been a gradual internationalisation of copyright – recently regulated within the WTO by the TRIPs agreements (1994) – and aimed at creating a statutory framework that is valid and applicable in the global marketplace.[17] As we shall show below, the differences in scope of the laws – international for copyright versus national for antitrust – can give rise to ambiguity and conflict.

Today, copyright protects original works of authorship, fixed in any tangible medium of expression. Ownership of the right grants the author or her licensee an exclusive right to the exploitation of the work through its reproduction, the distribution of copies, its public performance and the creation of derivative works. In addition to the above rights, which are of an economic nature, copyright also confers moral rights which are not, however, of practical relevance for the purposes of economic analysis.[18]

The theoretical justification for copyright law rests on the thesis of the 'incentive to create', and seeks to prevent a different type of market failure from that addressed by antitrust. In fact, because ideas are by their nature public goods – characterised by non rivalry in consumption and non exhaustibility, and by very low marginal costs of reproduction/diffusion – they can be easily imitated by free-riders who do not, however bear the production costs. This circumstance does not therefore permit the existence of an efficient market of ideas.[19] Copyright is one artifice for converting copyrightable works into private goods and securing for creators appropriate profits deriving from their activity. In a manner significant for the economic analysis, it gives owners the right to exclude other individuals from accessing the protected information good, save upon payment of a price. In other words, it grants authors a statutory monopoly over the copyrightable work which they have created. This legal monopoly confers – at least potentially – a certain amount of market power to the copyright owner. It is worth noting that, although the mere existence of copyright does not necessarily per se confer significant market power to owners or their licensees, the success of a given item on the market and the exclusive exploitation of the right imply market power. This point needs to be made for several reasons. First, according to Nordhaus' (1969) seminal contribution, the optimal incentive to create for the individual – not for the society (ref. Arrow, 1962) – is represented by monopoly profit.[20] In addition, a large part of the economic literature on copyright maintains the standard assumption of monopoly profits, and this will constitute the reference for the present work (Besen, 1986; Landes and Posner, 1989).

Secondly, market power is conferred by the poor substitutability of most information goods.[21] Note that this presumption is consistent with the assumption of the welfare enhancing effects of a variety of ideas.

The specificity of individual information goods is indirectly recognised by copyright when it endeavours to encourage their creation. If copyrightable works were not so manifold and diverse, there would be no need to set up such a complex system of incentives. In other words, if information goods were near or perfect substitutes for each other – as would be necessary to cancel out the market power – due to their low marginal costs of reproduction and non-exhaustibility there would be no need to produce a number of different ideas and the copyright mechanism wouldn't make sense, since it would be easier and more affordable to provide direct incentive to only one (or a few) creators.

Moreover, there is the objective fact that many goods are different from each other due to 'natural' differentiation effects, i.e. which depend on the specific nature of the information, such as its meaning and its symbolic value. The Bible is not a substitute for the Koran, but neither is a Spice Girls CD a substitute – other than a very poor one – for a recording of Pavarotti singing Umberto Giordano's Andrea Chénier.[22] This type of differentiation is set in motion by specific characteristics of the preferences ordering and the action of complex phenomena such as network effects on the demand.

The exogenous market power is then strengthened by the competitive strategy adopted by copyright owners and by the specific characteristics of the information goods. On the one hand industries producing such goods frequently exhibit special features such as economies of scope and scale and/or network externalities (i.e. economies of scale on the demand side) which confer market power in and of themselves, at least in the short run. On the other hand, the production process of such goods often entails endogenous sunk costs which chiefly serve the purpose of differentiating items by quality (thereby creating market power) and which, according to the literature (Sutton, 1998; Carlton and Gertner, 2002), lead to highly concentrated markets in which a few firms hold significant market power.[23] The empirical evidence confirms these assertions.[24]

All these characteristics, taken together, create a market structure that strongly steers the competitive behaviours of firms, and hence the performance of the market, in the direction of reduced competitiveness. It is paradoxical that copyright, created to overcome the market failure arising from the existence of public goods, lays the groundwork for the market failure which is instead addressed by antitrust law.[25]

This fact introduces a fundamental difference between antitrust and copyright which must be taken into account. Whereas the former, given the property rights and market structure, simply targets the behaviours of firms by specifying what cannot be done, the latter defines the property rights, that is to say the goods and the market structure, creating a precise system of incentives.[26]

Therefore it is worth repeating that the framework of property rights is critical to antitrust evaluations: there is a deterministic relation between property rights on the one hand, and market structure and modes of competition on the other.

7.3   COSTS AND EFFECTS OF COPYRIGHT: A DIFFERENT PERSPECTIVE

The economic evaluation of copyright and its competitive impact requires a careful consideration of the costs. The standard theory of copyright set out in the preceding section rests on the assumption that the social cost of the monopoly granted by the right is effectively less than the expected benefits, with a positive balance that maximises welfare. In other words, the static inefficiency associated with the monopolies granted by the right is offset by the expected dynamic efficiency resulting from the production of an optimal level of new ideas.[27] However this assertion raises some questions, due to the rather perfunctory and narrow description which it gives of the sectors involved and the effects of copyright in shaping industrial configurations and behaviours.

Added costs

There is first of all the logical difficulty of accepting the concept of injecting a certain amount of inefficiency into an economic system today to promote only its possible efficiency tomorrow; this is in effect an anomalous passage for the economic theory, and worth paying attention to as of now. The desired outcome is not guaranteed, but rather lies in the ability '[to] achieve the proper balance between the incentive needed to call forth productive activity, and the access to existing works upon which this activity builds' (Cotter, 1999, p.218). Therefore, for the purposes of creating the correct system of incentives for any given idea, category by category fine tuning would appear more appropriate. Instead, copyright today provides virtually identical protection to information goods that differ vastly in their nature and production costs, making it a rather coarse – and not necessarily efficient – stimulus for creative activities. Indeed, the theory of the mechanisms has shown that for an incentive to function correctly it must be opportunely tailored to the production costs. Otherwise, the outcome will be haphazard. For example, if the incentive is higher than necessary, even ideas that are inefficient will be produced (Scotchmer, 1998).

However, little consideration has been given to these aspects in the copyright field, not even for what concerns the correct use of parameters such as the scope and duration of the right (Barton, 1997). On the contrary, copyright grants equal protection to the most diverse ideas, with a duration that in many cases is as high as 70 years *post mortem autoris* (i.e. author's life plus seventy years)[28] – an arbitrary and decidedly excessive term for the purposes of incentive.

Similarly, no consideration is given to the 'incremental creation' costs which result from monopolistic rationing. In fact, because creative processes inevitably follow a cumulative procedure – yesterday's ideas become the inputs for the ideas of today[29] – the rationing of ideas through copyright increases the costs for follow-on creators and excludes certain individuals from creative activities (Scotchmer, 1998).[30]

And finally, there are the transaction costs generated by copyright. Some of these are classifiable as administrative costs, for example those connected with the set up and management of collecting societies (Landes and Posner, 1989; Gordon and Bone, 1999). Then there is the special category of legal costs and infringement monitoring costs – which are often overlooked despite their considerable impact on those operating in the market.[31] It is important to note that, at times, the enforcement of a copyright depends precisely upon the owner's ability to sustain such costs, and therefore the competitive process will also be affected by their existence.

In short, it seems clear that the welfare impact of copyright will certainly be different if we include the above described costs in the evaluation. In some cases the outcome might even be negative, and the incentive will not work. This is a first, elementary (though important) conclusion. However it is not the main object of the argument.

Rather, it is interesting to introduce a second observation: the implementation of copyright also produces the understandable side-effect of shaping the industrial sectors involved, generally by weakening the degree of competition. The design of an incentive that is disproportionate to the needs, such as the copyright of today, with its duration of 70 years *post mortem autoris*, the elevation of costs for follow-on creators which tends to block the potential competitors of tomorrow, and the exponential growth of transaction costs which mean that copyright is only fully accessible to those able to sustain long and expensive legal battles – all this effectively indicates that there exists a cost dimension to copyright that is measured in terms of a gradual erosion of competitiveness.

Variations on the theme of competition

We reach the same conclusion if we examine the model of competition put forward by the economic theory of copyright. This is generally represented as a dynamic Schumpeter-style innovation race, which continually generates an efficient level of new copyrightable works. Through the expected profits, copyright creates an endless succession of winner-takes-all (and competitive) races which inject an optimal quantity of copyrightable works into the market.[32]

Nevertheless, this model does not truly fit the copyright industries. On closer examination, there is little dynamic about the proposed model, which is an intertemporal transposition of a static competition whose output is measured in terms of quantity of copyrights. For example, an innovation race presupposes the ongoing possibility of leapfrogging by competitors, who can therefore claim the reward at any time, irrespective of their history. But recent theoretical developments (Shapiro, 2000) have clearly shown how this is not the case for information industries where, on the contrary, pockets of monopoly power (which copyright creates) can be competitively exploited to secure or reinforce monopolistic positions. This is borne out by the studies of specific industries, which have found that the majority of information goods markets follow a pathway of progressive concentration, at both the national and international levels.[33] This dynamic can in part be explained by the existence of scale economies and scope economies on the supply side, and of network externalities on the demand side. But the excluding and self-reinforcing effects of copyright still contribute to creating and strengthening dominant positions and consolidations.

The overall outcome of the described phenomena contributes to creating markets that bear little relation to the Schumpeterian characters – except perhaps during the first few rounds of the race[34] – and which instead exhibit all the symptoms of a weakened, or at any rate significantly altered competitive scenario.[35] One persistent trait is the existence of non-price competition, in which the sunk cost component has the dual role of consolidating and increasing demand and/or creating barriers to entry for potential competitors. A possible model for this scenario is for example a vertically differentiated oligopoly, in which the presence of sunk costs also explains the high degree of concentration.[36] The leitmotiv of the strategies adopted by copyright owners is the attempt to strengthen market power.

If we then combine differentiation practices with the inherently poor substitutability of goods protected by copyright, the effect is to create a peculiar competitive context in which price plays a limited role, exerted for the most part in relation to direct demand.

Note that, the 'natural' differentiation of ideas and that effected by copyright strategies means that each information good can be interpreted – at least to some degree – as a 'separate market'. Therefore, the owner of several copyrights is, to a certain extent, in a similar position to a multi-product company or conglomerate, whose relationships with competitors are in good measure still ambiguous and in any case difficult to interpret.[37]

The nature of these behaviours is often precariously balanced between legitimacy and unlawfulness, and the standard IO still does not offer sufficiently robust tools for supporting antitrust evaluations. Although – since US case United Shoe Machinery[38] – the antitrust authorities have acknowledged, for example, that the accumulation of intellectual property rights (patents in this case), though legal in itself, can be used to suppress competition by creating barriers to entry and foreclosing competitors (Anderson, 1998), and economic theory has backed up these findings with specific models,[39] there is still no robust method for detecting and interpreting the alleged anti-competitive practices.

In the following section we shall seek to extend this consideration to the copyright field.

A simple model for altering the competitive paradigm

Behind the interpretation of copyright as a pro-competitive tool lies the assumption that copyrightable works, once created, confront each other symmetrically in a competitive marketplace. In other words, the monopoly created by the right is temporary and disappears in a short time, whereas the innovation race is renewed at each step in a competitive manner (ref. for example Kingston, 1990). However the hypothesis of symmetry is not only unproven, but also misleading: to the extent that copyright provides an incentive in the form of a monopoly, it is rational for the owner to adopt behaviours aimed at strengthening and preserving the monopoly. But such behaviours cannot then be automatically deemed unlawful, since they take place within a sphere where competition is already restrained. While the success of one expression of idea over others may be the result of historical accident, the persistence of dominant firms is often a consequence of market imperfections which in our case are introduced by copyright (Williamson, 1977).

To better understand this assertion, let us consider a simple model representing a market in which there exists a producer who, for whatever reason, has the exclusive faculty of producing a catalogue of copyrights characterised by conditions of uncertainty. The reasoning set forth below is that this asymmetry, which is exogenous for the purposes of the analysis, can under certain structural conditions alter the competitive scenario to the advantage of the incumbent, to an extent that potentially creates barriers to entry.

The stylised facts represent a static market in which the incumbent has the ability to create a (horizontal) catalogue of n copyrights at time t_0. Naturally, this reasoning can be extended to the dynamic case in which the incumbent has a stock of n_t copyrights at times $t = 1, 2..., T$ (a sort of vertical catalogue).

In the static case, therefore, the incumbent creator has the ability to produce and distribute a catalogue n of information goods ($n > 1, n \in \Re^+$). This scenario, which is realistic for many information goods markets, might arise because the incumbent already operates in the market and therefore possesses skills and a production inertia that are impossible for a newcomer to match.[40] However there are no barriers to entry for a potential competitor, who can therefore enter but only producing a limited number of copyrights. For simplicity, only one. This hypothesis in effect reflects the reality of many information goods sectors in which new producers must necessarily start off with only one product.

For simplicity, let us assume that for both contenders the production costs are zero, and that there are sunk entrance costs which are positive and constant ($SC > 0$), i.e. which do not depend on the number of products put on the market. The simplest way to understand this hypothesis is to imagine that it corresponds to the creation of a distribution network. This is a sort of 'admission ticket' to the market whose price does not vary significantly as a function of the number of copyrights produced.[41] The ability to create a distribution network is crucial for entering the market.[42] The difference in costs is necessary for representing the conjectured asymmetry between newcomers and incumbents in terms of skills and production inertia. The fact that SC does not change as a function of n can instead be interpreted as an extreme instance of subadditivity of the cost function, attributable for example to economies of scale and/or scope.

Let us furthermore assume that all $n+1$ products have the same probability of success, defined as $P(S) = 1 - p$, or of failure, defined as $P(F) = p$, with $0 < p < 1$. The idea behind this hypothesis, in line with the structure of the information goods markets which, as mentioned previously, are generally vertically differentiated oligopolies, is that each product within a given quality segment has an approximately equal probability of success.[43]

Finally, the success (and hence the failure) events for each $n + 1$ copyright are statistically independent, that is to say the success on the market of one title does not depend on the success or failure of the others.[44] Note that this is the least favourable hypothesis for the incumbent, since it puts her copyrights on the same plane as those of the competitor. A further development of the analysis, which is not pursued here, could in any case examine different probability distributions, perhaps ascertaining whether they can be influenced by specific strategic behaviours.

According to the standard economic theory of copyright cited above, the profit of each product in case of success will be Π_M which represents the gross monopoly profit, that is to say without having subtracted the costs SC. This profit is conjectured to be equal for each product.[45] We therefore assume that each intellectual work is not in direct competition with the others, and that it faces its own demand curve. This condition follows from the observation, set out previously, that copyrightable works are considered poor substitutes for each other. And in any case it is consistent with the reality of the markets, in which firms offer catalogues and stocks with many titles. Such variety would not be rational if the different titles were interchangeable, because this would mean that the firms wish to engage in internal competition.

If the producers of information goods are neutral to risk, they will seek to maximise the expected profits, that is to say the weighted mean of the probability of profit and loss, which therefore represents the incentive to create. Now it is clear that each nth work, considered singularly, will promise an expected profit given by

$$E_n(\Pi_M) = (1 - p)\Pi_M - SC$$

For the producer to have an incentive to create the item it is necessary to satisfy the participation constraint[46]

$$E_n(\Pi_M) \geq \Pi_0$$

where Π_0 is the profit obtained from an alternative activity. If the above condition is met the information good will be produced and therefore the economic theory of copyright would appear to be validated: each idea created is promised an equal reward.

However, if we consider the initial asymmetry, a substantially different picture emerges: the new entrant will face a higher overall risk of failure than the incumbent, and this will substantially alter the system of incentives. In fact, because he produces only one item, her probability of failure, and hence of losing SC, will be that defined previously, $P_{nc}(F) = p$. Conversely the probability of failure for the incumbent, thanks to the possibility of offering a catalogue, will be given by the joint probability of failure of her n copyrights, expressed as

$$P_{inc}(F) = \prod_{i=1}^{n} P(F) = p^n$$

which measures the probability that all n products will simultaneously fail. Now, because the probability of failure of one item is $p < 1$, the effective risk of loss for the new entrant is always greater than that faced by the incumbent, due to the initial asymmetry. The final order of probability will be as follows: $P_{nc}(F) > P_{inc}(F)$, since $p > p^n$.

The proposition is validated by the fact that the incumbent's risk of failing to cover the costs SC, given by the joint probability $P_{inc}(F)$, decreases with increasing numbers of copyrights, with the limiting case being that of an infinite number of titles. In this case

$$P_{inc}(F) = \lim_{n \to \infty} \prod_{i=1}^{n} P_n(F) = 0.$$

This assertion appears consistent with the findings of other studies in the field.[47]

Note also that, in the scenario thus described, the production of a high number of copyrights answers the need to minimise risks. Consider for example the production of a large number of products. According to the above, this strategy increases the likelihood of success of at least one copyright, which represents the minimum probability of success.

In the borderline case where the incumbent has an infinite number of products, the minimum probability of success will be

$$P_{inc}(S) = 1 - \prod_{i=1}^{n-1} P_n(F) = 1 - p^{n-1} \text{ with } \lim_{n \to \infty} P_{inc}(S) = 1.$$

In this case, because at least one copyright will be successful, there exists a lower bound on the profits. This bound is of course given by the profit from exactly one successful copyright – i.e. the gross monopoly profit – minus the sunk costs. We can therefore state that the expected profit for an incumbent with an infinite catalogue is at least equal to the lower bound, i.e.,

$$E_{inc}(\Pi_M) \geq \Pi_M - SC$$

This expected profit satisfies the participation constraint, assures coverage of fixed costs and in general puts the incumbent at an advantage with respect to new entrants.

The situation described therefore confirms the preceding assertion: that the existence of asymmetries distorts the competitive model of the innovation race and favours the incumbent.[48] The effective structure of the incentives is different from that which is assumed by the mainstream literature, that is to say there is an innovation race where every creator has an equal incentive. In actual fact, however, the ranking of incentives is as follows $E_{inc}(\Pi_M) > E_{nc}(\Pi_M) > \Pi_0 > 0$. Hence a second consequence will follow from the consideration that the following new condition applies

$$(1-p)\Pi_M < SC < \Pi_M$$

In this case the incumbent will produce her own copyrights and the newcomer will be kept out of the market. Now, if the condition is exogenous and depends on the state of nature there are no particular problems. If instead the costs SC are determined endogenously by the incumbent, the definition of a level of SC for which $E_{inc}(\Pi_M) > \Pi_0 > 0 > E_{nc}(\Pi_M)$ is true would in practice effect a strategy of market foreclosure against the newcomer. Now, many authors have repeatedly observed strategies similar to that described, especially with regard to distribution costs which require a high level of sunk investments.[49]

We note also that the incumbent adopts an economic logic of cross-subsidy, which can introduce a certain degree of inefficiency into the market. For example, if we assume that the profits for the different items are variable, or that the success/failure probability distribution is different for each item, the consideration of joint profits by the incumbent will lead him to produce items which would not be produced in the Schumpeterian race. This peculiarity might explain, at least in part, the high rate of failure observed in many markets for information goods, even for large firms: the expectation of sufficiently high profits on a large catalogue can reduce efforts expended on the selection of the individual copyrightable works and the production of the individual titles. There is therefore also a risk of excessive differentiation.

The scenario described also explains, on the one hand, the elevated birth/death rate of small newcomer enterprises and the stability of a small number of incumbents, and on the other hand the high level of concentration – phenomena which several authors have observed in industries for information goods.[50] The progressive action of this mechanism tends to strengthen dominant positions and favours consolidation.

Finally, it is important to note that diversification into other, often complementary, production sectors provides an opportunity to make new profits on secondary markets (consider the case of home videos or television rights for films), making it easier to recover the costs and possibly further reducing the risks.[51] In this connection it has been observed (De Vany and Walls, 1999) that the existence of such practices can significantly alter the system of incentives, so that revenues from secondary markets become essential for permitting the production of certain items with a high production budget.

On the one hand, therefore, diversification and cross-subsidy practices can constitute an optimal strategy to be adopted in situations of uncertainty. On the other hand, however, they significantly alter the competitive balance of the market.

7.4 PRODUCT DEFINITION: THE AMBIGUOUS CASE OF TYING ARRANGEMENTS

Another sphere in which traditional antitrust analysis applied to information goods protected by copyright can come up against interpretative difficulties is that of tying arrangements. In fact, as shall be discussed below, in such a case the straightforward enforcement of antitrust law can even arbitrarily influence creative activities.

The definition of tying arrangements refers to practices which force the purchaser of a given product to acquire another product in conjunction with it. Tying is deemed unlawful by antitrust law when the sellers have sufficient market power over the 'tying' product to restrict competition in the market of the 'tied' product.[52] In this case, we speak of 'leverage of tying', because the strategy described is pursued with a view to monopolise a different market (Whinston, 1990, 2001).

The application of this practice is relatively old, and there are historic antitrust cases which testify to its anti-competitive effects in the specific sector of copyright. In the celebrated Paramount Pictures case of 1948, the tied products were groups of films licensed to theatres by the major movie studios, and a similar suit, but involving the licensing of films for television, was brought a few years later against Loew's Inc.[53] In both cases it was alleged that the combined sale of information goods had the purpose of foreclosing the market to competitors. But once again, this didn't lead to the creation of robust analytical tools, while the interpretation of these practices in the digital domain can be even more ambiguous.

Generally speaking, tying can be effected in two different ways, which are sometimes used jointly. In one case, the agreement is of a contractual nature: the parties explicitly or implicitly agree to the sale, and the buyer is forced to make the joint purchase (from which he may at times obtain a private benefit). By way of example, to stay within the information goods sector, this is what Microsoft has done by forcing computer manufacturers to install Internet Explorer in order to purchase licences of the Windows operating system (and because the cost of the browser is zero, this entails no private cost to the purchaser).

There is also a second, more technical formula for implementing tying which is achieved through the integration of products. In this case we speak of physical tying. This procedure can either render the two products complementary (e.g. a printer and its spare cartridge) or, in the case of intellectual property, it can create a new integrated product.

In the literature, the competitive evaluation of this type of tying is uncertain because it can create value and hence not impact negatively on welfare (Whinston, 2001). Within the context of information goods, the evaluation is even more uncertain, also because of the effects which it can have on the innovation process.

In the Microsoft case, for example, Bill Gates' decision to integrate the Internet Explorer browser into Windows was interpreted as physical tying of an anti-competitive character. This judgement was borne out by the concurrent existence of contractual tying.

Now, without entering into the merits of the decision, we note that this interpretation effectively has a prejudicial flavour, inconsistent with the particular production context, and which even risks altering the structure of incentives created by copyright law.

In fact, as those who have some programming experience will know, there are two schools of thought concerning the best architecture for a software program. At one extreme there is the 'open' architecture, consisting of a central interface (an application) which controls a set of separate routines (other applications), while at the other extreme we have the 'closed' architecture, in which a single extended application encloses all the functions within itself. According to traditional antitrust analysis, these two systems are equivalent for the user; however they are not so for the author and the law, because the adoption of an open architecture can presuppose the creation of as many copyrights as there are components (for example, the popular Word software program incorporates within itself a spell-checker application, an editor for mathematical formulas, etc.), which makes it a form of contractual tying. What's more, it is possible for an originally open product to be subsequently converted into a closed product. This operation can be interpreted by the antitrust authorities as physical tying, with the ensuing anti-competitive implications, as happened for Windows and Internet Explorer. However, because there are two different reasons why this practice might be implemented, one effectively anti-competitive while the other is pro-efficiency,[54] the intervention of antitrust law also changes the incentives in this respect. A rational agent, aware that he would be incurring antitrust penalties, might decide *ex ante* to adopt a closed architecture, or might decide not to integrate the products even when this would benefit efficiency. In both cases, the consequence would be an alteration of the system of incentives defined by copyright. This indicates a first point of conflict between the two statutory frameworks.

A second point of conflict arises from the different direction of the laws. In the case of copyright, the system of incentives influences the behaviours of the owners of the rights. The latter are profit maximising agents who pursue, as is normal, their own exclusive interests. Therefore it is reasonable to expect choices consistent with their objectives, including opting for creative solutions which are able to secure greater market power. The logic of attempting to secure market power is also what pushes owners to adopt differentiation strategies and is triggered by the nature of copyright, which confers a legal monopoly as a reward for innovation and is implicit in the information sector (Schmalensee, 2000). The system of property rights defined by copyright encourages owners to create a new product in exchange for a monopoly. Then – and inappropriately so, because it interferes with the self-same innovative process – antitrust law makes a value judgement on the new product which, because it is produced by the combination of two other products, is deemed to be potentially detrimental to competition.

Nevertheless, the creation of market power is the reward promised by copyright to creators, and the potential disappearance of certain markets (for example that for browsers, which become a feature of the operating system) is implicit in the concept of innovation race. Therefore, if for whatever reason we wish to alter the rational actions of the economic agents, in terms of their behaviours in response to a specific system of incentives, it is on the latter (i.e. the 'incentives system') that we must intervene. The use of antitrust law to correct the conceptual errors of copyright is in fact an inefficient (and costly) way of proceeding, and leads to a schizophrenic system that on the one hand encourages certain behaviours while on the other hand it punishes them.

Within the domain of information goods, both due to the incentives created by copyright and the nature of the products themselves, tying has a strongly competitive dimension and has been generally accepted. In the case of products different from software (music, literature, etc.), the fact of forcing consumers to acquire 'tied' or extended products has always been placidly accepted. When a consumer purchases a CD he is forced to purchase a set of songs, often in order to listen to only one of them. Such a purchase could in part damage the purchase of other songs. A similar argument could be made for a collection of novels, or for the chapters of a book on industrial economics. One might object that such a practice is made necessary by the technology which dictates a particular format for the 'cans'.[55] But such an assertion is debatable, also because the cans in question can be of different sizes.

And in any case, given the technological trend toward the progressive disappearance of the physical medium, how are we to interpret such practices? A creator who wishes to continue selling combined products might for example define a group of songs as an original work of authorship (a sort of 'suite'), and the tying would disappear. Nor would it be feasible for an antitrust authority to order a separation of the components, as this would most probably infringe the right to integrity of the work which is one of the many rights (moral rights, in the case in point) that make up copyright.

If the above considerations, taken together, substantiate the existence of a conflict between copyright and antitrust law with regard to tying, it is sufficiently clear that the resolution of this conflict in this setting must directly implicate copyright.

7.5   ATTEMPTING TO SKETCH OUT SOME GENERAL POLICY GUIDELINES

In the previous sections we have shown how the system of rights and incentives created by copyright defines goods and rules of behaviour in such a way that the rule of competition does not prevail in those markets. The nature and goals of these practices are often precariously balanced between legitimacy and unlawfulness. This renders their evaluation difficult and uncertain, even to the extent of producing unsatisfactory outcomes in terms of social welfare.

However intervention by antitrust authorities only raises further questions with regard to effectiveness and results. Such actions can follow two different courses: law enforcement, i.e. detecting and penalising unlawful behaviours to restore competition, or regulation, i.e. altering the competitive scenario through structural decisions. Note that this second line of intervention is somewhat more complicated and, at least in the European system, subject to specific institutional restrictions.[56]

Restoring competition?

The first course, which is the most important and well-established in antitrust experience, presupposes the possibility of ascertaining unlawful behaviours. In fact, the results which economic theory considers inefficient, or at any rate indicative of limited competition, are not sufficient to presume the guiltiness. Antitrust decisions are judicial acts, and as such must be based on hard evidence or well founded charges of unlawful behaviours. This certainly constitutes a limitation, from the economic standpoint. But there are also other limitations, some of a general character and some specific to copyright.

Let us consider for example the case of co-operative behaviours. As is known, agreements – particularly if formal – are not very frequently discovered today. Antitrust must therefore operate in the grey area of tacit collusion. Now, ascertaining tacit collusion is particularly difficult, because it implies use of the 'parallelism plus' method which not only requires showing that the outcomes are compatible with a collusive scenario, but that they cannot be otherwise explained (ref. Yao and De Santi, 1993). Nor has economic analysis yet developed a sufficiently robust theory for describing how the firms in an oligopoly can set up facilitating devices.[57] These circumstances create a certain degree of structural weakness for the general enforcement of antitrust. Since copyright industries are highly concentrated as a consequence of the legal incentive system, they are continually facing this ambiguous situation.

In addition there are further complications specific to copyright. Consider for example the Fimi/Vendomusica[58] antitrust case in Italy, concerning agreements and concerted practices in the phonographic market, in which the five major labels were charged with price fixing and other co-operative behaviours. The verdict of the trial confirmed the accusations, inflicting a penalty on the firms involved, but without however addressing two crucial points. On the one hand, the behaviours in question were in any case consistent with the market structure defined by copyright, and therefore rational even in a context without agreements. In consequence, although the antitrust action could perhaps eliminate the agreements, it could not substantially alter the market result or its structural inefficiency. On the other hand, the international scale of the firms charged with collusion (a global oligopoly with a concentration rate for the first five firms, $CR_5 > 80\%$) compared to the domestic scope of the antitrust proceeding and remedies – i.e. the Italian market – preclude any form of pro-competitive effectiveness.

The other context in which law enforcement is applied is abuse of dominant position, and more specifically exclusionary practices, of which the Microsoft case has been the most sensational example. The difficulty of evaluating such practices in markets for information goods has been repeatedly pointed out in this paper. The monopoly granted to the owner of the copyright cannot in itself constitute a violation, nor can its proper exercise be considered a monopolisation attempt. Rather, the problem arises when a firm that has secured a dominant position in one market seeks to extend it to other markets, restraining competition. In this situation, however, the concepts of product, market and competition – as has been extensively discussed – are ambiguous and escape many of the standard theoretical classifications, which are based on paradigms developed for the traditional manufacturing industries.

Regulating the market? The uneasy case of the essential facility

An interesting example of indirect regulation is the specific application of the essential facility doctrine within the sphere of antitrust intervention. This doctrine, defined within the context of public utilities, maintains that when a private resource becomes 'essential' for competition and cannot be duplicated by competitors, the antitrust authority under certain circumstances may force the owner to grant access to competitors on the grounds of the welfare-enhancing effects of competition itself.[59] In general, the facility in question is a physical investment whose unlimited use is called into question by antitrust.

The transposition to the copyright case is therefore based on the thesis that access to a given information good is often a crucial element for the existence of competition in a specific market, and might be exploited for effecting exclusionary practices against potential competitors. Many antitrust cases have implicitly adopted the concept of essential facility for information goods, even though this principle has rarely been enunciated.

In the Microsoft case, for example, the Windows operating system is treated de facto, although not de jure, as an essential facility for competition in the Internet browser market by the Federal Trade Commission (Cotter, 1999). Therefore, when the FTC adopts the remedy of forcing Microsoft to distribute Windows with its own Explorer browser and the competing Netscape Navigator browser included, it weakens the exclusive rights conferred by copyright to Bill Gates' company, and which define a private property, in order to permit competition on the browser market in line with the precepts of the doctrine.

Likewise, the follow-up of the Napster case, even given the uncertainty of the pre-trial phase, will still presumably hinge upon this concept, since the refusal of the major record labels to license their catalogue of phonograms for digital distribution effectively precludes access to an 'essential and not readily duplicable' facility for competition in the online music distribution market.

In Europe, too, the concept of essential facility has been adopted – for the most part implicitly – in a number of measures. This has been the case for the many suits involving the pay-TV[60] industry, where the antitrust authorities have once again applied this doctrine, at least in substance if not in form, by forcing the licensing or limiting the exercise of monopoly power over certain premium content – such as blockbuster movies and key sports events – to which access is a necessary condition for contending the market (Nicita and Ramello, 2002).

In a few rare cases, recourse to the essential facility doctrine has been explicit. One of these was the community NDC Health/IMS Health[61] case, in which the European Commission explicitly applied this theory to impose mandatory licensing of a data base in the pharmaceutical sector.

This generalised lack of conviction by the antitrust authorities in explicitly espousing the essential facility doctrine in copyright markets gives further cause for thought. Even if this doctrine offers a practicable solution for stimulating competitive effects in these sectors, the question of advisability in adopting such a doctrine extensively is raised.[62] As we have shown previously, copyright operates at the structural level, by defining property rights, whereas antitrust enforcement operates at the level of behaviours. Now the emergence of inefficient behaviours in the markets for information goods depends in good measure on the system of incentives created by copyright. Therefore, a continuous recourse to essential facility – directly or indirectly, as it seems to be the case for copyright – can substantiate a sort of legal schizophrenia which on the one hand weakens competition to sustain innovation, and on the other hand penalises innovation, violating the newly granted exclusive right in order to promote competition. Such a vicious circle does not promise efficient results.

In addition, the antitrust authorities can only apply the essential facility principle *ex post*, since it seeks to curb monopolistic positions created by copyright and reinforced by the particular conditions discussed previously. In this prospect, it can only have narrow and limited effects. Nor is it possible to propose an *ex ante* action, as this would be in blatant violation of copyright law; neither can it be generalised, because this would eliminate the incentive to create, which is an essential part of copyright. Unlike the cases of public utilities, its non-marginal application would be in direct conflict with an entire system of rights that have been artificially defined.

Changing copyright?

The direct route for avoiding or attenuating these inefficient outcomes is to alter copyright itself – i.e. to change the incentives system set up by the law –, reducing the degree of protection conferred especially in situations where the costs clearly outweigh the benefits. One model for implementing such a policy is already provided by the fair use doctrine (ref. Gordon and Bone, 1999), which permits the duplication of information goods without a licence in certain specific circumstances.

Innovation processes in contiguous markets, such as hardware or digital distribution, reinforce the stated position, based on the conviction that preserving broad scope for technological change is in the interests of consumers and society. Essentially, the dynamic process of discovery driven by individual self-interest represents another important dimension of the competition process, which makes it possible to introduce new products and new markets.[63] Now a firm which enjoys a strong dominant position in a copyright market might even control and direct innovation in contiguous industries. This in fact is the charge raised against the recording majors for digital distribution in the new Napster case (Picker, 2002).

In contrast, technology today offers accessible solutions for the trade-off between competition and incentives: thanks to digital storage and communication systems, we can finally envisage a system of information that is freely accessible against payment of a fair royalty, avoiding the monopolisation of downstream markets (that is distribution) according to the model proposed by Arrow (1962). And hence the need to overhaul the copyright system also appears to be entrained by technological change.

A number of recent theoretical developments bear out the idea that there can also be alternative systems for rewarding creators, which do not entail negative effects on competition.[64]

To summarise, if in the past the costs of the copyright system – also in terms of reduced competition – could find strong justification in light of the beneficial effects on creative activities, today they are less acceptable both because there are new possibilities for rewarding creators and because they risk weighing down the competitive dynamics and the innovation process. Several scholars have also underlined the threat to competition and innovation which exists when intellectual property rights are over-broadly defined (Anderson, 1998).

Therefore, all in all, the simplest measure to adopt for pursuing the goal of efficiency and minimising the negative impacts on competition is to reduce the burden of copyright where possible, paying specific attention to the effects of this right on the market dynamics.

We must in any case bear in mind that the institutional dynamic is a slow process, which in this context is further complicated by the existence of multilateral international conventions and agreements. And to this we must finally add the resistance by lobbies which are investing considerable sums to obtain measures that are exactly the opposite of those proposed here.

7.6   CONCLUSIONS

This paper analyses the relationship between competition and copyright law. In particular, it examines the points of conflict which seem to create interferences between the two statutory frameworks. On the one hand copyright regulates the market by introducing, as a solution for achieving its welfare enhancing aim, incentives and constraints which limit competition and constitute a second best. On the other hand, competition law and antitrust attempt to direct markets toward their first best solution, eliminating all possible obstacles to competition. This structural diversity creates a dialectic between the two frameworks which does not appear rectifiable. There are in fact specific characteristics of information goods and specific incentives created by copyright which lead to the emergence of inefficient behaviours in this context. The penalisation of such behaviours by the antitrust authority, in cases where they are found to be unlawful, would in any case have only doubtful effects on the competitive dynamic, whereas it would definitely impact on the system of incentives created by copyright, altering it. In certain cases it is possible to use the essential facility doctrine for effecting targeted actions, but such a practice constitutes an infringement of property rights and is therefore in conflict with copyright.

Moreover, the national scale of antitrust intervention conflicts with the international scope of the copyright industries, raising an issue of inconsistency.

It is also interesting to note how technological change is concurrently altering the structure of the markets, weakening and at times eliminating certain strategic elements crucial to the monopolistic exercise of copyright, such as control over distribution networks. In light of this observation, the previously mentioned suits – the Microsoft case and the Napster case in its antitrust aspects – can be interpreted as an initial outcome of this change, in the sense that the alteration of the industrial configuration, exogenous for the purposes of the behaviours of copyright owners, pushes them to expose the anticompetitive aspects of their strategies and puts them more clearly – when this is the case – in a position of unlawfulness.

Given this scenario, an acceptable antitrust policy for the information goods sector would appear to be one of minimum, contingent and non-systematic intervention, which does not attempt to steer technological change and does not propose a different and contradictory system of incentives. A corollary to this assertion is the observation that, if effects detrimental to efficiency exist, these arise for the most part from the system created by copyright. Therefore, the rule of reason suggests that, when this is necessary, we should intervene principally on copyright itself, taking care not to further aggravate its negative effects.

NOTES

1. In the interests of simplicity the term copyright is used here to refer to actual copyright as well as to author's right. For the same reason we will refer indifferently to competition law and antitrust law.
2. Several scholars share this view. Among others see Cotter (1999) and Anderson (1998). Note that even if the abuse of intellectual property is not directly alleged, intellectual property and the exclusive rights which it confers have been the pivotal point of the anti-competitive practices and hence of the antitrust proceedings.
3. Microsoft argues that the licence restrictions are legally justified because, in imposing them, Microsoft is simply 'exercising its rights as the holder of valid copyrights' Appellant's Opening Br. at 102 [...]. The company claims an absolute and unfettered right to use its intellectual property as it wishes: '[I]f intellectual property rights have been lawfully acquired', it says, then 'their subsequent exercise cannot give rise to antitrust liability.', Appellant's Opening Br. at 105 *USA v. Microsoft Corp*, US DC Court of Appeals, N. 00–5212 consolidated with 00–5213.
4. This was the question addressed by Judge Marylin Hall Patel who, after having repeatedly ruled against the peer-to-peer file-sharing system invented by the young student Shawn Fanning, also opened an investigation into alleged anti-competitive behaviour of the plaintiffs – the major record labels – against the company Napster (see Picker, 2002).
5. The pre-trial phase ends on 10 January 2003, and it is therefore necessary to wait for the developments of the case.
6. The debate has blazed increasingly over the past year. The seminal case in Europe has been the *Magill* case (*Radio Telefis Eireann, RTE, and Anor. v. European Commission*, 1995 EC I-743), concerning a copyright holder's refusal to license a television programming list (a subject matter in Eire) with the consequence of stifling competition on the television programming market. And many other cases have further fanned the flames of this debate. For instance, see the numerous cases in the pay-TV sector: European Commission 94/922/CE, *MSG Media Service*; UK MONOPOLIES AND MERGER COMMISSION, *BskyB/Manchester Utd*, 1999; Italian 'Autorità Garante della concorrenza e del Mercato' *Groupe Canal+/Stream*, n.10176, 13/05/2002.
7. US FTC and DOJ (1995), Antitrust Guidelines for the Licensing of intellectual property, par. 1.
8. Ref. Audretsch (1999, p. 229) and Neumann (2001, p. 32). The US courts were already dealing with violations of competition rights as early as 1890. However it was with the Sherman Act (1890), and the succeeding Clayton and Federal Trade Commission Acts (1914), that the American lawmakers introduced two new and important types of violation: agreements between undertakings and abuse of dominant position. In addition to this, an effective system of law enforcement was set up, headed by the Department of Justice and the Federal Trade Commission (Neumann, 2001, pp. 31–37).
9. The oligopoly theory was developed between the first and second half of the nineteenth century by Cournot and Bertrand, but in reality was consolidated in mainstream economic

theory only in the next century. For the evolution of IO and antitrust theory ref. also Neumann (2001) and Viscusi *et al.* (1995).

10. Consider for example the case of parallel behaviours and tacit collusion, in which a competitive equilibrium is not readily distinguishable from an unlawful situation (ref. for instance Neumann, 2001).

11. Several scholars share this opinion (Carlton and Gertner, 2002; Evans and Schmalensee, 2001).

12. The need of setting up a theory for these industries and markets is witnessed by the appearance of recent publications lamenting the application of standard theory (ref. for instance Shapiro, 2000 or Audretsch *et al.*, 2001) and trying to systematise the feasible theory in one homogenous *corpus* (ref. for instance Oz, 2001; Shapiro and Varian, 1998).

13. Consider the concepts of scale economies, growing marginal costs, price competition, etc.

14. This implementation of antitrust law in different countries has sometimes introduced novelties and differences (see Neumann, 2001).

15. The origins of copyright are older than those of antitrust. A precursor to copyright law can even be found in the privilege granted in 1487 by the Republic of Venice to Marcantonio Cocci, known as Sabellicus, to 'print and sell' copies of his work *Rerum Venetarum ab urbe condita ad Marcum Barbaticum libri XXXIII* (Ulmer, 1987).

16. Ref. Ulmer (1986).

17. Note that the TRIP Agreement indirectly confirms the tension between intellectual property and competition, recognising the possibility of anti-competitive practices in the exploitation of intellectual property. However they do not set out specific standards for dealing with them (Anderson, 1998).

18. For a rapid overview of copyright, among others ref. Gordon and Bone (1999). The moral rights concern the sphere of authorship and protect the paternity, the integrity of the work and the right to publication.

19. For an overview of the economics of copyright ref. Watt (2000).

20. Note that, even though the real-world profit may be lower than the monopoly profit, the effectiveness of the incentive requires significant market power. The incentive to create is directly correlated with private profit, decreasing with it and dropping to zero in the case of perfect competition.

21. Of course, this enounced non-fungibility is less than absolute and specific copyrightable works may sometimes present a certain degree of substitutability, especially at the margin. This however does not contradict the main assertion.

22. The fact that another *Andrea Chénier* performed by José Carreras can be substituted for the one by Pavarotti does not invalidate the proposition: the information is in large part the same (the same opera), though with certain elements of differentiation that are to some extent endogenous (they depend on the choice of the two singers and the quality associated with each) and therefore constitute a successive strategy, as will be discussed below.

23. Note that in industries which produce information goods, endogenous sunk costs can include advertising, fees for stars, and even the set-up and maintenance of specific distribution channels. In fact, due to the presence of network externalities, even this last-mentioned aspect is strategic for building the perceived quality of the products, which is crucially dependent upon their propagation and, hence, upon the distribution network.

24. The record industry exhibits a high level of concentration, both in the domestic and international markets and in production and distribution; see Silva and Ramello (2000) and Black and Greer (1987). High concentration is likewise found in the pay-TV (Armstrong, 1999) and motion picture industries Marvasti (2000).

25. In this connection see the ideas of McGowan (1996).

26. See Picker (2002).

27. For a detailed presentation see, for example, Landes and Posner (1989) and Watt (2000).

28. This term, for instance, as requested by the Council Directive 93/98/EEC harmonising the term of protection of copyright and certain related rights, has been adopted by European countries. The current United States law has adopted the same duration term (Gordon and Bone, 1999).

29. It is important to underline that creative activities feed upon those produced at time $t-1$. This is very clearly the case in the software industry, where writing programs relies upon the study of, and therefore access to, listings of previous programs, and is one of the motivations behind the Open Source movement, which upholds the need to make software source code freely available. But in general all cultural development takes place through processes that are imitative, albeit virtuously so.
30. Taking these costs into account is especially important in view of the global scope of today's knowledge markets: blocking access to certain information goods may preclude incremental creation in entire nations, thereby aggravating disparities in the international arena.
31. In this connection we can say that, for intellectual property lawyers, copyright unquestionably provides a different incentive from the incentive to create.
32. This appears to be the view of Evans and Schmalensee (2001).
33. See supra note 24.
34. This would explain, for example, the apparently higher degree of competitiveness of the software industry, as compared with the cinematographic or phonographic industries.
35. It is interesting to note that the owners of rights are often, and in open contradiction with the copyright model, quite reluctant to accept fundamental innovations in adjoining domains. In fact the legal records show how the main opponents of important technological innovations such as video recorders, MP3 players, etc. have been the audio-visual major Universal Pictures and the Recording Industry Association of America, that is to say the trade association of phonographic labels (Ramello, 2001).
36. For an in-depth discussion see Silva and Ramello (2000).
37. The difficulty in evaluating these types of firms from the antitrust viewpoint is asserted by Viscusi *et al.* (1995).
38. *US v. United Shoe Machinery*, 110 F. Supp. 295 (D. Mass, 1953) aff'd *per curiam*, 347 US 251 (1954).
39. See for instance the case of *sleeping patents* by Gilbert and Newbery (1982) or *brand proliferation* by Schmalensee (1978) .
40. This hypothesis is consistent with many markets for information goods, from music (ref. Autorità Garante della Concorrenza e del Mercato, 1997, par. 5–8) to films (ref. Marvasti, 2000), in which there are firms that consistently produce a certain number of titles per year and which moreover also hold a stock of already-produced items.
41. Many information goods sectors exhibit characteristics compatible with this hypothesis, with high distribution and *set up* costs that generally do not depend on the number of products, or which in any case are subject to strong economies of scale/scope. For the phonographic sector ref. Black and Greer (1987); Silva and Ramello (2000). For the cinematographic sector ref. Marvasti (2000); De Vany and Eckert (1991).
42. The literature quoted in the preceding note supports this assertion. These writings stress the point that it is not rational for the incumbent to distribute the newcomer's items, except with a view to directly or indirectly achieving control of the copyrights, which leads to further market concentration.
43. The industrial organisation of these markets and the probability distribution hypothesis are discussed extensively by Silva and Ramello (2000).
44. The debate concerning the probability of success of a product in an information goods market is complex, and gives rise to conflicting views. Note however that over time, and in different industrial sectors, a large number of authors concur that at least products in the same market segment face a substantially equal degree of uncertainty, and that the individual products are, however, poorly substitutable for each other (ref. for example from Conant, 1981 to Silva and Ramello, 2000).
45. For products competing within the same market quality segment, the expected demand is the same, as are the profits for a given level of costs (ref. Silva and Ramello, 2000).
46. Such a constraint, standard in incentive design, represents the necessary condition to participate for the information producer and means that she must expect a non-negative payoff, which otherwise would imply a negative reservation level of utility. For a survey ref. Varian (1992, chap. 25).

47. The statement is consistent with the findings of De Vany and Eckert (1991) for the case of the cinematographic industry. Nor does it conflict with the sector's high level of uncertainty. In this connection, De Vany and Walls (1999) have identified the optimal strategy to be the diversification of activities into a portfolio of films.
48. Note that the proposition applies also for values of *n* that are not infinite but sufficiently high.
49. For the former ref. Black and Greer (1987); Alexander (1994). For the case of the film industry, Marvasti (2000, pp. 102 and sgg.) emphasises how the production and marketing costs and even the high salaries paid to stars could be used as barriers to entry, leading to the progressive consolidation of the market.
50. Ref. again Black and Greer (1987); Alexander (1994); Silva and Ramello (2000); De Vany and Walls (1996).
51. Ref. Vogel (1986). This also seems to be one of the reasons for the growing diversification of the media and communication industries into complementary production activities, as testified by the recent rash of mergers and *joint ventures*, such as the agreement – opposed by various *antitrust* authorities – between Time-Warner and AOL.
52. The Intellectual Property Guidelines of the DOJ and the FTC also underline that the tying arrangements must have a significant adverse effect on market competition and that there must be justifications on the grounds of efficiency (par. 5.3).
53. *United Sates v. Paramount Pictures Inc.*, 334 U.S. 131 (1948); *United Sates v. Loew's Inc.*, 371 U.S. 38 (1962).
54. In fact Microsoft argued that the decision to integrate the browser in the OS was analogous to preceding software upgrade operations for enhancing the functionality of its product.
55. The definition is taken from Edison, inventor of the phonograph, who spoke of 'canned sound' (ref. Ramello, 2002).
56. For example it is not possible for one body to amend regulations issued by another body higher up in the juridical scale (Parliament, the Government, etc.).
57. See Neumann (2001).
58. *Associazione Vendomusica/Case discografiche Multinazionali-FIMI*, n. 5385(I/207), 24 October 1997.
59. Under US law, the *antitrust* authority must intervene in cases where there is: '1) control of the essential facility by a monopolist; 2) a competitor's inability to practically or reasonably duplicate the essential facility; 3) denial of use of the facility to a competitor; and 4) the feasibility of providing the facility' (*MCI Communications Corp. v. AT&T Co.*, 708 F.2d 1081, 7th CI 1983, 1132–1133). The EU law similarly considers that the emergence of such situations can be likened to abuse of dominant position, and therefore also justifies regulatory intervention for access to the facility in exchange for fair payment on the part of the antitrust authority (Neumann, 2001).
60. See supra note 5.
61. European Commission, 3/7/2001, COMP D3/38.O44.
62. The 'essential facility doctrine', entering the domain of regulation, has to be adopted only in 'exceptional circumstances' as asserted for instance in the so called Magill case (ref. C-241/91 P and C-242/91 P, *Radio Telefts Eireann and Independent Television Publications Ltd v. European Commission*).
63. Ref. Neumann (2001) p. 29.
64. Ref. the reward system proposed by Shavell and Ypersele (2001) and the Open Source movement (Lerner and Tirole, 2001).

REFERENCES

Alexander P.J. (1994), 'New Technology and Market Structure: Evidence from the Music Recording Industry', *Journal of Cultural Economics*, **18**,

113–123.

Anderson R.D. (1998), 'The Interface between Competition Policy and Intellectual Property in the Context of the International Trading System', *Journal of International Economic Law*, **4**, 655–678.

Armstrong M. (1999), 'Competition in the Pay-TV Market', *Journal of Japanese and International Economies*, **13**, 257–280.

Arrow K.J. (1962), *Economic Welfare and the Allocation of Resources for Invention, in NBER, The Rate and Direction of Incentive Activity: Economic and Social Factors*, Princeton: Princeton University Press.

Audretsch D.B. (1999), 'Industrial Policy and Industrial Organization', in Mueller D.C., A. Haid and J. Weigand (eds), *Competition, Efficiency, and Welfare. Essays in Honor of Manfred Neumann*, Dordrecht: Kluwer.

Audretsch D.B., W. J. Baumol and A. E. Burke (2001), 'Competition Policy in Dynamic Markets', *International Journal of Industrial Organization*, **19**, 613–634.

Autorità Garante della Concorrenza e del Mercato (1997), 'Associazione Vendomusica/Case Discografiche Multinazionali-Federazione Industria Musicale Italiana Provvedimento n. 5385 (I/207)', *Presidenza del Consiglio dei Ministri*, Bollettino, anno 7, **41**, 5–64.

Barton J.H. (1997), 'Paradigms of Intellectual Property Competition Balances in the Information Sector', *European Competition Law Review*, **18**, 440–447.

Besen S.M. (1986), 'Private Copying, Reproduction Costs, and the Supply of Intellectual Property', *Information Economics and Policy*, **2**, 5–22.

Black, M. and D. Greer (1987), 'Concentration and Non-Price Competition in the Recording Industry', *Review of Industrial Organization*, **9**, 85–98.

Carlton D.W. and R.H. Gertner (2002), 'Intellectual Property, Antitrust and Strategic Behaviour', *NBER Working Paper*, n. 8976.

Conant M. (1981), 'The Paramount Decrees Reconsidered', *Law and Contemporary Problems*, **44**, 79–107.

Cotter, T.F. (1999) 'Intellectual Property and the Essential Facility Doctrine', *The Antitrust Bulletin*, **44**, 211–250.

De Vany, A.S. and R. Eckert (1991), 'Motion Picture Antitrust: The Paramount Cases Revisited', *Research in Law and Economics*, **14**, 51–112.

De Vany, A.S. and W.D. Walls (1999), 'Uncertainty in the Movie Industry: Does Star Power Reduce the Terror of the Box Office?', *Journal of Cultural Econmics*, **23**, 285–318.

European Commission (1998), 'Difference between Primary and Secondary Innovation', *OECD, DAFFE/CLP*, **98**, 18.

Evans D.S. and R. Shmalensee (2001), 'Some Economic Aspects of Antitrust Analysis in Dynamically Competitive Industries', *NBER Working Paper*, n° 8268.

Gilbert R.J. and D. Newbery (1982), 'Preemptive Patenting and the Persistence of Monopoly', *American Economic Review*, 72, 514–526.

Gilbert R.J., T.N. Gallini and M.T. Trebilcock (1998), 'Intellectual Property Rights and Competition Policy: a Framework for Analysis of Economic and Legal Issues', in Anderson R. and N.T. Gallini (eds.), *Competition Policy and Intellectual Property Rights in the Knowledge-Based Economy*, Calgary: University of Calgary Press.

Gordon W.J. and R.G. Bone (1999), 'Copyright', in Bouckaert B. and G. De Gest (eds), *Encyclopedia of Law and Economics*, Cheltenham and Northampton, MA: Edward Elgar.

Kingston W. (1990), *Innovation, Creativity and Law*, Dordrecht: Kluwer.

Landes W.M. and R.A. Posner (1989), 'An Economic Analysis of Copyright Law', *Journal of Legal Studies*, 18, 325–363.

Marvasti A. (2000), 'Motion Picture Industry: Economies of Scale and Trade', *International Journal of the Economics of Business*, 7, 99–114.

McGowan D. (1996), 'Regulating Competition in the Information Age: Computer Software as an Essential Facility Under the Sherman Act', *Hastings Comm. and Ent. Law Journal*, 18, 771–851.

Neumann M. (2001), *Competition Policy. History, Theory and Practice*, Cheltenham and Northampton, MA: Edward Elgar.

Nicita A. and G.B. Ramello (2002), 'Exclusivity and Competition in the European Pay-TV markets.Whither Policy Options in the Convergence Era?', mimeo.

Nordhaus W.D. (1969), *Invention, Growth and Welfare*, Cambridge: MIT Press.

OECD (1998), Competition Policy and Intellectual Property Rights, *OECD*, DAFFE/CLP(98)18.

Oz S. (2001), *The Economics of Network Industries*, Cambridge: Cambridge University Press.

Patterson L.R. (1968), *Copyright in Historical Perspective*, Nashville: Vanderbilt University Press.

Picker R.C. (2002), 'Copyright as Entry Policy: The Case of Digital Distribution', *The Antitrust Bulletin*, Summer-Fall, 423–463.

Ramello G.B. (2001), 'Napster et la musique en ligne. Le mythe du vase de Pandore se répèterait-il?', *Réseaux*, 19, 131–154.

Ramello G.B. (2002), 'Author's Right, Copyright and the Market', *Revue MIF, Management, Information et Finance*, 2, 26–45.

Schmalensee R. (1978), 'Entry Deterrence in the Ready-to-eat Breakfast Cereal Industry', *Bell Journal of Economics*, 9, 305–327.

Schmalensee R. (2000), 'Antitrust Issues in Schumpeterian Industries', *American Economic Review*, **90**, 192–196.

Scotchmer S. (1998), 'Incentives to Innovate', in Newman P. (ed.), *The New Palgrave Dictionary of Economics and the Law*, London: Macmillan.

Shapiro C. (2000), 'Competition Policy in the Information Age', *Foundations of Competition Policy*, London: Routledge.

Shapiro C. and H. Varian (1998), *Information Rules. A Strategic Guide to the Network Economy*, Harvard: Harvard Business School Press.

Silva F. and G.B. Ramello (2000), 'Sound Recording Market: the Ambiguous Case of Copyright and Piracy', *Industrial and Corporate Change*, **9**, 415–442.

Sutton J. (1998), *Technology and Market Structure*, Cambridge, MA: MIT Press.

Ulmer E. (1987), *Copyright and Industrial Property*, Dordrecht and Boston: Martinus Nijhoff.

US FTC and DOJ (1995), *Antitrust Guidelines for the Licensing of intellectual property*.

Varian H.R. (1992), *Microeconomic Analysis*, New York: Norton.

Viscusi W.K., J.M. Vernon and J.E. Harrington (1995), *Economics of Regulation and Antitrust*, Cambridge MA: MIT Press.

Vogel H. (1986), *Entertainment Industry Economics*, Cambridge, Cambridge University Press.

Watt R. (2000), *Copyright and Economic Theory: Friends or Foes?*, Cheltenham and Northampton: Edward Elgar.

Whinston M.D. (1990), 'Tying, Foreclosure and Exclusion', *American Economic Review*, **80**, 837–859.

Whinston M.D. (2001), 'Exclusivity and Tying in U.S. v. Microsoft: What We Know, and Don't Know', *Journal of Economic Perspectives*, **15**, 63–80.

Williamson O.E. (1977), 'Predatory Pricing. A Strategic and Welfare Analysis', *Yale Law Journal*, **87**, 284–340.

Yao D.A. and S.S. De Santi (1993), 'Game Theory and Legal Analysis of Tacit Collusion', *The Antitrust Bulletin*, **38**, 113–141.

8. Self-help Systems: Good Substitutes for Copyright or New Barriers to Competition?

Joëlle Farchy and Fabrice Rochelandet[1]

8.1 INTRODUCTION

Information and communication technologies (ICTs) are often viewed in the cultural industries as being conducive to copyright infringements. By enabling the reproduction of protected works, they give rise to free riding problems. Non-rivalry in the consumption of cultural goods and the difficulty of shutting out copiers has been an issue since the development of analogue recording technologies (Adelstein and Peretz, 1985). But because digital technologies make it possible to copy material with no loss of quality and to distribute it at very low marginal costs, they take the phenomenon to new heights. There are various forms of copying: from individuals copying files online and burning CDs (for their own personal use) to industrial-scale piracy (for commercial gain). The 'dematerialisation' (digitisation) of cultural goods makes it very hard for suppliers to prevent non-paying users from gaining access to original artistic works. Online sharing of cultural goods centres mainly on free – and for the most part unauthorised – peer-to-peer networks.

Free riding may well render copyright impossible to enforce in the digital economy. Indeed, much hacking and unauthorised online sharing prove hard to detect, creating a large amount of free riding against which copyright law is helpless. Barlow (1994) is quick to brand it a 'relic' of the pre-digital age. But the absence of copyright would be a loss to artists and producers alike. How else can they find the sizeable amounts of investment needed to finance cultural content? A number of economic solutions already offer alternative ways for producers to cover their fixed costs without the benefits of copyright (Shapiro and Varian, 1998). These tend to be either commercial (indirect appropriability through bundling, cross-subsidies, tied sales, etc.) or technological (with digital technologies no longer poisoning copyright but serving as a remedy to unauthorised sharing and piracy).

This paper aims to go beyond the simplistic poison/remedy tandem. In the first part, it underscores the limits of the 'contractual paradigm' dominating a share of the digital economy debate and according to which technological protections give content producers a lever which, regardless of copyright, empowers them to obtain contracts with users, and that could render copyright law unnecessary.[2] The second part of the paper shows how producers can use these 'cure-all technologies' to erect new entry barriers, a solution that would, as it happens, run counter to the interests of the artists and the users.

8.2 PROTECTION TECHNOLOGY-BASED CONTRACTS ARE NOT A WHOLESALE SUBSTITUTE FOR COPYRIGHT

The alleged benefits of the contract

According to some economic literature, to some extent, contracts can substitute for copyright. In some cases, copyright involves sacrificing a share of contractual freedom. It imposes many constraints not only on publishers and producers, but also on all parties concerned in the future. In many countries, copyright laws create some important exceptions such as the fair use doctrine in the USA and the exception of parody, citation and private copying in the French law. Those exceptions prevent many contract opportunities. Furthermore, by contrast to the US copyright law, French *droit d'auteur* imposes some important constraints upon contract relationships between the authors and their economic partners (publishers, record producers, etc.). For example, as a general rule, a writer could not license in advance to a publisher her future works. Moreover, a remuneration proportional to the sales is legally presumed for all kinds of contracts between authors and producers in the cultural industries. Finally, in many countries, compulsory licences obviously limit contractual process.

A contract freely entered into, on the other hand, affects none but the contracting parties. With the development of ICTs, a number of economists and legal experts (Meurer, 1997; Bell, 1998; Stefik, 1997; Friedman, 1996; Dunne, 1994) have been challenging the usefulness of the constraints that copyright brings to bear on contracts (compulsory clauses, exceptions, etc.). ICTs lead to a considerable reduction in transaction costs, which should in turn generate an increase in contract-based commerce.

Contracts may eventually replace copyright on digital networks (Dunne, 1994; Dommering, 1996; Friedman, 1996). Suppliers would negotiate directly with the users and nobody would have to put up with copyright restrictions. By acting as exclusionary barriers to free riding, technological defence devices would allow content to be protected through privately formed contracts rather than through copyright. So, according to Fisher (1998), 'the creators of intellectual products suitable for distribution on the internet will soon come to rely less and less on intellectual-property law to enable them to charge consumers who wish access to their products and more and more on a combination of contractual rights and technological protections.'

Protection technologies are now described as 'self-help systems' (Dam, 1999; Schlachter, 1997). Just as an individual creating a physical object might seek to protect his or her new property by placing it in a safe, for example, cultural goods producers use a software system to defend their property against attempts at unauthorised appropriation.

Let us assume that self-help systems prove an effective means of protection, i.e. impenetrable at each and every stage of the commercial chain. A contract-based regime would then offer a good many advantages. First, decentralised electronic contract management provides a high degree of control over usage, with self-reporting – automatic forwarding of data to producers every time their content is accessed on a digital network – enabling electronic traceability. Next, there is the potential for greater market value enhancement: content providers can set a different price per category of user and use, and can maximise their revenues through price discrimination (Meurer, 1997; Bell, 1998). Finally, there is room for less costly and more competitive bargaining. Both sides can settle a contract quickly with the help of standardised contractual instruments. Contracts, being non-predetermined and freely negotiated, are more flexible than copyright in the digital economy. Such a contractual paradigm then would tend towards the ideal Paretian world of mainstream economics.

Information asymmetries and a shortage of trust

There are a number of factors that serve to bring this optimistic picture into perspective. For a start, the contract is not quite as flexible as this new paradigm might like to make out. Online contracts basically involve subscribing to terms and conditions predefined by the content provider (Merges, 1997; Lemley, 1995). The 'click to accept' buttons usually figuring in software (shrinkwrap licences) or on the Internet may well resemble a bilateral contract. But such contracts actually boil down to an opening page, offering users an opportunity to peruse the terms and conditions and, if they agree, to hit the 'accept' button. The only freedom of contract they have is to accept or refuse.

Furthermore, content is used by thousands of intermediary users around the world for an enormous variety of purposes that often call for specific bargaining and contracts (Merges, 1996). The absence of a universal registry and the risk of breaks in the chain of transfer are just two of the factors that can be conducive to the spread of opportunist behaviour. Despite the fact that data protection and traceability technologies are, without a shadow of a doubt, potentially powerful, they can only protect the content traded if there is a continuous economic link between the seller and successive users throughout the value chain. Once decrypted, the content escapes the control and protection of its producer (Merges, 1997).[3] As W. Gordon (1989, p.1420) has suggested, copyright and contract are not equivalent from this perspective:

> At bottom, copy-privilege [the abolition of copyright] and copyright lead to different results because of the many occasions on which persons have access to copyrighted works without needing to purchase them and thus have the means to copy independent of a contractual nexus. Wherever one could have access to a copyrighted work without asking consent … ordinary contract rules would not support restricting what the person with access can do with what he receives. The person has had access without needing to ask the creator's permission and thus has been free of the creator's leverage. Since this potential consumer or copier has already received what he wants, the work's originator has nothing with which to bargain.

Moreover, parties are not always negotiating with the same partners; and users and providers alike are confronted by information-related problems: acts of fraud, ignorance or negligence. One party may, intentionally or otherwise, circulate copies of works containing false information on the identity of the original producer. Introducing contract security can serve little purpose given the extent of information asymmetry. ICTs help facilitate the bargaining, but the market offers providers with no safeguards whatsoever against the 'moral hazard' risk. For even if users agree to the terms and conditions, how can providers ensure that they are keeping to their side of the bargain or check how the content is actually being used? They can, of course, seek to acquire a self-help system. But the effectiveness of that solution can be undermined by its cost, its vulnerability or a refusal on the part of users to adhere to such a means of surveillance.

We share the view of Merges (1997) that ICTs do not reduce transaction costs far enough to allow for the emergence of a world where contracts are more valuable than regulations. ICTs may well lead to lower search costs (building databases of producers, works, etc.), but they have less of an impact with respect to other costs: bargaining (e.g. specific contractual clauses), *ex post* (supervision of contractual commitments, renegotiation, etc.). As Merges (1997, p.136) has observed:

> The reference to Newton in the title is meant to invoke the conventional image of a mechanical 'clockwork' universe where friction plays no role. This is the image that comes to mind when cyber-enthusiasts tout the contractarian basis of exchange in the online economy where all sources of transactions costs have been eliminated. This essay contends that the image, while powerful, is incomplete. Bilateral contract will be ubiquitous in cyberspace, but it is unlikely to displace completely state-backed property rights for two reasons. First, breaks in the chain of privity mean that the 'safety net' of a property right may still be necessary to protect adequately investment by creators of digital content. Second, certain limits on the rights of intellectual property owners are best seen as immutable, i.e., outside the ability of contracting parties to waive or vary. While elegant, the Newtonian world came to be seen as incomplete. In the same way, the notion of purely contract-based commerce in cyberspace, while appealing, is too simple to be true. The complexities of enforcement costs and contracting externalities inevitably intrude. Like classical Newtonian mechanics, the world of pure contract must remain only a starting point.

Digital networks – given the speed and omnipresence of multiple transactions, not to mention the anonymity and heterogeneity of contracting parties – are high-risk environments governed by what Orléans (1994) calls 'the incompleteness of pure market logic'. Many contracting parties, therefore, turn to third parties for arbitration and underwriting.[4] The greater the asymmetries, the more important it may be to have some form of institutional regulation.

An endless technology race

The more watertight the self-help system the greater the guarantee that providers can protect their content against copying and minimise the value lost to unauthorised users. As we are regularly reminded in the news, however, protection systems are far from invulnerable.

Producing technologies may take time, skills and abilities and material and human investment. But they can be *assimilated* at low cost by anyone who is computer-literate; all the more so given the considerable synergies that they foster among actors belonging to Internet forums. With respect to protection systems, content providers and copiers thus find themselves engaged in a technology race. As Dam (1999, p. 402) points out: 'one can view the copier as the attacker, with the content provider responding to copying by using "defensive" self-help systems. Then offensive techniques will arise to overcome the defences to copying (or to alterations) not authorised by the content provider, and so on ad infinitum.' The outcome of that race is unclear.

Copiers are seeking to make some form of gain, be it material (resale of pirated content or circumventing technology) or symbolic.[5] They can therefore be involved in a race in which they are competing against each other via copiers' coalitions or clubs, where some are pirating the original content and others are purchasing it.

From the content producers' point of view, the technology needs to be sufficiently well developed to enable them to make returns on their investment. They do not mind losing some stages of the race if they emerge as the overall winners – with the help of the other means they have of capitalising on their content. As for those distributing content via the Internet, the technology needs to be infallible when it comes to ensuring that rights to use that content are authenticated and respected. They have to win each and every leg of the technology race, for defeat will put them out of the running. So, if they are legally bound to a strict liability regime, website hosting companies and Internet service providers can ill afford to lose because any victory on the part of hackers will leave them with a dead loss.

8.3 NEW ENTRY BARRIERS IN THE CULTURAL INDUSTRIES

In theory, digital technologies can be regarded as an alternative to copyright for protecting content. Technology plus contract can substitute for copyright. In practice, the major companies are currently using them to reinforce their copyrights rather than as a replacement. In this case, technology supplements copyright. Either way, whether ICTs serve to reinforce copyright or replace it with contract law, they give rise to issues of standards and compatibility.

Experiences with defensive self-help systems are many and varied. Given the diversity of operators, it is highly unlikely that a single standard can be enforced. What is more, technologies that are viable for one type of content are not necessarily universally applicable and will serve to generate distinct installed bases by significantly rising switching costs. In the event of head-on competition, there may be a number of different standards hinging on content type or the extent of oligopoly in the marketplace. The absence of a single standard raises two questions. First, does a diversity of competing technologies not serve merely to undermine efforts to protect content and manage copyright? Second, is there any strategic manoeuvring involved in the proliferation of incompatible systems?

Some problems associated with incompatibility

The coexistence of competing self-help system projects is akin to that of competing standards. One of the key issues with respect to standardisation is the matter of compatibility. As a rule, the market has two alternatives for fostering inter-standard compatibility: either the actors voluntarily seek consensus and define common standards through standard-setting committees; or individual actors enforce their own standards.[6] In every event, IT firms often have to arrive at an agreement when launching new products, given the highly complementary nature of content, data transmission networks and storage media.

Having a diversity of competing systems seems to be unhealthy from the point of view of content providers and users alike, for it incurs information costs as well as multiple adoption costs. Technical conflicts are likely to result from the same content being protected by different systems at different stages in the value chain. Users would have to 'subscribe' to a number of different security and decryption systems, and to switch to others in line with developments in the technology race between producers and copiers. What is more, there is the risk of creating 'angry orphans' (David, 1987): copyright owners or content providers having adopted a system that is subsequently abandoned due to obsolescence or if the developer goes out of business. From the intermediary users' point of view, the coexistence of different authentication and protection systems generates inefficiencies stemming from information-gathering costs. Furthermore, interoperability must extend beyond national frontiers. If every national grouping of copyright owners independently adopts its own standard, it will give rise to the risks of incompatibility and non-interconnectability, which is bound to create problems given the instantly global scale of exploiting works via the Internet (Hoeren, 1995).

Competition between technologies may have short-term advantages, not least because it stimulates innovation. But a fundamental precondition of its longer-term efficiency is that systems developed in parallel be interoperable.[7] Some projects – the EC's Copyright in Transmitted Electronic Documents (CITED) project, for instance – provide solutions geared to interoperability. Providers seeking to protect content must be able to shift it from one system to another without incurring significant switching costs: the cost of changing format as well as opportunity costs. What if the technology were to prove a failure (due to an insufficient installed base, for example)? Would the content still be protected when switched to another?

Minimising switching costs would call for the adoption of common standards with respect to identifiers and metadata. An identifier code has to be recognised by every system, irrespective of its traceability and anti-copying techniques. This corresponds to the gateway technology concept within the realm of economics of compatibility and standards.[8] It is a matter of having an alternative to universal standards, one that provides for *ex post* compatibility. These gateway technologies help foster an increase in demand by producing network effects between previously incompatible systems.

Yet de facto incompatibility and non-interoperability can also be seen as an attempt to lock in the installed base[9] by the developers. Network effects lead to efforts to secure a market lock-in: if the competing technologies are incompatible, abandoning a network can result in considerable switching costs and, hence, force the system owner into *ex ante* calculation. The installed base of each firm represents a strategic entry barrier (Cohen, 1996). Competition can therefore prove harmful to content producers, especially when the guiding principles of a network such as the Internet facilitate a basic minimum of compatibility and interoperability (Barrow, 1996).

Strategic goals of the producers

Content protection technologies represent a new competitive weapon that could boost the market power of the dominant producers and publishers.

The installation of defensive self-help systems goes hand-in-hand with co-operation between the content providers benefiting from complementary potentialities. Indeed, the latter seek to acquire 'additional strategic means geared to gaining or re-establishing competitive advantage' (Monateri and Ruffieux, 1996, p.102). Meanwhile, however, such 'co-operative' developments give rise to both latent and open conflict between providers seeking to impose their own standards. The development and installation of self-help systems is actually very costly in terms of investment (research, standardisation, etc.), risky alliances and high-speed obsolescence. Not every actor can afford such investments in isolation. Large organisations seem to be the only ones capable of mustering the necessary competencies and financial resources to keep on developing and upgrading these systems. The levels of investment required represent an entry barrier that runs the risk of smaller producers being excluded. Producers with less efficient systems cannot ensure that their rights will be respected as thoroughly as those that benefit from a system securing higher appropriability. Independent producers and publishers can, of course, approach specialised technology suppliers, but they are then subject to information asymmetries: how can the degree of effort actually made by service providers be assessed with a view to improving their systems' performance?[10]

The coexistence of a variety of different protection standards represents an additional factor of competition. In answer to the second of the two questions posed earlier, the cultural industry majors have been deliberately creating and promoting incompatible systems in an effort to secure a dominant position as market intermediaries. Creators would prefer to go through them because they provide a guarantee of higher earnings.

The process of competition/co-operation between dominant firms is illustrated by the music industry's Secure Digital Music Initiative (SDMI) consortium. SDMI was set up in 1998 in order to develop technological specifications for online music so as to counter MP3 and create an anti-piracy protection standard. So it amounted to a standard-setting committee whose aim, according to those taking part, was not to impose a single standard from above but to negotiate common formats with a view to standard interoperability. Rather than produce *ex ante* compatibility standards that ran the risk of rapidly becoming obsolete, SDMI wanted to create gateway technologies for *ex post* compatibility.

Yet beneath the surface of this ambitious project, competition has continued to rage between the majors. It has mainly served as an arena bringing the majors into contact with the large IT industry players. The majors were seeking alliances so that each could develop its own online distribution system. Competition between the majors has therefore continued via efforts to seek the best possible appropriability-oriented technology. The most effective standard within the realm of enclosure (establishing *technological barriers* and preventing them from being circumvented) secures improved appropriability and a dominant position in the field of online music.

In May 1999, Microsoft (one of the leading promoters of the SDMI) put forward its own system with a view to cornering the downloadable music systems market. Its MS Audio 4.0 format, however, proved far from compatible with the standard SDMI format and, unfortunately for Microsoft, was quickly circumvented by software circulating on the Internet. The same month, Universal announced an alliance external to the SDMI consortium with InterTrust (Digibox). And Universal and BMG (the GetMusic joint venture) entered into an alliance with ATT and Matsushita: the two majors supply the content, while ATT develops online distribution and billing systems and Matsushita focuses on an anti-copying system. This coalition spurred Sony into joining forces with Microsoft, also in May 1999, with a view to distributing content using Windows Media 4.0.

These opportunistic alliances[11] account for the delays in the SDMI schedule and the discontent of producers of equipment for downloading and listening to music. Indeed, competing services have been developed to enable the illegal trading of music files. These have worked fully to the advantage of

MP3 technology. The Napster or Gnutella systems, for instance, have encroached upon the potential client base of firms such as Liquid Audio, AudioSoft or RealNetworks. The SDMI project was well and truly scuppered by the failure of its anti-piracy solutions.[12]

More recently, in 2001, this interplay of alliances and competing standards was further stimulated by the appearance of two rivalling coalitions in the music industry: MusicNet, associating AOL-Time-Warner, BMG-Napster and EMI with RealNetworks; and PressPlay, a joint venture launched by Vivendi Universal-MP3.com, Sony, Yahoo and MSN. Both aim to distribute music online via a combination of subscriptions and security processes. Each is developing its own protection system. The problem is that access to the works on each site is restricted to the content produced by the majors taking part in the respective projects, while the consumer chooses neither the companies nor self-help systems, but the artists and musical genres. A similar phenomenon exists in the film industry: the majors are currently seeking a means of extending their business activities to digital networks. In the final analysis, the development of electronic commerce is hindered not so much by copyright as by the strategic manoeuvring of majors, which may end up producing non-interoperable and incompatible technologies.

8.4   CONCLUSION

Purely technological solutions seem ill suited to resolving free riding problems. Maintaining rules and institutions appears to be a must. Self-help systems are not neutral. They become competitive arms that are not within reach of every producer. Majors could reinforce their control over users as well as creators. Here, we partly share the point of view of Lessig (1999, 2001). Conversely, copyright may well be open to criticism, but it stands on more equitable grounds: nobody is excluded from this 'invisible technology' whose adaptation costs (costs of implementation and regulation) are borne by the community at large. What is more, unlike strictly technological solutions, copyright guarantees a certain number of exceptions for users. Indeed, their 'rights' – as defined by those exemptions – must be safeguarded in order to limit the scope of overprotection by technology (Cohen, 2000); self-help systems can, for instance, extend to content that is no longer protected by copyright or that falls within the realm of copyright exceptions. Further, the US Digital Millennium Copyright Act of 1998 and the EU copyright directive adopted in May 2001 could represent a genuine threat to users (Rochelandet, 2002). In providing legal protection for self-help systems, these two laws actually place major restrictions on the users' rights. In any case, whatever the prevailing situation – copyright reinforcement by ICTs or copyright abolition in the favour of self-help systems – these regulations may well break the balance between creators, users and publishers by strongly reinforcing the bargaining and market power of the majors.

NOTES

1. A first draft of this paper has been published in Revue d'Economie Industrielle, Paris, 2002. The authors owe special thanks to Wendy Gordon for her very helpful comments.
2. To illustrate this idea, one could refer to many authors. Hugenholtz (1995) defines the contractual (and disintermediation) paradigm as follows: 'The emerging digital networked environment is creating exciting new possibilities of solving the complexities of licensing a multitude of rights. Perhaps, the built-in intelligence of the superhighway will enable individual right holders to grant and administer licenses to users directly, without any intervening mechanism. Works disseminated over the superhighway might carry identifying "tags", inviting prospective users to automatically contact right owners, or "permission headers", with pre-determined licensing conditions to which users may agree in real time. Such a system of "self-administration of rights" might eventually replace collective or co-operative licensing. If so, the digital network would bring back to right holders what they (nearly) lost in the age of mass copying: the power to transact directly with information users.'
3. More specifically, Merges (1997) raises the issue of legal ties between the provider and the various transferees throughout the property transfer chain. If party A enters into a contract with party B and B does likewise with party C, and if A wishes to take legal action against C for a breach of the contract agreed with B, then some tie or another must exist between A and C at some point in the chain. Any legal action will be focused on party B. But a host of problems arises if B is representing a number of other parties, some of whom are not subject to A's jurisdiction while others are insolvent. The fact is that under a strictly contract-based regime, A cannot pursue C for breach of contract because they have not directly entered into an agreement with each other. Merges (1997) argues that application of contractual clauses hinges on an unbroken legal tie imposing obligations on the initial contracting party and all successive users throughout the commercial chain.
4. Orléans (1994) points to three alternatives: oath, reputation and contracts. The first two are somewhat vague when it comes to digital networks. The oath is ill suited to an information society that lacks any meaningful means of monitoring whether individuals are adhering to or complying with a given moral prescription. As regards reputation, Friedman (1996) and others may believe the electronic signature system to be an adequate means of creating the necessary conditions for it to have an influence, but the extent of that influence remains hard to gauge. And unless there are third parties, the contract is just as problematic.
5. A repressive institutional framework can increase the chances of providers marking a victory by increasing the average cost of copying for 'commercial' copiers.
6. Another solution, of course, would be de jure standard-setting on the part of the state.
7. 'It is generally recognised that without a high degree of interoperability between the various proposed schemes for copyright control (Cryptolopes, COPYSMART, etc.) the market will remain fragmented and costs will be too high for an acceptable service (except perhaps in some specialist, high value areas).' (LITC, 1996, p. 45).
8. See Greenstein (1997), Choi (1996), Farrell and Saloner (1992), Bunn and David (1988). Bunn and David (1988, p. 170) argue that 'some means (a device, a convention) for effectuating technical connections (technical compatibility) between distinct production subsystems are required in order for them to be utilized in conjunction, within a larger integrated production system'. Farrell and Saloner (1992) single out a number of gateway

types that differ according to whether the owner can benefit, unilaterally or otherwise, from additional network externalities.

9. In technologies competing models (Arthur, 1989; Farrell and Saloner, 1986; Katz and Shapiro, 1985), the size of the installed base – the number of the adopters of a given technology – could lead economic agents not to adopt a new technology. In doing so, an installed base acts as a source of inertia.

10. There may be a number of competing firms in the market. A producer whose earnings are lower that those of its competitors is not always capable of distinguishing its share of responsibility in a failure (e.g. flawed editorial approach) from the influence of inefficiency in the system adopted.

11. The firms in question work together in standard-setting committees. When each has competencies that the others lack, they co-operate fully in the process. The risk of opportunistic coalitions comes to the fore when their areas of competency overlap. In such cases, the nature of their co-operation in the upstream reaches of the market becomes technical – geared to market creation – and strategic – geared to dominating the market (Ledortz and Lequeux, 2000).

12. SDMI set a challenge in autumn 2000 by offering a $10,000 reward to anybody who could unpick the electronic watermarking incorporated into music files without any loss of sound quality. Alarmed at how quickly a number of research teams managed to achieve this, the consortium sought to protect the security of its protection system by threatening to sue a university professor and his team if they went ahead with their aim of publishing their findings.

REFERENCES

Adelstein, R.P. and S.I. Peretz (1985), 'The Competition of Technologies in Markets for Ideas: Copyright and Fair Use in Evolutionary Perspective', *International Review of Law and Economics*, **5**, 217–218.

Arthur, W.B. (1989), 'Competing Technologies, Increasing Returns and Lock-in by Historical Events', *The Economic Journal*, **99**, 116–131.

Barlow, J.P. (1994), 'Selling Wine Without Bottles: the Economy of Mind on the Global Net', *Wired*, March, 84–86, document available online at www.hotwired.com/wired /2.03/features/economy.ideas.html)

Barrow, E. (1996), 'Rights Clearance and Technical Protection in an Electronic Environment', Conférence ICSU Press/UNESCO *Electronic publishing in science*, Paris, February 19–23, online document: www.library.uiuc.edu/ icsu/barrow.htm.

Bell, T.W. (1998), 'Fair Use vs. Fared Use: The Impact of Automated Rights Management on Copyright's Fair Use Doctrine', *N.C. Law Review*, **76**, 557–620.

Bunn, J. and P.A. David (1988), 'The Economics of Gateway Technology and Network Evolution: Lessons From Electrical Supply History', *Information Economics and Policy*, **3(2)**, 165–202.

Choi, J.P. (1996), 'Standardization and Experimentation: *Ex Ante* Versus *Ex Post* Standardization', *European Journal of Political Economy*, **12(2)**, 273–290.

Cohen, W.E. (1996), 'Competition and Foreclosure in the Context of Installed Base and Compatibility Effects', *Antitrust Law Journal*, **64**, 535–569.

Cohen, J.E. (2000), 'Copyright and the Perfect Curve', *Vanderbilt Law Review*, **53**, 1799–1819.

Dam, K.W. (1999), 'Self-Help in the Digital Jungle', *Journal of Legal Studies*, **28(2)**, 393–412.

David, P.A. (1987), 'Some New Standards for the Economics of Standardization in the Information Age', in Dasgupta, P. and P. Stoneman (eds.) *Economic Policy and Technological Performance*, Cambridge: Cambridge University Press, 206–239.

Dommering, E.J. (1996), 'Copyright Being Washed Away Through the Electronic Sieve. Some Thoughts on the Impending Copyright Crisis', in Hugenholtz P.B. (ed), *The Future of Copyright in a Digital Environment*, La Hague: Kluwer Law Intenational, 1–12.

Dunne, R.L. (1994), 'Deterring Unauthorized Access to Computers: Controlling Behavior in Cyberspace Through a Contract Law Paradigm', *Jurimetrics Journal*, **35(1)**, 1–15.

Farrell, J. and G. Saloner (1986), 'Installed Base and Compatibility: Innovation, Product, Preannouncement and Predation', *American Economic Review*, **76(5)**, 940–955.

Farrell, J. and G. Saloner (1992), 'Converters, Compatibility and the control of Interfaces', *Journal of Industrial Economics*, **40(1)**, 9–35.

Fisher III, W.W. (1998), 'Property and Contract on the Internet', *Chicago-Kent Law Review*, **73(4)**, 1203–1252.

Friedman, D. (1996), 'A World of Strong Privacy: Promises and Perils of Encryption', *Social Philosophy And Policy*, **13(2)**, 212–228 (document available online at http://www.davidfriedman.com/Academic/Strong _Privacy/Strong_Privacy.html).

Gordon, W. (1989), 'An Inquiry into the Merits of Copyright: The Challenges of Consistency, Consent and Encouragement Theory', *Standford Law Review*, **41**, 1343–1469.

Greenstein, S.M. (1997), 'Lock-in and the Costs of Switching Mainframe Computor Vendors: What do Buyers See?', *Industrial and Corporate Change*, **6(2)**, 247–273,

Hoeren, T. (1995), 'Long Term Solutions for Copyright and Multimedia Products', European Commission, online document: http://www2.echo.lu/ legal/en/hoerlic2.html

Hugenholtz, P.B. (1995), 'Licensing Rights in a Digital Multimedia Environment', *Information Society: Copyright and Multimedia*, LAB, European Commission, 57–62, online document: http://europa.eu.int/ ISPO/legal/en/lab/950426/hugen.html.

Katz, M. and C. Shapiro (1985), 'Network Externalities, Competition and Compatibility', *American Economic Review*, **75(3)**, 424–440.

Ledortz, L. and F. Lequeux (2000), 'Dynamique Concurrentielle et Coopération dans le Cadre d'une Industrie Émergente: L'exemple du Multimédia', in Bellon, B. et al. (eds) *La Coopération Industrielle: Diversité et Synthèse*, Paris: Economica.

Lemley, M.A. (1995), 'Shrinkwraps in Cyberspace', *Jurimetrics Journal*, **35(3)**, 311–376.

Lessig, L. (1999), *Code, and Other Laws of Cyberspace*, New York: Basic Books.

Lessig, L. (2001), *The Future of Ideas: The Fate of the Commons in a Connected World*, New York: Random House.

Merges, R.P. (1996), 'Contracting into Liability Rules: Intellectual Property Rights and Collective Rights Organizations', *California Law Review*, **84(5)**, 1293–1393.

Merges, R.P. (1997), 'The End of Friction? Property Rights and Contract in the 'Newtonian' World of On-Line Commerce', *Berkeley Technological Law Journal*, **12**, 115–136.

Meurer, M.J. (1997), 'Price Discrimination, Personal Use, and Piracy: Copyright Protection of Digital Works', *Buffalo Law Review*, **45**, 845–889.

Monateri, J. C. and B. Ruffieux (1996), 'Le Temps de la Quasi-Intégration: Une Approche Dynamique.', in RAVIX, J-L. (ed.), *Coopération Entre les Entreprises et Organisation Industrielle*, Paris: CNRS éditions.

Orléans, A. (1994), 'Sur le Rôle de la Confiance et de L'intérêt dans la Constitution de L'ordre Marchand', *Revue du MAUSS*, **4**, 17–36.

Rochelandet, F. (2002), 'Le Droit D'auteur Européen à L'ère Numérique: Quelles Leçons Tirer de L'expérience Américaine du Digital Millennium Copyright Act?', in Baslé, M. and Pénard, T. (eds.) *Europe.com: La Société Européenne de L'information*, Paris: Economica.

Schlachter, E. (1997), 'The Intellectual Property Renaissance in Cyberspace: Why Copyright Law Could be Unimportant on the Internet', *Berkeley Technology Law Journal*, **12(1)**, online: www.law.berkeley.edu/journal/btlj/12-1/schlachter.html

Shapiro, C. and H. Varian (1998), *Information Rules: A Strategic Guide to the Network Economy*, Cambridge MA: Harvard Business School Press.

Stefik, M. (1997), 'Shifting the Possible: How Trusted Systems and Digital Property Rights Challenge us to Rethink Digital Publishing', *Berkeley Technological Law Review*, **12(1)**, 137–156. Document available online at http://www.law.berkeley.edu/journals/btlj/articles/12-1/stefik.html

9. The Market for Intellectual Property: The Case of Complementary Oligopoly

Francesco Parisi and Ben Depoorter[1]

9.1 INTRODUCTION

Today's market for intellectual property is characterised by an increasing degree of composite creation and innovation. Digital technology and ever growing back catalogues have allotted a greater creative role to the combination of intellectual property works in the creative process. Digital production tools enable artists to produce derivative works of art that combine cut and paste processing of samples, images, and sound effects from other creative works. For example, in the case of DJ-mix compilations, artists innovate by combining other artists' tracks in an original version.[2]

Building on Cournot's (1838) intuition on complementary duopoly and the more general framework developed by Buchanan and Yoon (2000), Schulz, Parisi and Depoorter (2000, 2002), we illustrate the economic case of complementary creative inputs in the context of the market for intellectual property.

9.2 RETHINKING COMPLEMENTARITIES AND COMPETITION

In 1838 Cournot considered the case of complementary duopoly.[3] Cournot's model shows that a single monopolist producing a composite good will charge a price lower than the sum of the prices that would be charged by two complementary duopolists selling the single component parts. Suppose that two separate individuals each hold intellectual property rights over the two rights, A and B, respectively, which are used as inputs of production for a composite good C. Because of their strict complementarity as inputs of production, the demand for each depends on the price of both. A move from complementary duopoly over intellectual property rights to a concentrated monopoly will decrease price and increase output, thereby increasing overall welfare. In the case of complementary duopoly, unlike the traditional case of duopoly over substitute goods, both producer and consumer surplus are diminished compared to the alternative monopoly outcome. In the standard duopoly case for substitute goods, the strategic pricing of the duopolists leads to lower prices, with an increase in consumer surplus and overall welfare. In the case of complementary duopoly, the strategic pricing of the duopolists leads instead to higher prices, with a decrease in *both* consumer surplus and overall welfare.

As was pointed out by Buchanan and Yoon (2000) and Schulz, Parisi and Depoorter (2000), the intuition behind this result is surprisingly simple. Take the example of two copyright holders who have autonomous exclusion rights over two distinct works (primary works). In our hypothetical case, the copyrighted primary works are complementary inputs for the production of a derivative work, such as an anthology or review essay on the topic of the Coase Theorem. Such compilation requires the inclusion of passages from the relevant primary sources on the same subject (e.g., the 1960 Coase paper, the 1972 Demsetz paper, and the 1972 Calabresi-Melamed one, etc.), each of which is essential to the success of the anthology and therefore can be thought of as strict complementary inputs in the production function of the final derivative work (i.e., the anthology). We will refer to these factors of production as non-substitutable inputs.[4] In the absence of a fair use defence, a third party who wishes to utilise passages from the above mentioned primary sources needs to obtain the consent of all copyright holders. In our example, the editor or author of the derivative work has to purchase copyright licences from all relevant parties. Because their works are strictly complementary, the demand for each intellectual property right depends not only on the price set for his own licence, but also on the price charged by the other property right holders. This implies that any change in the price or quantity supply of the complementary good by one duopolistic intellectual property seller will have external effects for the other intellectual property seller. Each party maximises his profits, without regard for any effect on the profits of other property owners.[5] When one seller decreases output and raises the licence price, the demand curve for the other intellectual property owners will be negatively affected, and vice versa. However, a concentrated monopolistic seller of intellectual property rights would internalise these price or output externalities.

A simple illustration is useful. Suppose two firms, A and B, each produce one of two complementary components. Consumers combine the components in a strict one-to-one ratio. Each firm must make a decision about price without knowing what the other firm will do. To simplify, suppose there are only three pricing options: the price a single monopoly producer would produce, P_M, a price greater than P_M, or a price less than P_M. The following game matrix in Figure 9.1 illustrates the incentives facing each firm.

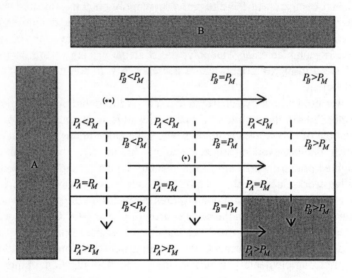

Figure 9.1 Game matrix

Each cell would contain the payoff (profit) to Firm A and Firm B from the corresponding combination of their pricing decisions. Firm A is a row player, and its Nash strategy given each of Firm B's choices is indicated with the dotted, vertical arrows.[6] Firm B is a column player, and its Nash strategies given each of A's potential choices are indicated with the solid, horizontal arrows.[7]

Here, given the cross-price effects present in this complementary duopoly, both firms would have a dominant strategy, with a single Nash equilibrium, indicated by the shaded area in Figure 9.1. The firms will choose to price above P_M, to the detriment of both the producers' profits and the overall (i.e., producers' plus consumers') welfare. The cells corresponding to the profit maximising prices and the welfare maximising prices are respectively marked with a single asterisk (*) and a double asterisk (**), in Figure 9.1.

It should be noted that in the standard duopoly case, the strategic behaviour of the parties leads them to choose pricing strategies $P_A = P_B < P_M$. This constitutes an improvement over the monopolistic pricing with respect to social welfare, but a Pareto inferior outcome with respect to the firms' profits. In our case of complementary duopoly, instead, another set of strategies $P_A = P_B > P_M$ is obtained in equilibrium. Also in this case, the firms' strategic pricing renders the maximising monopoly profit unobtainable in equilibrium. The firms' pricing, however, pushes the equilibrium in the opposite direction compared to the standard duopoly case, with the interesting result of generating an equilibrium (i.e., the shaded area in Figure 9.1) that is inferior both privately and socially to the alternative monopoly outcome (in the standard case, the duopoly outcome is inferior to the monopoly outcome, with respect to the firms' profits, but is superior to the monopoly alternative with respect to social welfare). The outcome of the complementary duopoly thus represents a classic prisoner's dilemma.[8]

The game theory intuition exposes the differences between the standard case of duopoly with substitutable goods and the duopoly model with complements. Compared to monopoly, duopoly (and to an even greater extent, oligopoly) leads to more efficient competitive equilibria when involving substitutes. The reverse holds true when complementary goods are involved. Thus competitive or oligopolistic supply of strict complements would paradoxically lead to higher prices, smaller output, and reduced welfare, compared to an alternative co-ordinated monopolistic pricing. The monopolist is no longer an endpoint on the spectrum of market models because complementarity pushes duopoly to higher prices and greater quantity restrictions than monopoly.

9.3   A MODEL OF COMPLEMENTARY OLIGOPOLY

In the previous section we have illustrated how the independent pricing of intellectual property rights from two complementary duopolists likely results in an equilibrium that is worse for both the private parties, and society at large. We shall illustrate this point for the more general case of n oligopolists, showing that the extent of the deadweight loss also depends on the number of suppliers of complementary inputs. An increase in the number of copyright holders exercising independent control on the price of their respective licences exacerbates the degree of underutilisation. Suppose that n individuals hold intellectual property rights over n components, which can be used as inputs of production for a composite good, Q. Because of their strict complementarity as inputs of production, the demand for each depends on the price of all others. P_Q is the sum of the prices of the n separate intellectual property rights

$$\sum_{i=1}^{n} P_i .$$

Each owner of a specific input of production thus has a profit function that can be written as

$$\pi_j = P_j D(P_Q) = P_j D\left(\sum_{i=1}^{n} P_i\right) \tag{9.1}$$

Differentiating the profit functions with respect to the corresponding price variable yields these first order conditions

$$\frac{\partial \pi_j}{\partial P_j} = P_j D'(P_Q) + D(P_Q) = 0 \tag{9.2}$$

Summing the first order conditions yields the equilibrium price for the composite good when the intellectual property rights are held by separate producers, operating in complementary oligopoly.

$$P_Q D'(P_Q) + n D(P_Q) = 0 \tag{9.3}$$

We can now compare these conditions with those that characterise the supply of a single concentrated monopolist (or by separate owners, who can effectively co-ordinate prices). In the case where a single monopolist produces the composite good, the profit function will take the following form

$$\pi = P_Q D(P_Q) \tag{9.4}$$

By differentiating this profit function with respect to the price, we determine the first order conditions for the single monopolist

$$\frac{\partial \pi}{\partial P_Q} = P_Q D'(P_Q) + D(P_Q) = 0 \tag{9.5}$$

The interesting comparison is between the optimal price in equations (9.3) and (9.5). One finds that the optimal price under a single monopolist (equation (9.5)) is actually lower than the total price of the composite good under a complementary oligopoly (equation (9.3)). A move from complementary oligopoly over intellectual property rights to a concentrated monopoly will decrease price and increase output, thereby increasing overall welfare. It is also interesting to look at the comparative statics of equation (9.3) with respect to the number of oligopolistic firms. By inspection, it is possible to see both the overall price, and overall deadweight loss, increase in *n.* This is the inverse of the traditional case of oligopoly over substitute goods, in which the strategic pricing of the oligopolistic sellers leads to lower prices, with an increase in consumer surplus and overall welfare. However, in the case of complementary oligopoly, the strategic pricing of the oligopolists leads to higher prices: both producer and consumer surplus are diminished compared to the alternative monopoly outcome.

This result is consistent with that of a previous model of anticommons pricing applied to the case of copyright protection (Depoorter and Parisi, 2002) which demonstrates that the extent of deadweight losses from concurrent copyright protection increases monotonically with the number of independent sellers. The greater the number of individuals who independently price complementary inputs, the higher the equilibrium price that each of these individuals will demand for his own right. At the margin, as the number of intellectual property owners approaches very large numbers (or infinity), complete abandonment of valuable resources will result. Interestingly, the 'oligopolistic' supply of intellectual property rights leads to higher prices than those that would be charged by a single concentrated monopolist.

9.4 COMPLEMENTARITIES AND COMPETITION IN INTELLECTUAL PROPERTY

The examples above illustrate how the independent pricing of complements into the production of a final derivative work can result in a sub-optimal equilibrium. We should note that the above equations assume a strict complementarity of the inputs (in our narrative, of the copyright licences) as factors of production for the final work. A more general model which allows, but does not require, the strict complementarity of the inputs can be shown to produce qualitatively similar results. The relationship between various factors of production could, indeed, vary. Furthermore, the interconnection between the copyrighted inputs may instead reveal partial (or less-than-perfect) complementarity in the production of the derivative work. The case of strict complementarity thus represents a special case of the more general anticommons problem discussed in Schulz, Parisi and and Depoorter (2000).

Cases of less-than-perfect complementarity are more realistic in ordinary copyright situations. Unlike the exceptional cases of essential production inputs, most inputs in the production of derivative work can, with more or less ease, be substituted with other comparable sources. With imperfect complementarity, withholding a copyrighted input reduces, without eliminating, both the ability to produce a derivative work, and its final value.

The cases of strict complementarity and perfect substitutability of the inputs can be seen as the dual end points along a continuum, where the relevant variable captures the cross-price effect between the pricing of the copyrighted material. In the case of strict complementarity, as we have seen above, copyright owners can impose substantial external costs on the sellers of other complementary inputs, due to the effect that an increase in the price of one copyright will have on the demand for the bundle of complementary copyrights. Conversely, in the case of perfect substitutability, the external cost of one copyright owner's price choice will be limited to the cross-price effects of a standard Bertrand-type competition between sellers of substitutable goods.[9]

We can think of these two hypotheses as the end points around the case of a single owner of all copyrighted inputs. Such a concentrated monopolist fully internalises the costs and benefits in the pricing and withholding of copyright licences. The external effects of the decisions of the copyright holders are the root cause of the deadweight losses that increase monotonically with the number of inputs to production.

9.5   SUBSTITUTES AND COMPLEMENTS DISTINGUISHED

This paper's analysis reveals the surprising result that price co-ordination and monopolistic pricing do not produce inefficient equilibria in all circumstances. More specifically, the effect of monopolistic price co-ordination on the efficiency of the equilibrium pricing depends on the nature of the various copyrights as factors of production.

The failure of the various copyright holders to co-ordinate prices has ambiguous effects with respect to the resulting social deadweight loss. If the copyrights are in a relationship of complementarity in the production of a derivative work, the competitive Nash equilibrium would generate an anticommons pricing problem, making both society and the individual copyright holders worse off. The anticommons equilibrium pricing is simply the outcome of a prisoner's dilemma that individual copyright sellers face when pricing their copyrights independently. As in a traditional prisoner's dilemma, the inability of copyright holders to co-ordinate prices produces both private and social inefficiencies. Quite strikingly, in this case the competitive outcome is socially inefficient, even if compared to the alternative monopoly equilibrium. Competitive pricing of complementary goods generates a substantially larger social loss than the monopolistic equilibrium.

If the copyrights are substitutes in the production function of the derivative work, the inability of the copyright sellers to co-ordinate their prices will also be detrimental for them. As in the previous case, the independent and unco-ordinated pricing of the copyrights renders the monopolistic pricing unsustainable in a Nash equilibrium, with a loss of profit for the various sellers. Unlike the complementarity case considered above, however, the competition among copyright sellers would be beneficial for society at large. In this case, in fact, the substitutability of the copyrights as inputs of production leads to the usual negative price effect. The resulting equilibrium – albeit Pareto inferior for all the players – is socially preferable to the alternative monopoly outcome.

The analysis above applies even when parties can negotiate agreements at no cost concerning the transfer of copyright licences from authors to users. If strategic behaviour is not prevented by the ability of users of copyrighted work to obtain copyright licences without effort, for instance by the purchase of copyrighted material from the Internet in a 'click and pay' manner, sub-optimal equilibria may still result from the independent pricing of copyright licences for the production of a final derivative work. In light of this, the defence of fair use retains an important, albeit residual, role in minimising the deadweight losses, even where the digital market allows individual copyright owners to enter into transactions and to collect licensing fees at low cost.

9.6　THE EFFECT OF PRICE CO-ORDINATION

In an ideal world where copyright owners could effectively co-ordinate on-line licensing efforts, the above result would be considerably changed. If the fragmented group of copyright holders could co-ordinate the pricing of their licences – when each copyrighted material serves as complementary input in the production of a final good, such as in our review essay example – they would clearly be able to act as a monopolist, maximising gains. In fact, one important aspect of many on-line licensing initiatives is the co-ordination by intermediaries that have collected a broad portfolio of copyrighted works. In this setting, it may be important to consider the impact of copyright databases, such as those held by copyright collectives, rather than that of individual copyright owners, on the two equilibrium hypotheses discussed above.

For this purpose we focus in particular on the two main performance right organisations in music, the American Society of Composers, Authors and Publishers (ASCAP) and Broadcast Music, Inc. (BMI).

9.7　THE ROLE OF COPYRIGHT COLLECTIVES

An essential consideration in the study of the role of intermediaries is their authority and practical ability to set prices. As a matter of law, copyright collectives, such as ASCAP and BMI do not have exclusivity in the sale of copyright licences. Potential licensees can choose to contract directly with the author ('direct licences'), with syndicates that secure rights from the author ('source licences') or copyright collectives ('intermediary licences'). The consent decree in *United States v. ASCAP*[10] explicitly guarantees ASCAP members the authority to issue source licences for their work.[11] This allows for potential competition between original owners and copyright collectives. The potential competitive supply of 'direct licences' or 'source licences' has dual effects in the two cases considered above.

In order to study the impact of copyright collectives and non-exclusivity rules on the pricing (and resulting efficiency) of the licences, we need to proceed in two steps, first considering the dual effect of intermediaries on licence prices and subsequently considering the impact of the potential competition between 'direct licencing' and 'intermediary licencing' in the process.

The role of copyright collectives and intermediaries

Copyright collectives and other intermediaries often retain the independent power to specify the price for individual transactions. This power is limited by antitrust constraints, which result in ASCAP's inability to conduct first or second degree price discrimination between licensees that are similarly situated (ASCAP does not price discriminate in licence rates, terms or conditions between similarly situated users).[12] These institutions, however, regularly engage in third degree price discrimination, charging different prices to various broad categories of licensees (e.g., profit/non-profit, number of seats in a venue, number of listeners of the radio station, voltage, etc.).[13]

In this respect, copyright collectives are not simple agents of copyright holders, maintaining some independence in the pricing and packaging of their product. Such independent authority to fix the price of licences has an obvious effect on the two equilibria considered above. In the complements scenario, the intermediary would choose prices that are lower than the prices copyright holders would have chosen if pricing independently from one another. The salient point is that the lower price charged by the intermediary is beneficial to all individual copyright sellers, since it allows them to maximise the total profit from the sale of their licences, improving upon the alternative anticommons result reached in the absence of price co-ordination. The paradox – that the intermediaries' price is lower than one that would have been chosen by the owners and yet it increases their total profits from the sale – can be understood by recalling that the anticommons equilibrium pricing is the direct outcome of a 'prisoner's dilemma' that individual copyright holders face when pricing copyrights independently. While individual sellers could not co-ordinate prices, intermediaries serve this function, providing a benefit for society as well as for the owners.

Opposite conclusions are reached in the case of substitutes. Here, an intermediary with independent price-fixing authority renders monopolistic pricing sustainable in a Nash equilibrium. The resulting equilibrium favours copyright owners, who are able to maximise total profit from the sale of their licences, as would happen in a cartel. But such co-ordination is socially inefficient compared to the alternative competitive (or oligopolistic) equilibrium, since it prevents beneficial competition with the creation of a social deadweight loss.[14]

Source licencing and non-exclusivity of intermediary licencing

Recent antitrust rulings require copyright owners to retain the ability to issue licences ('direct licences') for their work. Potential licensees can choose to contract directly with the author, allowing for potential competition between owners and intermediaries offering licences.[15] The competitive supply of 'direct licences' and 'intermediary licences' has different effects in the two cases considered here.

In the 'complements' case, owners have no incentive to deviate unilaterally from the co-ordinated pricing equilibrium induced by the intermediary. Owners will not be able to sell for more than the 'collective' equilibrium price and, given the complementarity of the licences, they have no incentive to sell for less. The competition between source and intermediary licences would thus have no effect on the equilibrium price. The consent decrees' provisions on this point are therefore ineffective.

In the 'substitutes' case, owners have quite different incentives. Given substitutability, both source and direct licences compete with the intermediary licences. Each copyright owner will have an incentive to lower the price of the licences, and deviate unilaterally from the co-ordinated pricing equilibrium induced by the intermediary. In turn, this will induce the copyright collectives to lower the price of their offering, in order to preempt the oligopolistic competition of the individual sellers. The competition between source and intermediary licences thus has beneficial effects on the equilibrium price. In this case, the antitrust rulings are valuable.

The practice of blanket licences

The question arises whether our analysis applies also to tying practices. ASCAP and other comparable performance right institutions only offer blanket licences (covering the right to perform the collective's entire repertory) and to a small extent per-programme licences (a blanket licence that covers use of the repertory in a specific radio or television programme, while requiring the user to keep track of the use). As a practical matter, per-program licences are rendered unattractive by ASCAP and BMI, because of a cumbersome procedure and the threatened enforcement of non-intentional infringement. Also, it is questionable whether source and direct licences provide alternatives to the preeminent system of blanket licences in performing rights. The viability of source licences is hampered, for syndicates generally tend to split-off performance rights to the collective performing rights associations; while original copyright holders are reluctant to licence their works individually.[16] In fact, the collectives have objected to anything but blanket licences and have been ostensibly unwilling – despite efforts by the antitrust authorities – to implement item-specific licences (e.g., right to use a particular song once).

The most obvious explanation for this reluctance lies in transaction costs saving arguments (cf. Besen, Kirby and Salop, 1992; Merges, 1996). The analysis above provides an additional rationale for the strategy of collectives with regard to blanket licences. By tying all licences together, copyright collectives are able to shield their market power from the potential competition of individual source licences. Tying, in other words, is instrumental to the sustainability of the concentrated monopolistic pricing of the copyright collectives. Bearing in mind the previous discussion, this has dual effects from an efficiency point of view. In the 'complements' case, this prevents the tragic outcome of the anticommons pricing. However, in the 'substitutes' case this has the effect of preventing desirable competition.

The traditional concern of tying should thus be re-appraised in light of the beneficial effects of 'packaging' complementary goods, to avoid the undesirable pricing problems discussed above. At first impression, bundling may be the result of the successful co-ordination of suppliers of complementary goods, who have overcome the hold-out strategies that generate the complementary oligopoly problem discussed in this paper.

The rationale of per-use licences

One word should be spent here to verify whether the tying rationale would also assuage the traditional antitrust concern with ACAP and SMI's reluctance to offer per-use licences (e.g., a licence to buy the performance right to just *one* song), and practice to offer all-or-nothing licences.[17] The answer to this question is quite straightforward. While practices of bundling may be appreciated as evidence of a successful solution to the firms' strategic problem, this justification would not extend to the practice that excludes per-use licences from the available options. If the underlying problem is one of complementary oligopoly, the supply of per-use licences would reflect higher per-unit prices, compared to the alternative bundle. As long as consumers may acquire cheaper bundled licences, the availability of a per-use licence does not constitute an impediment to the solution of the complementary oligopoly problem. The reluctance to offer per-use licences cannot find support on the sole basis of the model presented here.

9.8   CONCLUSION

This paper has applied the case of complementary oligopoly and anticommons pricing to intellectual property rights. Our model reveals the dramatic result that price co-ordination and monopolistic pricing do not in all circumstances produce inefficient equilibria. Because complementary inputs push oligopoly to higher prices and greater quantity restrictions, monopoly may paradoxically represent a second-best alternative. That is, an improvement with respect to the alternative Nash equilibrium. As illustrated, the welfare effects of competition and price co-ordination with regard to works of intellectual property depend on the degree of complementarity and the nature of the intellectual products involved.

This paper concluded with remarks on the implications of this analysis on the practices of copyright collectivisation and relevant antitrust regulation. It was noted that the preservation of competition between 'direct licences' and 'intermediary licences', as provided by antitrust regulation, produce dual effects from an efficiency point of view. In the case of intellectual property rights that are complements in a composite creation, such competition remains ineffective. However, with regard to substitutes the antitrust regulation retains its relevance by inducing a lower equilibrium price. Similarly, copyright collectives' blanket licensing policies have ambiguous effects from the antitrust policy perspective. Not all practices generally regarded as anti-competitive in the standard case of substitutable goods are undesirable when applied to complementary goods. Practices of price co-ordination and mergers solve the strategic pricing problem discussed in this paper, to the mutual advantage of producers and consumers. The outcome is not the best social optimum, but is an improvement – both privately and socially – over the alternative Nash equilibrium.

NOTES

1. The authors would like to thank Clair Smith for elaborating on the similarities between the anticommons problem and Cournot's (1838) model of complementary duopoly.

2. One of the most current DJ-mix albums today, '2 Many DJ's', combines 46 songs of various artists. Reportedly, the clearance of the rights on the songs, featured on the album, lasted three years, involving 865 emails, 160 faxes and hundreds of telephone calls. In the end 72 tracks were omitted from the album because the rights could not be obtained in time for those tracks (see http://breedband.telenet.be/muziek/dossiers/2manydjs/, last visited 12 May, 2002).

3. Cournot considered the case of two monopolists producing complementary goods: zinc and copper. These two products can be combined to make brass. See Cournot (1838).

4. Other primary sources are less essential to the completion of the anthology, since it would be easy to substitute any one of those less essential sources without compromising the quality and success of the final product. We will refer to this category of less essential inputs as substitutable inputs.

5. Because the inputs of production are strict complements, there is no offsetting substitution effect; when the price of one component goes up, the consumer purchases fewer units of each of the component goods.

6. The same logic would hold if the firms were allowed to control output, rather than price. Here however, there would be a substantial difference, likely to facilitate firms' co-ordination. Because consumers use one of each component together, neither firm can sell more than the lesser firm's output. Furthermore, neither firm would have an incentive to produce more than the single monopolist's output level. If one firm did produce output greater than the monopolistic output, Q_M, the other firm would be free of the complementarity constraint, and would also produce at Q_M to maximise profits. On the other hand, if one firm produces less than Q_M, the other firm would maximise profits by also producing less than Q_M.

7. In a Nash strategy a player cannot benefit by changing her strategy while the other players keep their strategies unchanged.

8. Note that the conditions for the prisoner's dilemma are satisfied by assuming that each complementary duopolist prefers the other party to price low, while setting higher prices for himself. In Figure 9.1, the ranking of payoffs satisfies the conditions of the prisoner's dilemma, as indicated by the direction of the arrows (pointing from least preferred to most preferred outcome for each party).

9. One point worth noting is that the situation in which each of two copyright holders can separately license would create a Bertrand duopoly, unless they can agree to join forces, acting as a monopolist.

10. *United States v. ASCAP*, 1940-1943 Trade Cas. (CCH) 56, 104 (S.D.N.Y. 1941), superseded by 1950 Trade Cas. (CCH) P 62,595. A similar consent decree was entered into by BMI, 1966 Trade Cas. (CCH) P 71,941 (1966).

11. See Section IV., Art. B. of the proposed new consent decree in *United States of America v. ASCAP*. The consent degree declares that 'ASCAP is [...] enjoined and restrained from:.... Limiting, restricting, or interfering with the right of any member to issue, directly or through an agent other than a performing rights organization, non-exclusive licences to music users for rights of public performance.' The Decree is available online at http://www.ascap.com/press/afj2final.pdf (last visited 22 November, 2000).

12. In response to increasing antitrust concerns by courts for the monopolistic powers of ASCAP within the music industry, a consent decree was issued, see *United States v. ASCAP* (1940-1943 Trade Cas. (CCH) 56, 104 (S.D.N.Y. 1941)). A new consent decree was recently proposed, see http://www.ascap.com/press/afj2final.pdf (last visited 22 November, 2000).

13. For further reference see http://www.ascap.com, (last visited 20 November, 2001). In an amendment to the original consent decree, the United States District Court for the Southern District of New York is assigned to adjucate disputes on what constitutes a 'reasonable fee' (*United States v. ASCAP*, 1950–1951 Trade Cas. (CCH) 62, 595 (S.D.N.Y. 1950)). More recently, the Sensenberger Amendment, in attachment to the Copyright Term Extension Act of 1998, allows non-broadcasters to initiate — less cost intensive — binding arbitration under the rules of the American Arbitration Society (Sec. 203 HAMDT 532, amendment to H.R.

2589, 105th Cong. (1998)), available on http://thomas.loc.gov (last visited 20 November, 2000).

14. Bundling and price co-ordination is always in the interest of those who have control over these practices (sellers), even though this may not always create desirable equilibria for society at large. This, in turn, generates a pooling equilibrium which prevents us from using revealed preferences to distinguish between the two hypotheses.

15. This fact was conclusive in *Buffalo Broadcasting Co. v. ASCAP*, where the US Court of Appeal for the Second Circuit held that the blanket licences offered by ASCAP to local TV stations did not constitute an unreasonable restraint on trade; see *Buffalo Broad. Co. v. ASCAP*, 744 F.2d. 917 (2d Cir. 1984). See also *Columbia Broadcast System, Inc. v. Am. Soc. of Composers, Authors and Publishers*, 620 F.2d 930, 936 (2d Cir. 1980), cert. denied, 450 U.S. 970 (1981): '(I)f the opportunity (to purchase individual licences) is fully available, and if copyright owners retain unimpaired independence to set a competitive price for individual licences to a licensee willing to deal with them, the blanket licence is not a restraint of trade.'

16. These arguments are set forth in Hillman (1998). Hillman criticises the flawed remedial role of consent decrees in performance rights associations' alleged anti-competitive conduct.

17. See in this regard the litigation in *Buffalo Broad. Co. v. ASCAP*, 744 F.2d. (2d Cir. 1984) and *CBS v. ASCAP*, 620 F.2d 930 (Distr. 1980), both discussed in Hillman (1998, 747–757).

REFERENCES

Besen, S., S. Kirby and S. Salop (1992), 'An Economic Analysis of Copyright Collectives', *Virginia Law Review*, **78**, 383–411.

Buchanan, J. and J. Yoon (2000), 'Symmetric Tragedies: Commons and Anticommons Property', *Journal of Law and Economics*, **43**, 1–13.

Cournot, A. (1838), *Researches into the Mathematical Principles of the Theory of Wealth*, Nathaniel Bacon, trans. Macmillan (1927).

Depoorter, B. and F. Parisi (2002), 'Fair Use and Copyright Protection: A Price Theory Explanation', *International Review of Law and Economics*, **21**, 453–473.

Hillman, N.L. (1998), 'Intractable Consent: A Legislative Solution to the Problem of the Aging Consent Decrees in *United States v. ASCAP* and *United States v. BMI*', *Fordham Intellectual Property Media & Entertainment Law Journal*, **8**, 733.

Merges, R. (1996), 'Contracting Into Liability Rules: Intellectual Property Rights and Collective Rights Organizations', *California Law Review*, **84**, 1293.

Schulz, N., F. Parisi and B. Depoorter (2000), 'Duality in Property: Commons and Anticommons', in University of Virginia Public Law Working Paper Series # 00–8.

Schulz, N., F. Parisi and B. Depoorter (2002), 'Fragmentation in Property: Towards a General Model', *Journal of Institutional and Theoretical Economics*, **158(4)**, 594–613.

10. Are Copyright Collecting Societies Efficient Organisations? An Evaluation of Collective Administration of Copyright in Europe

Fabrice Rochelandet[1]

10.1 INTRODUCTION

This contribution examines the performances of copyright collecting societies (CCS), which play a key role in the field of copyright management. They are non-governmental non-profit organisations, which administer some of the rights of copyright holders. They negotiate licences with users and receive payments they distribute among their members.[2] CCS historically act as private institutions that minimise search and contracting costs between and among intermediary users and copyright holders (Merges, 1996). Nowadays, the question is, whether this idea still prevails with the dissemination of information and communication technologies. On the one hand, given the emergence of self-help systems, opponents of collective administration argue that ICTs permit to reduce transaction costs in such a manner that these private institutions turn out to be unnecessary.[3] On the other hand, even though ICTs permit some components of transaction costs to be reduced – for instance, by facilitating identification or by tightening up enclosure – they do not reduce them all.[4] So, by playing the role of intermediaries and representatives of their members, CCS can figure among the main private institutions that enable effective governance of transaction in the digital economy (Rochelandet, 2000).

Beyond this important current debate, it should be noted that CCS are also specific organisations. Thus, before drawing some general conclusions about the (in)effectiveness of the collective administration in the digital age, it is necessary to evaluate their performance as organisations. One possible method would be to measure and compare the performances of each kind of organisation likely to manage copyright, i.e. for-profit, public and non-profit organisations. Economic theory would then determine the efficient copyright arrangement according to a given criterion such as Pareto-optimal allocation of copyrights[5] and transaction costs minimisation. This study, however, is based on another perspective. It attempts to compare *existing* organisations with similar features by isolating the respective impact of ownership structure and legal supervision on their performance.

I elsewhere highlight performance dispersions between French CCS (Rochelandet, 2001). Among the main factors to explain these results are ownership concentration and copyright administration complexity.[6] However, these results have been established with no possibility of isolating the very impact of legal supervision on CCS performance. Drawing on meaningful data on three major European CCS, the current study tries to fill this gap. It addresses thereby three questions: (1) Which organisations are characterised by the best performance? (2) What relationship is there to be found between ownership structure, legal control and performances in the case of CCS? (3) Under what legal system will we observe better results for collecting societies? At the time of important discussions about copyright management methods, this study could help European regulators to specify what kind of regulation should be implemented in European countries.

10.2 THE COLLECTIVE ADMINISTRATION OF COPYRIGHT: AN AGENCY PROBLEM

Collective administration of copyright figures among the different methods to administrate copyright, that is primarily individual administration, for-profit private management by publishers (who link this function with their business), collective administration and non-voluntary licences. Factors to explain the implementation of such methods are of economic nature (searching and contracting costs minimisation, respective bargaining power of authors, publishers and commercial users) as well as of historical nature (institutional path dependencies).[7] Each method displays some drawbacks, in particular in terms of monopolistic pricing and risk of abuse of dominant position through hold-up strategies. That explains in the case of CCS why legal supervision plays a key role in order to control their behaviour. In this section, these organisations are analysed through the lens of positive agency theory.

Hypotheses

The nature and running of CCS can be characterised by some hypotheses.

(H1) Divergence of interests between members and managers.

A general assumption underlying this study is that the interests of managers and members of CCS diverge. The former are supposed to maximise an objective function grounded on their remuneration, power, job security and status. Two complementary strategies make it possible for managers to achieve these goals: *boosting management costs* in such a way that copyright distributions are reduced in proportion and *maximising copyright collection* so that administration costs are automatically increased. As for the members, they are wealth maximisers in the sense that they expect their individual share in collected sums to be as great as possible.

(H2) Informational asymmetries and lack of significant market pressure.

However, large informational asymmetries make it generally impossible for the members of any CCS at zero cost to ensure that the managers will make optimal decisions from their viewpoint. Relinquishing controls would be favourable to opportunistic behaviour of managers. They would be all the more important if no effective market pressure such as product market competition and potential hostile takeovers forced CCS towards higher performances. The monopolistic position of CCS makes it very difficult to compare the results of each CCS with similar organisations. So managers have room for discretionary allocation of collected copyrights. In this case,[8] the more dispersed the membership is, the more managers are incited to raise their remunerations of all kinds far beyond their actual productivity and results.

How do members convince managers to minimise administration expenses and so maximise copyright distribution? How do they make sure that the managers do not boost the running costs and squander collected copyrights in acts and projects unrelated to the main objectives of the CCS? In short, how to solve this agency problem?[9] In fact, some governance mechanisms are likely to reduce these organisational rents by leading managers to act in the interest of members: on the one hand, ownership concentration and especially existence of large members; on the other hand, legal controls.

(H3) Divergence of interests between large and less important members.

As for large members, their market power gives them not only greater incentives to monitor managers but also the power to control managerial behaviour and, if necessary, to replace managers. In other words, many large members make it possible to reduce significantly managerial rents. Nonetheless, beyond their common goal of individual revenue maximisation, all members have not the same interest. From the large members' viewpoint, CCS have to specialise on the collection of the most valuable rights, i.e. those that are the less costly to administrate in comparison to their amount. By contrast, less important members expect their organisation to collect any right, even if it would be costly for a CCS to adopt such a development strategy.[10] In fact, this conflict is centred on the existence of cross-subsidies between highly valuable copyrights and costly-to-collect copyrights.

Although the presence of many large members could be effective in solving the agency problem, they may also inefficiently redistribute collected sums from members without any significant power to themselves. In this case as well as in the case of dispersed membership, an effective governance system supposes at first glance that legal supervision should be established. This legal supervision is all the more needed as in the spirit of law, copyright is not aimed to favour some copyright holders to the detriment of others. So copyrights should tend to their social value for all kinds of copyrighted uses and CCS should maximise the sums they collect *and* distribute. But the question then is, to what extent their intensity should be established.

(H4) A diversity of legal supervision national systems.[11]

The purpose of this study is to determine the impact of institutional supervision systems on the results of CCS. It is therefore necessary to highlight their nature. The extent of legal control of CCS differs among countries and especially among the European member states.[12] Two opposite cases are to be found. On the one hand, the less restricting national regulation is characterised by the absence of specific control: only competition and contract laws apply to CCS. Greece is a significant example. It looks like the American legal system, which mainly consists in supervising the pricing and licensing practices of CCS.[13] On the other hand, the most restricting system takes the form of a public administration of copyrights. The Italian system illustrates this case. Since the 1941 copyright law, the Italian CCS – the SIAE – has enjoyed a legal monopoly. In return, any statutory changes must be approved by a presidential decree in accordance with the main government ministries. The running of this public law association is subject to a permanent control of the prime minister. This control is strengthened by an auditors' division and some government officials sit on the SIAE board.

Between these two opposite cases are intermediary systems, which combine a control on the establishment of any CCS and a control of their activities. All of these systems take into account the interests of users (pricing and licensing contracts) and those of individual members (quality of the management, equitable distribution, etc.). Therefore, controls differ according to their intensity: no control, control at the request of users, founding control, permanent control and intense control.

The following table classifies European countries according to the control intensity.

Table 10.1 Legal supervision systems in European countries

Countries	Lack of control	Control at request	Setting up control	Permanent control	Extreme control
Germany			+++	+++	
Austria			++	++	
Belgium	+++*				
Denmark			+		
Spain			+++	++	
France		+	++	++	
Greece	+++				
Luxembourg			++	++	
Ireland		+++			
Italy					+++
Netherlands			++	++	
Portugal			+		
United		+++			
Kingdom			++		
Switzerland					

* Since 1994, the Belgium system has been significantly strengthened.
Sources: Hilty (1995), Sénat Français (1997)

Note that supervision is very intense in Germany, somewhat low in the UK and intermediary in France. In the German case, the establishment of any CCS requires to be jointly authorised by the German Patent Office and the Kartellamt. Their activities are placed under the control of these institutions. Not only can the Patent Office demand any information and attend board meetings, but they can also require the CCS to replace their manager or even forbid them to carry out their activity. Furthermore, any CCS can be legally bound to enter into contract with any user and to conclude blanket contracts with representative association of commercial users on their request. Finally, the Patent Office plays a role of arbitrator when CCS and users are in conflict. Only in case of failure, the dispute takes the form of a trial. By contrast, the British legal system is much less restrictive. It applies to the price setting by CCS and proceedings are undertaken only at the request of users when they litigate a claim towards the copyright tribunal. No specific control applies to their establishment and running. Finally, they are placed under the regime of competition law as anywhere in Europe. The French legal system is a go-between institutional environment, which consists mainly in heavy control of establishment and a moderate control of activity.[14]

Propositions

On the basis of the previous hypothesis, it is possible to make the following propositions.

(P1) Many large members can lead managers to minimise administration expenses.

Not only large members with market power have greater incentives to monitor managers but also they have the power to control their behaviour and, if necessary, to replace them. Therefore, many large members make it possible to reduce significantly managerial rents.

(P2) By contrast, dispersed membership can lead managers to boost their declared costs to the detriment of distributions to members.

In this case, managers have much more room for discretionary allocation of collected copyrights, for instance, by raising the running costs of the organisation in order to improve their own status.

(P3) The stronger the legal supervision is, the smaller managerial rents are likely to be.

This external governance is supposed to be all the more effective when internal control proves to be low (dispersed membership or informational asymmetries). I have tested propositions P1 and P2 in a previous study about French collecting societies by suggesting that the bargaining power of members – more or less concentrated ownership – affects sharply the performance of these organisations (Rochelandet, 2001). So internal governance appears to be a strong constraint in managerial behaviour. For instance, it explains the better results of producers' collecting societies in comparison to performers' ones. However, it doesn't highlight proposition P3. The impact of legal supervision obviously is impossible to determine because comparisons are made in the same legal system. So this study aims to analyse the impact of legal supervision systems on the results of CCS.

10.3 THE PERFORMANCES OF CCS AS ORGANISATIONS: AN EVALUATION

Data

In order to compare CCS, it is necessary to highlight the common features of the services they produce. Among the data generally available on a relevant period are the total copyright royalties they collect from content users P, the total revenues they distribute to their members R, the licensing and administration expenses C, their membership size M, the number of their employees E, and the amount of their cultural and social funds F. Then, a collecting society is characterised by

$$R = P - C - F + e_t ,$$

where e_t is a parameter that approximates the various sums collected – or distributed – by the CCS and added to – or deducted from – the collected sums during period t: financial revenues from invested non-distributable sums; collected sums during previous periods $t-1$, $t-2$... that are effectively distributed during period t; and non-distributable sums from periods t, $t-1$, $t-2$, ... This parameter could be of positive or negative sign and its components prove to be very difficult to get from CCS.

The present study focuses on copyright collecting societies that carry out their activities in radically different legal control systems. The data set includes organisations that manage the same kind of rights (musical rights) and benefit from a dominant position relative to the other national collecting societies. Most of the data have been obtained from the 1992-1999 annual yearbooks of the studied CCS and supplemented by official reports (BPLA, 1995, 1997; Sénat Français, 1997) as well as personal inquiries. The study is limited to the three largest European organisations, i.e. PRS, GEMA and SACEM. Indeed, analysing the other important international organisations raises specific problems that prevent any relevant comparison. For instance, the SIAE, which manages copyright in Italy, is a public law organisation and its repertoire covers musical rights as well as audiovisual, literary rights, and the like. As for the American ASCAP and BMI – which administrate more than 90 percent of collectively managed copyrights in the USA – their competition proves to impact positively their results (Sénat Français, 1997).

Two complementary methods: performance criteria and data envelopment analysis

Two methods are used in order to evaluate the performance of CCS. The first one is based on the elaboration and comparison of specific performance criteria and the second is a complementary dynamic evaluation through the data envelopment analysis.

Performance criteria analysis: advantages and limits

Several specific criteria can be built from the aggregates P, R, C, F, E and M. The first one, *OPTIC* (the 'optimisation criterion') assesses the ability of a CCS to maximise its collected sums at the lowest cost. It is given by

$$OPTIC = \frac{P}{C}$$

At first glance, this ratio estimates the performance of a given CCS regarding its collecting activity. It implicitly assumes that the higher the management costs in comparison with collections, the less effective the organisation. Thus, this criterion proves to relate more to cost optimisation than merely to cost minimisation.

Among its main drawbacks, however, figures the fact that the administration expenses C include costs incurred in the collection of rights – i.e., contract concluding, licensed users supervision, etc. – as well as costs relating to their distribution among members such as the determination of effective beneficiaries, right measurement and effective payments. One solution would be to identify these two components of C and therefore, to calculate two criteria: one would apply to the effectiveness of collection and the other would assess distribution activities. However, this task turns out to be extremely difficult for two main reasons: the lack of detailed accounts for all societies and the existence of joint costs. Thus, in the absence of relevant data, the criterion *OPTIC* proves a good approximation of the ability of a CCS to manage its members' rights at the lowest cost.

The growth rates of collections ΔP_t and of distribution ΔR_t allow the variation of collected and distributed sums from one year to another to be measured. For a year t, they are respectively given by

$$\Delta P_t = \frac{P_t}{P_{t-1}} - 1 \text{ and } \Delta R_t = \frac{R_t}{R_{t-1}} - 1$$

These dynamic ratios evaluate the productivity gains due to rationalisation strategies. But both have the same flaw: they depend too heavily upon specific growth of cultural markets where collectively managed copyrights are exchanged. Thus, it turns out to be very difficult to distinguish what is due to the effective efforts of CCS and what is explained by the fluctuations of content markets. A better criterion would incorporate a weighting according to the relative share of each market contributing to the collections made by CCS. Given the tangle of their repertoires, it would not be, however, an easy task to do.

Nevertheless, these two indicators make it possible to build a more interesting ratio, even though it has the same drawbacks as ΔP_t and ΔR_t. As an elasticity, it measures the additional amount of distributions when copyright collection increases by 1 percent. It is given by

$$ELRP_t = \frac{\Delta R_t}{\Delta P_t}$$

Another criterion, *GDRAT*, measures the gross proportion of distributed revenues over a given period in comparison with the effective collected sums. For a given CCS, it is given by

$$GDRAT = \frac{R}{P}$$

It evaluates the effectiveness of the distribution activity of a given CCS, i.e. its ability to distribute the maximum of the collected rights. It is based on the preferences of its members: the greater the proportion of collected sums they get, the greater their satisfaction. This ratio compares the final result (actual distributions) to the initially available sums (the collected sums from users).

But it raises two problems. On the one hand, it implicitly incorporates the dynamic factor e_t which relates to the distributable sums from one period to another. It can therefore be greater than 100 percent, in which case collected sums from previous years are distributed only the year this ratio is calculated. The calculation of an average ratio over the tested period reduces significantly this problem.[15] On the other hand, before being distributed, some proportion of the collected sums is allocated in professional, social and cultural actions (subsidies to festivals, pension funds, etc.). To overcome this difficulty, the net distribution ratio *NDRAT* takes into account these various funds, whether or not they are legally imposed to the CCS. For a given CCS

$$NDRAT = \frac{R+F}{P}$$

Symmetrically, the difference 1–*NDRAT* is the proportion of collected sums that are not allocated to the distribution or to the cultural and social funds. The greater the *NDRAT* ratio is, the more efficient is the CCS regarding its activity of distribution.

The proportion of undistributed copyrights *NONR* compares the distributable sums to the effectively distributed sums for a given year. Its evolution permits to assess the ability of a CCS to distribute the most part of the copyrights it has collected. It is given by

$$NONR = \frac{R_{pot}}{R_{eff}} - 1$$

where R_{pot} is the distributable sums and R_{eff} is the actual distributions. Unfortunately, the amount of R_{eff} is not available in all cases and over the whole period. It would be possible to approximate it through the amount of financial revenues – the invested sums correspond partly to the non-distributed copyrights – but this calculation requires the exact composition of the financial portfolios of the CCS and the respective share of financial interests yielded by the other components of their private assets.

The average productivity per employee *COPE* measures the collected sums per employee. In a similar way, it is possible to elaborate *DIPE*, i.e. the distributions per employee.

$$COPE = \frac{P}{E} \text{ and } DIPE = \frac{P}{E}$$

The higher are these ratios the more productive are the employees. However, it is difficult to infer systematically a greater performance from an increase of these ratios and vice versa. The collected sums could decrease more slowly than the number of employees and that could reveal a decreasing quality of services.

The average cost per employee *ACE* is a counter-performance criterion.

$$ACE = \frac{C}{E}$$

The higher is the cost of an employee, the higher is the *ACE* ratio. Nevertheless, explaining this criterion is problematical when comparing the various CCS. For instance, the impact of any technological change is not similar on every CCS, but it depends upon the structure of their respective repertoire. Moreover, the increase of this ratio could mean a higher quality of their services or the need for lawyers more and more qualified. Because of the heterogeneous competences and needs of CCS, this criterion was not adopted in the comparisons between French CCS (Rochelandet, 2000). By contrast, it proves to be more relevant in the current study based on CCS managing similar repertoires.[16]

The collected sums per member *COPM* and the distributions per member *DIPM* are respectively given by

$$COPM = \frac{P}{M} \text{ and } DIPM = \frac{R}{M}$$

The higher these indicators are, the more efficient is the CCS. They are much more 'profitability-orientated' since they take account of the average member viewpoint. From a dynamic perspective, they allow the improvement of production methods implemented by CCS to be evaluated. But their main limit is that they do not incorporate revenue dispersion. So if a CCS regroups only 'wealthy' – or more exactly 'valuable' – members, it would seem more efficient than a CCS regrouping all the copyright holders of a given repertoire.[17] This drawback raises many problems regarding comparisons between the CCS with many large members and the ones with dispersed membership.

Finally, variation indicators are made from *C*, *COPE* and *COPM* in order to retrace their trend, that is respectively ΔC, $\Delta COPE$ and $\Delta COPM$.

This comparison does not take into account either productivity measures such as capital intensity and R&D expenditure per employee – which appear to be difficult to obtain and somewhat irrelevant – or the traditional profitability ratios – which make no sense in the case of non-profit organisations. Table 10.2 shows the different tested criteria.

Data envelopment analysis: a more dynamic perspective

The basic problems with expressing the economic performance in separate single indicators like the previous method are manifold. First, it is impossible to aggregate and compare a number of non-commensurate performance indicators (for example, collections and membership) to one single performance measure and secondly, to establish a benchmark for comparing the performance of CCS. An alternative is data envelopment analysis (DEA),

Table 10.2 Summary of the performance criteria used in the study

Criteria	Formula	Relevance
OPTIC: management ratio	$OPTIC = \dfrac{P}{C}$	+++
ΔP_i: annual variation of collected sums	$\Delta P_t = \dfrac{P_t}{P_{t-1}} - 1$	+
ΔR_i: annual variation of distributable sums	$\Delta R_t = \dfrac{R_t}{R_{t-1}} - 1$	+
ELRP$_i$: elasticity of distributions compared to collections	$ELRP_t = \dfrac{\Delta R_t}{\Delta P_t}$	++
ΔC_i: annual variation of administration expenses	$\Delta C_t = \dfrac{C_t}{C_{t-1}} - 1$	++
GDRAT: gross distribution ratio	$GDRAT = \dfrac{R}{P}$	++
NDRAT: net distribution ratio	$NDRAT = \dfrac{R + F}{P}$	+++
COPE: collected sums per employee	$COPE = \dfrac{P}{E}$	+++
DIPE: distributed sums per employee	$DIPE = \dfrac{R}{E}$	++
ACE: average cost of an employee	$ACE = \dfrac{C}{E}$	++
$\Delta COPE_i$: annual variation of COPE	$\Delta COPE_t = \dfrac{COPE_t}{COPE_{t-1}} - 1$	++
COPM: collected sums per member	$COPM = \dfrac{P}{M}$	+++
DIPM: distributable sums per member	$DIPM = \dfrac{R}{M}$	+++
$\Delta COPM_i$: annual variation of COPM	$\Delta COPM_t = \dfrac{COPM_t}{COPM_{t-1}} - 1$	++
NONR: non-distributed copyrights	$NONR = \dfrac{R_{pot}}{R_{eff}} - 1$	+++

which is a non-parametric non-stochastic approach that uses a linear programming technique. It defines the best production frontier which serves as a benchmark and minimises the relative distance to this benchmark. The relative performance of any CCS is measured as the relative distance to the productive frontier. The DEA method is a multiple-input/multiple-output optimisation method that generalises the Farrell (1957) technical efficiency measure. Originally developed by Charnes, Cooper and Rhodes (1978) and extended by Banker, Charnes and Cooper (1984) to include variable returns to scale, this non-parametric non-stochastic approach is frequently applied in the field of non-profit organisations such as hospitals and schools.[18]

Applied to collecting societies, the DEA method makes it possible to consider many various cases. This study explores three complementary options according to an output maximisation/input minimisation test and the number of inputs to be considered in the analysis.

According to the first option, collections P and costs C are considered as inputs and distributions R as output. This case focuses only on the distribution activity. The underlying idea is that a CCS combines its collected sums with various factors, evaluated by C, to distribute them among its members. What is entering into the organisation is its collected copyright and its administration expenses and what is coming out of the organisation are the copyrights.

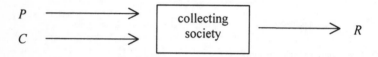

According to the second option, the number of employees E and members M (as an estimation of the repertoire size of each CCS) are added to inputs. The membership and employment levels are supposed to impact the output. Here, what is analysed is the joint impact of, on the one side, P and C and on the other side, the essential production factors of collective administration: labour and copyrights.

The third case considers two inputs (E, C) and two outputs (collected sums per member $COPM$ and R). It corresponds to a more productivity-orientated test.

In each case, efficiencies are tested under two complementary hypotheses: output maximisation and input minimisation. In each case, variable returns to scale are supposed to prevail and the production frontier is fixed at 100 percent.

Results and recommendations

The average criteria for the 1991-1998 period figure in Table 10.3 (in the appendix) and the results from the DEA method appear in Table 10.4 (in the appendix). As for the DEA results, the figures can be read as follows: for a given year, the more the indicators depart from 100 percent (indicating the production frontier), the less efficient is the CCS relative to the others. For instance, in the first table, '100.00 GEM96' means that by being on the production frontier (100%), the GEMA is more efficient than the SACEM in 1996 ('85.90 SAC96', i.e. 85.9%) and as efficient as the SACEM in 1992 ('100.00 SAC92'). According to both methods, the most efficient organisation is the GEMA, PRS comes second and SACEM is classified third.

Several conclusions can be drawn from these data. Given the fact that the most efficient organisation is the GEMA which carries out its activities in the most binding legal supervision system, a first conclusion is the following:

(C1) The most restrictive legal control gives rise to the lowest rents.

Accordingly, a first general recommendation could be made according to which it is in the interests of members to claim a large reinforcement of institutional controls. However, a second result qualifies such a recommendation. For the same period, the results of the PRS, which runs in the less restrictive legal system, are better than those of the SACEM and, above all, not so far from those of GEMA as Tables 10.3 and 10.4 show. In other words, implementing low supervision (UK) is better than setting up intermediary control (France). Therefore, a second conclusion could be that:

(C2) No general positive correlation can be made between the intensity of legal supervision and the results of CCS.

Should we therefore recommend a large reduction in the intensity of legal control? Indeed, lightening supervision could generate social savings in terms of reduced regulation costs, though the interests of members would be less respected. So, in a social welfare perspective, the gains from a reduction in supervision overcome the social loss of CCS' members due to lower revenues.

However, such a recommendation is difficult to defend. As a matter of fact, the PRS differs from the two other CCS by the greater power of its members. Publishers play a key role in the UK system of copyright. Accordingly, their internal governance proves to be sufficient to compensate a low legal control.

A third conclusion is that:

(C3) Intermediary levels of supervision appear to be imperfect and a source of inefficiencies.

The managers of SACEM are supposed to benefit from monopolistic rents due to an easing of external and internal control relatively to the GEMA and PRS. So two general recommendations can be made:

1. supervision reinforcement should be implemented only for CCS with dispersed membership.
2. correlatively, competition law is supposed to be sufficient to compel CCS with large members to act in the interest of their members.

Further comments

All these conclusions and recommendations are based on the SACEM results relative to the two other CCS. However, these results can be challenged by two facts: on the one hand, a CCS could strategically limit the scope of its repertoire in order to focus on its more valuable rights, i.e. those for which the management costs are significantly lower than the collected fees. For instance, these strategies can consist in only controlling and collecting copyrights from the biggest, easy-to-identify users. Limiting the scope of copyright management in such a manner can certainly imply better performance. In fact, it could also be interpreted as a socially inefficient specialisation to the detriment of copyright law spirit.

On the other hand, by offering its members the most equitable and diversified services, a CCS can incur higher costs of collection and distribution. In my point of view, this idea is essential but it requires a more meticulous study through, for instance, specific audits. It would consist in determining such things as homogeneous classes of members according to their revenues, management costs by specific piece of repertoire, and the number of members who actually perceive copyrights relative to the total membership. By definition, a CCS would be efficient if and only if it collects more copyrights and distributes them 'better' than its members. Of course, it could be costly to allocate equitably, but in this case, evaluating a given CCS would necessitate to include the criterion of quality of service in its objectives. Providing members with more equitable and diversified services can be costly and imply lower performance. In fact, there is a trade-off between costs and quality, especially in the case of collecting societies for which members are both owners and customers.

Beyond a purely productive efficiency analysis, it would thus be necessary to introduce some qualitative factors to compare collecting societies: quality of services to members as well as to users; equity of distributions among members; and correlation between development strategies of CCS and copyright law purposes.

Furthermore, testing this hypothesis would require to take into account the features of each cultural market in which CCS operate. Indeed, for a similar national market, PRS collects much less copyrights than SACEM (its collected sums are about 60 percent of those of PRS for the period 1990–1998). PRS is then likely to be more selective regarding the copyrights it administrates. In this perspective, a significant proof is the greater number of employees of the SACEM. At first glance, this greater number could be perceived as a bureaucratic bias or a strategic objective of managers in order to entrench themselves into their organisation. However, another viewpoint is to consider this greater number as an indicator of the quality of the services the SACEM supplies for its whole membership. A more detailed investigation would therefore be necessary to evaluate the relation between quality and costs in these non-profit organisations.

Finally, the sole criteria of costs minimisation and productivity turn out to be insufficient to evaluate the performance of a given CCS. No definitive conclusion could be made if the quality of provided services – assessed by the collection of *any* copyright and the improvement of their distribution – is not integrated into the analysis. There is a very delicate balance between the purpose of cost minimisation and the provision of valuable services in terms of quality and equity. Nevertheless, the impossibility of comparisons with similar for-profit organisations requires a more detailed investigation of the CCS as non-profit organisations. Thereby, members are not confined to their role of owners, but they are also considered as consumers of the whole production of CCS (Rochelandet, 2000).

10.4   CONCLUSION

Among the key factors to explain the performance of copyright collecting societies are the concentration of ownership and the intensity of institutional control. First of all, the bargaining power of their members and hence the more or less concentrated structure of ownership are proposed to affect sharply their performances. A previous comparison between French collecting societies suggests that internal governance appears to be the stronger constraint in all cases (Rochelandet, 2001). This explains the better results of societies that represent producers in comparison to performers' societies. By contrast, the impact of legal supervision is much more problematical to determine. Although the current study is still an exploratory paper, with more data to analyse in futures studies, initial results are very encouraging. The measure of the performance of three collecting societies with all the same repertoire in contrasted but complementary legal systems suggests several conclusions. First, the stronger control in Germany explains the best results of the GEMA. On the contrary, the worse results of the SACEM are certainly due to the intermediary level of supervision in France. Compared to the intermediary results of the PRS, this suggests that a strong internal control is sufficient to overcome the potential failure inherent in limited institutional constraints. But in the case of failure of this internal governance mechanism, the strengthening of legal supervision should be recommended.

However, all these results are essentially grounded on productive efficiency. Further investigations are needed to take into account the quality of delivered services and the non-profit nature of CCS. In addition, one must isolate the key institutional factors to determine which one affects the most CCS performance. Moreover, another question is whether ICTs do not challenge these results nowadays. At a first glance, these technologies reinforce the various controls on collecting societies by enabling better information, which benefits their members as well as the authorities. ICTs will enable the CCS to improve their performance by reducing management costs and allowing members to receive their remuneration more rapidly. In addition, they represent a new form of market governance through an extension and a renewal of competition in the field of copyright management (Rochelandet, 2000). Another objective drawn from this research is therefore to study in which way these technologies are adopted by the CCS and to determine their impact on the effectiveness of collective administration of copyright.

APPENDIX

Acronyms and abbreviations

ASCAP: American Society of Composers, Authors and Publishers
BMI: Broadcast Music, Inc.
BPLA: Bureau de la Propriété Littéraire et Artistique [*Copyright division of the French ministry of culture*]
CCS: Copyright Collecting Societies
GEMA: Gesellschaft für musikalische aufführungs-und vervielfatigungsrechte

PRS: Performing Rights Society
SACEM: Société des auteurs, compositeurs et éditeurs de musique
SIAE: Società italiana degli autori ed editori

TABLES

Table 10.3 Average Ratios for the period 1991–1998

M$ and %	relevance	GEMA	SACEM	PRS	most efficient
OPTIC	+++	738%	446%	594%	GEMA
GDRAT	++	86.4%	73.7%	83.5%	GEMA
NDRAT	+++	89.1%	79.9%	83.5%	GEMA
ELRP	++	0.98	0.43	1.28	PRS
ACE	++	0.089	0.084	0.068	PRS
ΔACE	+++	8.7%	3.6%	5.2%	SACEM
ΔC	++	5.9%	4.1%	2.2%	PRS
COPE	+++	0.651	0.374	0.408	GEMA
DIPE	++	0.563	0.277	0.343	GEMA
ΔCOPE	+++	8.6%	3.5%	10.3%	PRS
COPM	+++	0.020	0.008	0.010	GEMA
ΔCOPM	++	-2.2%	0.4%	2.4%	PRS
DIPM	+++	0.017	0.006	0.008	GEMA

Table 10.4 Efficiencies from DEA method (1991-1998 period, variable returns to scale used)

Input minimisation radial model			Output maximisation radial model		
Inputs: P, C / Output : R			Inputs: P, C / Output : R		
85.90	86.13	87.12	78.32	83.36	85.16
SAC96	SAC95	SAC97	SAC91	SAC93	SAC96
87.20	88.27	91.62	85.37	86.44	86.47
SAC98	SAC94	PRS93	SAC95	SAC97	SAC94
92.89	93.03	93.37	86.58	91.15	91.56
PRS92	PRS94	SAC93	SAC98	PRS93	PRS92
94.49	96.27	98.49	92.67	94.24	94.98
PRS96	PRS95	GEM98	PRS94	PRS96	PRS91
98.71	98.73	99.35	96.08	98.48	98.70
GEM93	GEM94	SAC91	PRS95	GEM98	GEM93
99.66	99.74	99.75	98.73	99.66	99.75
GEM92	GEM97	GEM95	GEM94	GEM92	GEM95
99.76	99.98	100.00	99.80	99.98	100.00
PRS91	PRS97	GEM91	GEM97	PRS97	GEM91
100.00	100.00	100.00	100.00	100.00	100.00
GEM96	PRS98	SAC92	GEM96	PRS98	SAC92

Table 10.4 (cont.)

Input minimisation radial model			Output maximisation radial model		
Inputs: P, C, E, M / Output: R			**Inputs: P, C, E, M / Output: R**		
87.20	88.31	90.32	78.32	83.36	85.16
SAC98	SAC97	SAC96	SAC91	SAC93	SAC96
91.60	93.25	94.14	85.37	86.44	86.47
SAC95	SAC94	PRS92	SAC95	SAC97	SAC94
94.43	94.80	95.93	86.58	91.15	91.56
SAC93	PRS93	PRS94	SAC98	PRS93	PRS92
97.72	98.71	98.73	92.67	94.98	96.08
PRS95	GEM93	GEM94	PRS94	PRS91	PRS95
99.85	100.00	100.00	96.63	98.70	98.73
PRS96	GEM91	GEM92	PRS96	GEM93	GEM94
100.00	100.00	100.00	100.00	100.00	100.00
GEM95	GEM96	GEM97	GEM91	GEM92	GEM95
100.00	100.00	100.00	100.00	100.00	100.00
GEM98	PRS91	PRS97	GEM96	GEM97	GEM98
100.00	100.00	100.00	100.00	100.00	100.00
PRS98	SAC91	SAC92	PRS97	PRS98	SAC92
Inputs: C, E / Outputs: R, COPM			**Inputs: C, E / Outputs: R, COPM**		
73.50	74.23	76.11	81.19	84.22	84.82
SAC98	SAC97	SAC95	SAC92	SAC97	SAC93
76.45	78.50	79.03	86.91	86.94	87.11
SAC96	SAC94	SAC93	SAC91	SAC95	SAC98
80.26	83.31	86.14	87.19	87.28	87.94
SAC92	PRS92	PRS93	SAC96	SAC94	PRS92
86.16	87.89	88.08	88.53	91.32	93.33
SAC91	PRS94	PRS91	PRS91	PRS93	PRS94
91.60	97.12	97.56	94.81	97.72	97.82
PRS95	PRS96	GEM94	PRS95	GEM93	GEM94
97.68	100.00	100.00	99.17	100.00	100.00
GEM93	GEM91	GEM92	PRS96	GEM91	GEM92
100.00	100.00	100.00	100.00	100.00	100.00
GEM95	GEM96	GEM97	GEM95	GEM96	GEM97
100.00	100.00	100.00	100.00	100.00	100.00
GEM98	PRS97	PRS98	GEM98	PRS97	PRS98

NOTES

1. Helpful suggestions by Didier Lebert (University of Paris 1 Panthéon-Sorbonne) are gratefully acknowledged.
2. Further, their activities extend to copyright claims, litigation, measurement, enforcement, defence of the moral interest of their members and sometimes social and cultural action.
3. And, according to the *contract law paradigm*, copyright law itself must vanish (Dam, 1999).
4. This is particularly true the greater the number of economic partners and the larger the informational asymmetries.

5. For instance, see Hollander (1984).
6. For instance, neighbouring rights are less costly to manage than author's rights. In the same way, collecting copyrights from national radios or through legal devices such as private copying levies is easier to run than collecting copyrights from nightclubs or in country festivals.
7. For example, in France, the initial domination of the SACEM regarding the administration of musical rights in the cafés-concerts has permitted its expansion in musical activities (Rochelandet, 2000). The implementation of non-voluntary licences in the USA – which are frequently adopted in this country – is undoubtedly explained by the political power of consumers and intermediary users' lobbies.
8. I assume that the very reputation of managers turns out to be an insufficient mechanism to solve this problem.
9. See Jensen and Meckling (1976, 1979), Fama and Jensen (1983), Schleifer and Vishny (1986).
10. Some of them – the less rich – prefer to earn something rather than nothing.
11. See Dietz (1978), Hilty (1995) and Sénat Français (1997). Since then, changes have occurred in some countries, for example Belgium.
12. In fact, Katzenberger (1995) emphasises the lack of harmonisation in Europe.
13. For instance, the 'ASCAP consent decree' prohibits the ASCAP to supply users with exclusive licences. However, no particular legal control is applied to the running of the CCS.
14. However, some reforms have recently been adopted in order to strengthen control. But they are not taken into account in the present study because they occurred after the analysed period.
15. Of course, the amount of undistributed sums is a relative indicator of the efficiency of a CCS over a given year. The delays of copyright distributions could be the sign of inefficient information processing and distribution schedule. An interesting fact here is that before announcing their results to their members, some CCS deduct from their administration expenses the financial incomes derived from the investments of undistributed sums. However, the importance of these investments and their incomes does not necessarily result from economies due to efficient rationalisation or from a fine portfolio management.
16. It assumes, however, that the cost of hiring a lawyer is more or less the same from one country to another.
17. It is possible to integrate this dispersion but this kind of data is not homogeneous amongst CCS and therefore does not allow a general comparison.
18. An introduction to the DEA model can be found at http://www.deazone.com/index.htm.

REFERENCES

Banker, R.D., A. Charnes and W.W. Cooper (1984), 'Some Models for the Estimation of Technical and Scale Inefficiencies in Data Envelopment Analysis', *Management Science*, **30**, 1078–1092.

Bureau de la Propriété Littéraire et Artistique (1997), *La Gestion Collective du Droit d'Auteur et des Droits Voisins en 1995 et 1996 par les Sociétés de Perception et de Répartition des Droits*, Paris: Ministère de la Culture.

Bureau de la Propriété Littéraire et Artistique (1995), *La Gestion Collective du Droit d'Auteur et des Droits Voisins*, Paris: Ministère de la Culture.

Charnes A., W.W. Cooper and E. Rhodes (1978), 'Measuring the Efficiency of Decision Making Units', *European Journal of Operational Research*, **2**, 429–444.

Dam, K.W. (1999), 'Self-help in the Digital Jungle', *Journal of Legal Studies*, **28(2)**, 393–412.

Dietz, A. (1978), *Das Urheberrecht in der Europäischen Gemeinschaft*, Baden-Baden.

Fama, E. and M. Jensen (1983), 'Separation of Ownership and Control', *Journal of Law and Economics*, **26**, 301–325.

Farrell, M.J. (1957), 'The Measurement of Productive Efficiency', *Journal of the Royal Statistical Society*, **120(3)**, 253–290.

Gesellschaft für musikalische aufführungs-und vervielfatigungsrechte, *Jahrbuch* (1993-1999), Berlin: Nomos.

Hilty, R.M. (ed.) (1995), *Die Verwertung von Urheberrechten in Europa – La Gestion Collective de Droit d'auteur en Europe*, Bale: Helting & Lichtenhahn, Bruylan, Carl Heymanns Verlag.

Hollander, A. (1984), 'Market Structure and Performance in Intellectual Property. The Case of Copyright Collectives', *International Journal of Industrial Organisation*, **2**, 199–216.

Jensen, M. and W. Meckling (1976), 'Theory of the Firm: Management Behavior, Agency Costs and Ownership Structure', *Journal of Financial Economics*, **3**, 305–360.

Jensen, M. and W. Meckling (1979), 'Rights and Production Functions: An Application to Labor-Managed Firms and Codetermination', *Journal of Business*, **52(4)**, 469–506.

Katzenberger, P. (1995), 'Les Divers Systèmes du Droit de Contrôle de la Gestion Collective des Droits d'Auteur dans les Etats Européens', in R. M. Hilty (dir.), *La Gestion Collective du Droit d'Auteur en Europe*, Bale: Helting & Lichtenhahn Verlag AG, 17–31.

Merger and Monopoly Commission (1996), *Performing Rights: A Report on the Supply in the UK of the Services of Administering Performing Rights and Film Synchronisation Rights*, London: MCC.

Merges, R.P. (1996), 'Contracting into Liability Rules: Intellectual Property Rights and Collective Rights Organisations', *California Law Review*, **84(5)**, 1293–1393.

Performing Rights Society, *Yearbook* (1992-1999), London: PRS Corporate Communications Department.

Rochelandet, F. (2001), 'La Mise en Œuvre Collective des Droits d'Auteur: Une Évaluation", *Réseaux*, **19**, n°110, 93–130.

Rochelandet, F. (2000), *Changement Technologique et Propriété Intellectuelle: La Mise en Œuvre du Droit d'Auteur dans les Industries Culturelles*, PhD thesis, University of Paris I.

Société des Auteurs, Compositeurs et Éditeurs de Musique, *Rapport d'Activité* (1992-1999), Paris.

Sénat Français (1997), *La Gestion Collective des Droits d'Auteur et des Droits Voisins*, Service des Affaires Européennes, Novembre.

Shleifer, A. and R. W. Vishny (1986), 'Large Shareholders and Corporate Control', *Journal of Political Economy*, **94(3)**, 461–488.

Index